Greek Cooking

SUSANNA TEE

Greek
Cooking

Love Food ® is an imprint of Parragon Books Ltd

Parragon
Queen Street House
4 Queen Street
Bath BA1 1HE, UK

Copyright © Parragon Books Ltd 2004

Love Food ® and the accompanying heart device is a trademark of Parragon Books Ltd

All rights reserved. No part of this publication may be reproduced, stored in a retrieval system or transmitted, in any form or by any means, electronic, mechanical, photocopying, recording or otherwise, without the prior permission of the copyright holder.

Created and produced by The Bridgewater Book Company Ltd.
Project Editor Nicola Wright
Project Designer Michael Whitehead
Photography Simon Punter
Home Economists Ricky Turner and Clare Nolan
Additional photography Max Alexander

The author, Susanna Tee, would like to thank the following for their help: Kate Smith, Fran Rodriguez, her husband Peter Hills, and her children Laura and James.

ISBN: 978-1-4075-6809-6

Printed in China

NOTES FOR THE READER

- This book uses imperial, metric, or US cup measurements. Follow the same units of measurement throughout; do not mix imperial and metric.

- All spoon measurements are level: teaspoons are assumed to be 5 ml, and tablespoons are assumed to be 15 ml.

- Unless otherwise stated, milk is assumed to be whole, eggs and individual vegetables such as potatoes are medium, and pepper is freshly ground black pepper.

- Recipes using raw or very lightly cooked eggs should be avoided by infants, the elderly, pregnant women, convalescents, and anyone with a chronic condition.

- The times given are an approximate guide only. Preparation times differ according to the techniques used by different people and the cooking times may also vary from those given.

contents

Introduction	8
In the Greek Kitchen	28

Mezzes & Soups   38
Hot Roasted Nuts *Pása Témpos*	46
Cucumber and Yogurt Dip *Tzatzíki*	47
Smoked Cod Roe Dip *Taramasaláta*	48
Split Pea Dip *Fáva*	50
Chickpea and Sesame Dip *Húmmous kai Tachíni*	51
Eggplant and Garlic Dip *Melitzanosaláta*	53
Smoked Red Bell pepper Dip *Piperiá Kapnistí*	54
Greek Sausages *Loukánika*	55
Deep-fried Squid *Kalamarákia*	56
Stuffed Vine Leaves *Dolmádes*	59
Hot Cheese Pastries *Tirópites*	60
Greek Garlic Sauce *Skordaliá*	64
Yogurt and Tomato Soup *Soúpa Yaoúrti-Domáta*	65
Consommé with Egg and Lemon Sauce *Soúpa Avgolémono*	66
Roasted Vegetable Soup *Soúpa Psitón Lahanikón*	69
Bean and Vegetable Soup *Fasoláda*	70
Chilled Cucumber Soup *Angourósoupa*	71
Fishermen's Soup *Soúpa tou Psará*	72
Fresh Herb Soup *Soúpa me Freska Mirodiká*	75
Olive Bread *Eliótsomo*	77
Sesame Crackers *Almirá me Sousámi*	78
Walnut Cheese Wafers *Gufrétes me Tirí kai Karídia*	81

Fish Dishes   82
Traditional Greek Baked Fish *Psári Plakí*	90
Broiled Red Snapper with Garlic *Psári Skordáto*	92
Fresh Sardines Baked with Lemon and Oregano *Sardéles me Rígani*	93
Pasta with Scallops and Pine Nuts *Macarónia me Thalasiná kai Koukounária*	95
Roasted Fish from Spetsae Island *Psária Spetsiótika*	96
Baked Mackerel Stuffed with Raisins and Pine Nuts *Skoubriá Gemistá*	99
Monkfish and Shrimp Kabobs *Souvlákia me Psári kai Garídes*	100
Fish Fritters with Greek Garlic Sauce *Psári me Skordaliá*	104
Fish in Egg and Lemon Sauce *Psári Avgolémono*	107
Skate in Mustard and Caper Sauce *Psári me Moustárda kai Cápari*	108

Pan-fried Fish with Lemon *Psári Tiganitó me Lemóni*	109
Seafood Pasta *Makarónia me Thalasiná*	111
Red Mullet Wrapped in Vine Leaves *Barboúnia me Ambelófila*	113
Shrimp Pilaf *Garídes Piláfi*	114

Meat & Poultry Dishes — 116

Smyrna Sausages in Tomato Sauce *Soudzoukákia*	127
Grecian Meatballs *Keftédes*	128
Lamb with Zucchini and Tomatoes *Arní me Kolokíthia*	129
Lamb and Eggplant Moussaka *Moussaká*	130
Lamb with Tomatoes, Artichokes and Olives *Arní me Domátes Angináres kai Eliés*	133
Marinated Lamb and Vegetable Kabobs *Souvlákia*	135
Cinnamon Lamb Casserole *Arní me Kanéla*	136
Roast Lamb with Orzo *Arní me Giouvétsi*	138
Rosemary Lamb in Filo Pastry *Arní me Dendrolívano se Fílo*	141
Lamb with Aubergine and Black Olive Sauce *Arní me Melitzána kai Eliés*	142
Lamb's Liver in Red Wine and Orange Sauce *Sikotakiá me Sáltsa*	143
Baked Pasta with Spicy Meat Sauce *Pastitsio*	144
Thick Beef and Pearl Onion Casserole *Stifádo*	149
Braised Veal in Red Wine *Moshári me Kókkino Krási*	150
Braised Pork with Fennel *Hirinó me Aníthos*	153
Pork and Romaine Lettuce in Egg and Lemon Sauce *Hirinó Avgolémono*	155
Grilled Chicken with Lemon *Kotópoulo Scharás me Lemóni*	156
Spicy Aromatic Chicken *Kotópoulo Pikántiko*	157
Phyllo Chicken Pie *Kotópita*	159
Chicken Kabobs with Yogurt Sauce *Kotópoulo Souvláki me Sáltsa Yaóurti*	160
Chicken with Goat Cheese and Basil *Kotópoulo me Tirí Próvio kai Vasilikó*	163
Chicken with Walnut Sauce *Kotópoulo me Karídia*	164
Roast Chicken with Oregano *Kotópoulo me Rígani*	165
Rabbit, Roast Tomato, and Sage Pie *Kounéli me Domáta kai Mirodiká*	166

Vegetables & Salads — 168

Braised Okra with Tomatoes *Bámies Kokkinístes*	176
Zucchini Slices with Greek Garlic Sauce *Kolokíthia me Skordaliá*	177
Crispy Roasted Fennel *Psitó Traganistó Aníthos*	179
Zucchini Pie *Kolokithópita*	181
Stuffed Cabbage Leaves *Láhano Dolmádes*	182
Baked Stuffed Eggplant *Melitzánes Gémistes*	184

Carrots à la Grecque *Karóta á la Grecque*	187
Roasted Vegetable Moussaka *Moussakás Lahanikón*	189
Spinach and Feta Pie *Spanakópita*	190
Artichoke Hearts with Fava Beans *Agináres me Koukiá*	194
Stuffed Zucchini with Walnuts and Feta *Kolokíthia Gemistá*	195
Roasted Red Bell peppers with Halloumi *Pipéries Gemistés me Hallóumi*	197
Greek Country Beans *Fasólia Yahní*	198
Tomato Pilaf *Piláfi me Domáta*	200
Tomato Salad with Fried Feta *Domatasaláta me Féta*	202
Traditional Greek Salad *Saláta Horiátiki*	203
Fava Bean Salad *Saláta me Koukiá*	204
Salad of Greens with Lemon Dressing *Hórta me Ladolémono*	206
Orange and Olive Salad *Saláta me Portokali kai Eliés*	207
Charred Bell pepper Salad *Saláta me Psités Piperiés*	209
Sweet Things	210
Baked Stuffed Honey Figs *Síka Fournóu me Méli*	218
Greek Shortbread Cookies *Kourambiédes*	219
Orange and Walnut Cakes *Melomakárona*	221
Butter Cookies *Koulourákia*	222
Doughnuts in Honey Syrup *Loukoumádes*	225
Walnut Custard Tarts *Tártes Karidión*	226
Honey and Lemon Tart *Siphnópitta*	229
Orange Cheesecake with Caramelized Lemon Slices *Cheesecake Portokáli me Karameloméno Lemóni*	230
Greek Rice Pudding *Rizógalo*	232
Oranges in Caramel Sauce *Portokaliá Karameloméno*	233
Lemon Ice Cream in an Ice Bowl *Pagotó Lemóni se Bol apo Págo*	234
Pistachio Ice Cream *Pagotó Fistíkia*	237
Walnut Pastries *Baklavás*	240
Semolina and Almond Cake *Halvás*	243
Apricot and Pistachio Cake *Kéik me Eginís kai Veríkoko*	244
Yogurt Cake *Yaourtópita*	247
Walnut Cake *Karidópita*	248
Almond Paste Pears *Achládia apo Pólto Amýgdalou*	251
Lemonade *Lemonáda*	252
Greek Coffee *Ellinikós Kafés*	253
Index	254

INTRODUCTION

Think of Greece and you think of blue skies and seas, tumbling vermilion and scarlet bougainvillea flowers, red and pink geraniums growing in cans that were once the home of feta cheese, twisted lemon trees, olive groves, cypress trees blowing in the wind, fishing boats bringing in their catch, and whitewashed houses perched on hilltops.

Each year, more and more people visit Greece. It could be to lie on the beach and bask in the sun, swim in the crystal-blue sea, study its history and architecture, sail from island to island, paint the landscape, study wild flowers, or enjoy its cuisine. The market stalls are laden with produce, the smell of fresh herbs and garlic fills the air, and people sit outside *tavernas*, eating and drinking, shaded from the sun by a vine.

The people of Greece are warm, generous, and hospitable. Food has always been a part of this hospitality and you could not visit a Greek home without being offered something to eat and drink. It would be considered impolite not to offer something to a guest and equally discourteous to refuse. The Greek lifestyle and the seasonal availability of ingredients are reflected in their national cuisine. Most importantly, however, eating in Greece is a social occasion.

The Greek mainland and its islands, of which there are around 2,000 (some, it is true, just a few bare rocks), lie on the far southeastern fringes of Europe. Greece borders Albania, Macedonia, the former Yugoslav Republic, Bulgaria, and Turkey and is surrounded almost entirely by the Ionian Sea, the Mediterranean, and the Aegean Sea.

This proximity to the water has had an enormous influence on Greek food for, by the very nature of where the population lives, either on the mainland or on one of the many islands, the seas that surround it provide a wealth of fish and shellfish. Fish is therefore eaten in abundance.

A mountainous range lies across a large part of mainland Greece and, much of the terrain being barren, there is very little good grazing land. This makes it difficult to raise cattle, so little beef is eaten and olive oil takes the place of butter. Calves are often slaughtered and eaten as veal as it is difficult for them to grow to maturity on the dry summer soil. Of the milk that is produced, most is used as milk and for yogurt with little used to make cream and butter. Sheep and goats are livestock that are more easily reared and are as important for their flesh as their milk, which is drunk as well as used to produce yogurt. Lamb therefore, followed by kid, is the most popular meat eaten in Greece. Poultry is also abundant and pigs are bred in most parts of the country so that chicken and pork are also popular meats, as is offal. Hen's eggs are common and are particularly used to thicken sauces and soups as in *avgolémono*, the well-known Greek egg and lemon sauce.

The people of Greece are warm, generous, and hospitable

Traditional Greek windmills make a striking silhouette against the clear blue sky

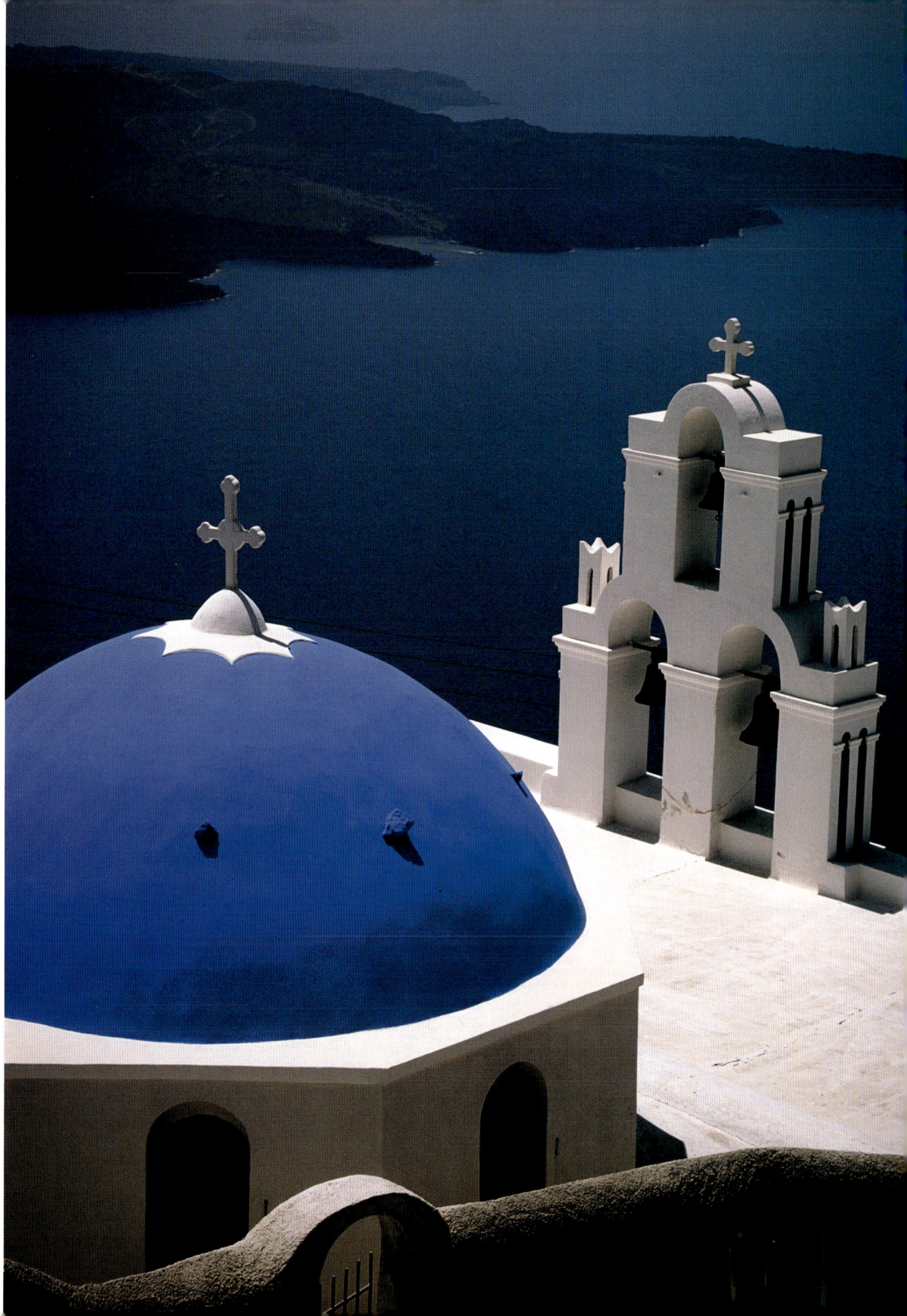

Blue and white—the quintessential colors of coastal Greece

Greece also has the best environment for the olive tree, which thrives in the hot, arid land. The cultivation of the olive tree has always been of great importance to Greece and as a result olives and olive oil are the cornerstones of Greek cuisine. There are also areas on mainland Greece and the islands where the soil is fertile and cultivated. Areas that are completely green in summer are covered with vineyards and tended for the cultivation of wine. Fields of tomato plants (especially from Santorini) are cultivated for the canning industry and the production of tomato purée and other products. Many other vegetables also flourish, including eggplant, zucchini, bell peppers, onions, and garlic. In numerous valleys, wheat, barley, corn, and oats can be seen billowing in the summer heat and then there are orchards of fruit trees, particularly fragrant lemons and oranges, filling the warm air with their scent, as well as walnuts, almonds, and apples. Other fruits that flourish in the fertile soil are quinces, pears, melons, and figs.

Many of the best-known Greek dishes such as *Fáva* (the dip made with yellow split peas, see page 50), *Soúpa tou Psará* (Fishermen's Soup, see page 72), and *Kotópita* (Filo Chicken Pie, see page 159), and the particularly famous *Soúpa Avgolémono* (the soup flavored with egg and lemon, see page 66), are found throughout Greece. There are, however, ten distinct regions within the country of which half are groups of islands, and many of these have their own specialties of food. From the island of Santorini come small, uneven tomatoes; Mykonos is known for its dried pork (*loúses*) and onion and cheese pie (*kremythópita*); Syros for its zucchini pie (*kolokythópita*); Sifnos for its honey pie (*melópita*) and chickpea casserole (*sifniótika revíthia*); Cos for its lemon tart and lettuces; Karpathos for its stuffed lamb and quinces; Chios for its mastic; Tinos for its sun-dried tomatoes; Crete for its graviera cheese, quinces, and artichokes; Hydra for its marzipan; and from Corfu come the Italian-inspired dishes of *Pastítsio*, Baked Pasta with Spicy Meat Sauce (see page 144), and *sofríto*, the dish of fried steaks cooked in a thick, richly flavored wine sauce.

Greek food is colorful, fresh, and bursting with flavor. It is basically simple and uncomplicated yet reflects the healthy Mediterranean diet that is popular today. Foods are eaten when in season and fresh—tomatoes at their ripest, fish when the fishing boat comes in, herbs and salad greens freshly gathered from the hillsides and fields, and lemons and figs as soon as they are harvested. Cooking styles are also relatively simple, for until fairly recently every village had its own communal outdoor spit and barbecue as well as a bread oven which was used by the community. Modern kitchens, with ovens, microwaves, and food processors, have replaced communal cooking but these traditional cooking methods still influence the Greek cook. Even today, both lamb and kid, which are eaten broiled and roasted all year round, are routinely spit-roasted for festive occasions.

Greek cuisine has a tradition that is as long as its history and much of the food that is eaten today, especially on the islands, probably does not differ greatly from that enjoyed by the ancient Greeks 2,500 years ago, although it could be argued that there may have been foreign influences from countries such as Turkey, Bulgaria, and Italy.

Greece also has the best environment for the olive tree...olives and olive oil are the cornerstones of Greek cuisine

Influences are mostly owed to the movement of travelers, armies, and merchant sailors. As a seafaring nation, it was particularly easy for the Greeks to travel by ship around the shores of the Mediterranean and many settled in communities in the large cities on the edge of the Mediterranean. There was also the movement of cargo ships and small boats around and across the mainland and islands. The necessity of taking on board new crew and fresh foodstuff that the sailors carried for selling or bartering at their next port of call encouraged the introduction of foods from foreign parts. There were, for example, pasta from Italy, beans from Egypt, almonds from France, lemons and oranges from China, rice from India, eggplant from southeast Asia, okra, dates, and onions from Africa, spinach from Persia, and, from the 16th century, tomatoes from Peru and beans and bell peppers from the New World. None of these ingredients was native to Greece but all have a natural affinity with Greece's own produce, dating from antiquity, of olives, figs, wheat, and grapes, which produced oil, bread, and wine. (Interestingly, grapes were not eaten as a fresh fruit in ancient times but were solely used for drying and for producing wine.)

When the Romans occupied Greece, wealthy Roman families would employ Greek tutors for their children and Greek chefs in their kitchens, so the Greeks came to influence Italian cooking. Then, for nearly four hundred years, Greece was occupied by the Turks. During this time the Greeks were forced to refer to their own dishes in the Turkish language so, although some dishes may be considered Turkish, they are in fact of Greek origin. During this time many learned Greeks, who were also good cooks,

Greek life and the country's cuisine are irrevocably linked with the sea that surrounds its mainland and many islands

introduction

observance of religious festivals has played a part in the development of many Greek dishes

took refuge in Orthodox monasteries where they created wonderful culinary concoctions. They wore black robes but to distinguish themselves from the monks they wore tall white hats instead of the black ones worn by the monks. These tall white hats are still worn by professional chefs throughout the world today.

The Greek diet is based on a predominance of vegetables and salads, broiled fresh fish and meat, fruit and yogurt, flavored and seasoned with a delicate, subtle combination of olive oil, lemons, wine, and herbs, such as thyme and oregano, found in plentiful quantities on the Greek hillsides and used in extravagant abundance in most dishes. Spices, such as cinnamon, cloves, allspice, and cumin, are also used sparingly and mainly in Crete, Rhodes, and the other Dodecanese islands where the Arabs left their influence. In almost all Greek kitchens you will find the staple ingredients of cheese, tomatoes, lemons, fresh and dried herbs, garlic, *rigani* (wild marjoram) and other fresh herbs, honey, brine-cured tuna and sardines, salted capers, olives, and olive oil. All are used in large quantities.

The observance of religious festivals has played an important part in the development of many Greek dishes and in the Greek Orthodox calendar there are many feast and fast days that are observed rigorously. The first festival of the year starts on January 1. It is celebrated by serving a large yeast cake flavored with cinnamon and sesame seeds called *vasilópita*, meaning St. Basil's cake, named after the founding father of the Orthodox Church. It is baked with a good luck coin inside. No meat is eaten on the first day of Lent, which is known as Clean Monday, and on this day green beans in oil, *Taramasaláta* (see page 48), *Dolmádes* (Stuffed Vine Leaves, see page 59), pita bread, fish, and *Halvás* (Semolina and Almond Cake, see page 243) are traditionally eaten. The two Sundays before Lent are known respectively as Meat Sunday and Cheese Sunday, which speak for themselves.

Easter is the most important feast to be observed in Greece. It is of even greater importance than Christmas and on Good Friday most shops and businesses are closed, and flags fly at half-mast in commemoration of Christ being taken down from the cross. On Holy Thursday, Good Friday, and Easter Saturday the whole family goes to church, and after church at midnight, when the Greek Lenten fast is broken, a traditional soup called *magirítsa*, made with the intestines and offal of a young lamb, is eaten. Some people also follow the tradition of eating red-dyed hard-boiled eggs, to signify the blood of Christ. These are carried to church in their pockets and the eggs are cracked and eaten, often with salt and pepper that they have brought with them. On Easter Sunday the Greeks enjoy spit-roasted or roasted spring lamb or kid. The meal begins at around noon with mezzes and includes the sharing of the Easter bread known as *lambrópsomo*. This rich bread is beautifully decorated with leaves and flowers made out of the dough and four red-dyed eggs. After plenty of food and wine, singing and dancing begin and last well into the late afternoon.

Christmas is celebrated with a roasted turkey and replaces the roasted stuffed capon that was once eaten. Small traditional brandy-flavored honey cakes

Sitting outside at café tables is a favorite way of socializing and relaxing in Greece

Overleaf *The Parthenon in Athens still stands as testimony to Greece's ancient history*

The vine is an important feature in Greece for the cultivation of both white and black grapes for eating fresh...and, of course, wine

called *finíkia* or *melomakárona* and Greek Shortbread Cookies called *Kourambiédes* (see page 219) are also eaten. *Christópsoma* is the Christmas bread flavored with orange peel and dried fruit, decorated with a cross of dough and topped with chopped nuts.

Breakfast is not an important meal in Greece; in fact the Greeks rarely eat breakfast. Instead they usually have a strong, sweetened cup of coffee in the morning, followed by another one at work in the middle of the morning, perhaps with a sweet pastry. Lunch remains the main meal of the day, although because of the summer heat, some Greeks prefer to eat a light lunch and to have their main meal in the evening. Lunch is usually eaten between 2 and 3 p.m. while dinner is often eaten late, between 9 and 10 p.m.

The mild climate of Greece allows the Greeks to eat out in the open air throughout most of the year. Lunch is enjoyed at a leisurely pace, when time allows, and is usually followed by an afternoon siesta. Food in Greece is served warm rather than hot, probably also because of the mild climate.

When it comes to eating out, there is a variety of different eating places to choose from. *Tavérnas*, once only frequented by men, are now the most popular and here you will find a good selection of mezze dishes, baked snacks as well as fish and meat dishes. Then there are restaurants, which tend to be more expensive than *tavérnas*, most of which offer a selection of ethnic Greek dishes as well as foreign dishes. *Psáriatavernas* are fish *tavérnas*, usually found on the islands and in coastal areas, and, as their name suggests, they specialize in fish and seafood dishes. Sometimes in these *tavérnas* you can select the fish you want to eat, still swimming in a tank, and soon afterwards it will be cooked and served to you! There are also *tavérnas* that specialize in grilled meat cooked over charcoal. These are served with salads, and mezzes are also offered. Some establishments only serve mezzes and these are eaten with a glass of wine, beer, or ouzo. Another traditional establishment that is popular with young people is the *ouzéri* which serves ouzo with a few mezzes. A coffee can be bought from a *kafeneíon*, and cakes and pastries from the *zaharoplastíon*. For fast food the Greeks buy grilled skewered meat (*souvlákia*) wrapped in pita bread with tomatoes, onions and *Tzatzíki* (see page 47) at a small café or stall, or there is always the familiar McDonald's or its Greek equivalents, Goodies and Hambo!

A Greek meal starts with a mezze. This is followed by a main course with salad and bread but unlike the heavy structured meal of many countries, the Greeks prefer a choice of several small dishes made with a variety of different foods. Vegetables are usually served after the main course, not with it, and the meal frequently ends with fresh fruit, a dessert, or ice cream. Cheeses, such as feta, find their way into salads, pastries, and mezze dishes, rather than being served as a course in their own right at the end of a meal. Pastries and cakes may be eaten some time after the meal, not at the dining table, with coffee. Sweetened coffee concludes the meal.

Good, crusty, freshly baked bread, which is traditionally round in shape, is served with all Greek meals and is frequently used to mop up any juices or dressing left on the plate. It may be plain or flavored

As well as idyllic beaches edging a clear blue sea, Greece boasts some spectacular mountain scenery

with such additions as olives as in the recipe for *Eliótsomo* (see page 77), cheese, sesame seeds, and nuts. For the mezze table there is always pita bread, the soft, flat bread, which in Greece is usually made large and round. It is used for scooping up various dips and sauces. In addition, of course, with its natural pocket, it is also ideal as a container for serving many salads and kabobs.

Other interesting breads are *peinirlí*, which are boat-shaped bread rolls filled with a feta cheese, egg, or meat mixture, and *tsourékia*, a sweet braided loaf or buns made for celebrations such as engagements, weddings, and the birth of a child.

Rice, which is thought to have been introduced to Greece from India by Alexander the Great in 300 BC, is the most commonly eaten grain. It is often served combined with chickpeas and in pilafs with the addition of vegetables such as spinach or tomatoes (see page 200), with chicken, lamb, or with seafood such as mussels or shrimp (see page 114).

Above *Preserved remains at Knossos, the temple and palace complex that was the seat of the Minoan civilization around 1900 BC on the island of Crete*

Left *Ruins of a Venetian fortress against a clear, blue sky at Réthymno, Crete*

For the mezze table there is always pita bread...used for scooping up various dips and sauces

the Mediterranean diet is a healthy way of eating. The Greek diet, with its abundance of vegetables and fruit, some fish, grains, and wine, a little meat, and plenty of olive oil is very much a part of this way of eating

Pasta is also a favorite dish, and some of the recipes which feature it reflect the influence of the Italians who controlled many of the Aegean islands during their history. (See, for instance, the recipe for *Pastitsio* on page 144.)

Coffee is the most popular drink in Greece and this is usually served sweetened, the sugar being added, according to taste, to the coffee grounds at the same time as the water. Greek coffee, or Turkish coffee as it is often called, is always served in small cups and left for a few moments to allow the coffee grounds to settle. It is accompanied with glasses of ice water and often served with a sweet cake or pastry. During the summer months *frappé*—iced coffee, shaken with or without milk and sugar—is an extremely popular drink. It is sold in most coffee shops and bars. Freshly squeezed fruit juices and lemonade (see page 252) are also widely consumed as is water, either from the tap or in bottles.

Ouzo is the traditional Greek apéritif. It is an anise-flavored, fiery alcoholic liquid that is drunk neat or with water, which makes it cloudy. As the Greeks seldom drink without food, ouzo is always served with a few mezzes. Brandy is another spirit that is widely drunk in Greece, the most popular brand being Metaxá, and a third is *koum-kouát*, an orange-colored brandy distilled in Corfu from the tiny oranges of the same name.

In Greece, wine is an everyday accompaniment to meals and most is drunk rather than used in cooking. Greece produces a variety of local wines of varying quality and until quite recently only a few vineyards produced sufficient quantities for export. Vineyards are located on the mainland and, of the Greek islands, Crete is the largest producer of wine. Now more and more Greek wines of top quality can be found in liquor stores and wine shops and these include sweet and dry red wines, mostly dry and light white wines and light rosé wines. Much of the wine produced in Greece, in Attica, the region of Athens, is the famous white wine, Retsina. (There is also a rosé version known as *kokkineli*.) Small pieces of pine resin are added to the wine during fermentation and it therefore smells and tastes of pine resin. It is an acquired taste!

Modern research has shown us the Mediterranean diet is a healthy way of eating. The Greek diet, with its abundance of vegetables and fruit, some fish, grains and wine, a little meat and plenty of olive oil is very much part of this way of eating. It is simple, good food and the Greeks enjoy good food.

Ancient Greeks had a word for a lover of good food, epicure, and even today Greek food reaches epicurean heights. Enjoy preparing the recipes in this book, either to rekindle memories of having eaten the dish in its native land or to introduce you to something new. More importantly, sit down, relax, and enjoy your meal; take a sip of wine and you too may feel like Zorba the Greek!

Gia mas! (Good health!)

Right *Narrow cobbled streets, offering welcome shade from the hot sun, wind between spotlessly clean, white-washed houses in a typical Greek town*

Overleaf *Dried herbs and spices for sale in a Greek market. A wide variety are added to Greek dishes*

in the greek kitchen

almonds
This nut is much used in Greek cookery. Popular dishes in which it features include *Skordaliá*, Greek Garlic Sauce (see page 64), and cakes and pastries.

anari
A blue cheese, made with goat's or sheep's milk.

basil
A popular herb, its Latin name of *basileus* means 'king' in Greek, and it is therefore known as the king of herbs. It is not an herb for cooking but is used for flavoring salads and is particularly good served with tomatoes.

beans
This is the collective name for dried peas, beans, and lentils. Fava beans, cannellini beans, chickpeas, black-eyed peas, lima beans, gigandes beans, butter beans, and brown lentils are all popular dried beans used in Greek cooking to make soups, casseroles, dips, and salads. Most need to be soaked prior to use. When cooking, do not add salt until the very end, as it tends to toughen the beans if added during cooking. If you live in a hard water area, add a pinch of baking soda to the cooking water to help soften them.

capers
These are the buds of the low-growing shrub that grows wild in Greece as in other parts of the Mediterranean. The buds are picked, left to dry for 24 hours, then pickled in brine. When their flavor has developed they are preserved in brine, vinegar, or olive oil. They are used as a mezze and to flavor savory dishes.

cilantro
This is an herb that has flat, slightly bitter-tasting leaves. It is used to flavor salads.

cinnamon
A spice used, in its ground form, to flavor lamb or veal stews and, in its stick form, to flavor syrups for use in cakes and pastries.

cumin
A spice used to flavor meat dishes.

dill
This is an herb with feathery leaves that imparts a mild, sweet, caraway flavor. It is added to dishes containing white beans (see the recipe for Artichoke Hearts with Fava Beans on page 194), to lamb and chicken dishes, and in the *avgolémono* sauce (see the recipe for Pork and Romaine Lettuce in Egg and Lemon Sauce on page 155).

fáva
The name of a dip made with a purée of yellow split peas and olive oil (see page 50). The best yellow split peas are said to come from the volcanic Greek island of Santorini where the soil is thought to give them a strong flavor. Yellow dal can be used as a substitute. Fava is also the American name for the broad bean.

feta cheese
Made from pasteurized sheep's and goat's milk, this is a moist, white, crumbly cheese. It is mainly used fresh in salads and as a filling in savory pastries (see the recipe for Hot Cheese Pastries on page 60). Its salty flavor comes from the brine in which it is stored. It is the most popular cheese and the traditional cheese used in Greek Salad (see page 203) and is also used in vegetable dishes, pastries, and mezze dishes. It varies in texture and saltiness from region to region but, because it is so salty, do not season with additional salt in a recipe. There is also a blue feta cheese which has a finer texture and a peppery flavor. Feta is also sold in jars, cubed and marinated in olive oil and

Fishing boats bring their catch to harbors daily

oregano. Choose authentic Greek feta cheese rather than any substitutes.

figs
A fruit which comes in black, green, white, and purple varieties, all with an intensely sweet flesh full of small, edible seeds. Dried figs are available as ready-to-eat varieties or compressed in blocks. Today, vine leaves are used to stuff various rice mixtures (see page 59) but in days of old fig leaves were probably used.

garlic
Greece's ubiquitous vegetable and the Greeks' favorite ingredient!

Fresh herbs are used by the handful in Greek cookery and are often freshly picked from the hillsides

grapes
The vine is one of the staple crops of Greece and thrives in the hot climate and dry soils. Varieties of vine produce both white and black grapes for eating fresh, for drying to produce sultanas, raisins, and currants and, of course, to make wine and spirits.

graviera cheese
This is a firm cheese made from sheep's milk that is similar in texture to the Swiss cheese, Gruyère. It is made on the island of Crete.

hallóumi cheese
A white cheese that is soft and springy when young and hard and salty when matured. It is made from a mixture of sheep's and goat's milk or cow's, goat's and ewe's milk and is often flavored with mint. It is much used in Greek cooking, and can be broiled, fried, baked, boiled, grated, or simply eaten on its own. Greek *hallóumi* is difficult to find outside Greece but the *hallóumi* cheese from Cyprus, where it has been made for centuries, is available.

halorini cheese
A cheese made from sheep's milk that is flavored with coriander.

halva
See the entry for sesame seeds.

herbs
Fresh herbs are used by the handful in Greek cookery and are often freshly picked from the hillsides and fields. For specific herbs, refer to the individual entries in the glossary. If you are unable to obtain a specific herb indicated in a recipe, dried herbs can often be used to replace them. As a rough guide, 1 teaspoon chopped fresh herbs is equivalent to $\frac{1}{2}$ teaspoon dried; 1 tablespoon fresh is equivalent

to 1 teaspoon dried and 3 tablespoons fresh are equivalent to 1 tablespoon dried.

honey
Honey is used in an enormous variety of Greek dishes. It is eaten with bread or yogurt, added to salad dressings and sauces, and syrups for pouring over all those traditional Greek pastries and cakes. Hymettus honey is considered to be the best and is made by bees from the nectar of the wild thyme that grows on Mount Ymitós.

kasseri cheese
Made from sheep's milk, this is a hard, salty, yellow Greek cheese, not dissimilar to Kefalotíri cheese (see entry below) but with a milder flavor and creamier texture. It is particularly suitable for grating and broiling. If you cannot find it, a good substitute is Italian provolone cheese.

kefalotíri cheese
This is a hard, dry, pale yellow, salty cheese made from a combination of sheep's and goat's milk, which has a tough rind. It is used in cooking and is ideal for grating and frying. Italian pecorino or Parmesan cheeses are suitable substitutes if you are unable to buy this cheese.

lemons
The lemon tree groves can be seen in abundance on the dry hillsides of Greece and the lemon is used extensively to flavor, marinate, and garnish most savory and sweet Greek foods. Very few of the recipes here do not include lemon in the list of ingredients. To extract the maximum amount of lemon juice from a lemon, roll it on a work surface with the palm of your hand prior to squeezing or heat it in a microwave oven on a high setting for 1-2 minutes. All Greek cooks do of course have a lemon in the house but should you be without a lemon and in need of some juice, in desperation bottled lemon juice can be used and a handy measurement to know is that 1 lemon yields about 3 tablespoons of juice.

manoúri cheese
This is a soft cheese, similar to cottage cheese, made from sheep's and goat's milk. Mixed with honey, it makes a delicious dessert, produced in seconds. It is also used in salads, pastries, and mezze dishes. If you cannot track it down, cream cheese, cottage cheese, or Italian ricotta cheese can all be used as a substitute.

marjoram
This herb belongs to the same family as oregano but tastes slightly sweeter. It is used both fresh and dried in Greek cooking. In Greece, wild marjoram is dried and used extensively in cooking. It is known as *rígani* (see separate entry).

mastic
A resinous gum produced from the mastic tree that grows on the island of Chios. The crystals are ground to a powder and used to flavor meat stews and confectionery and *Mastíha* (see entry below).

mastíha
This is a liqueur flavored with mastic powder and therefore anise-flavored.

mint
An herb, used both fresh and dried, to flavor salads.

okra

Also known as ladies' fingers and *bámies* to the Greeks, this is another popular vegetable in Greece although it originally came from Africa and the West Indies. When preparing okra be careful not to cut into the flesh or bruise them as this releases their gluey sap. The exception is when using them in stews as the sap helps to thicken the juices. Marinating okra in vinegar or lemon juice for a short time prior to cooking also helps to prevent them from splitting so they retain their sap.

> *It is thought that the origin of the first olive tree for cultivation was from Greece*

olive oil

Olive groves stretching as far as the eye can see are a well-known sight in Greece because they thrive in the arid land and produce the olive oil for which Greece has always been famous. It is thought that the origin of the first olive tree for cultivation was from Greece around 3000 BC and there are now more than sixty varieties of olive tree growing olives for either eating or for producing oil, the staple ingredient used in lavish quantities in Greek cooking. A single olive tree can hold up to 240 lb/100 kg of olives. The olives are harvested for oil when they are beginning to turn black. A few estates still pick the olives by hand, which prevents them from bruising, but most are shaken into cloths. Greek olive oil is green-gold in color, has a fresh flavor and is rated highly in the oil-producing world. It is considered that the best Greek olive oils come from the island of Crete and, on the mainland, from the Peloponnese. Extra virgin olive oil, made from the first cold pressing of olives usually from a single estate, is the best-quality olive oil and, for an oil to be described as extra virgin, it must by law have less than 1 per cent acidity. Its taste differs according to the climate of the area and the soil in which the olives grew. Virgin olive oil is made from cold-pressed oils from different estates and is considered the next best in quality. Pure olive oil is refined oil from a third or fourth pressing and most have been heat-treated. Use extra virgin olive oil in dressings and for drizzling over cooked dishes, and virgin olive oil for cooking, as extra virgin olive oil tends to spit when heated and loses its bouquet.

olives

Olives picked from the tree are bitter and must be processed, including being submerged in brine, before they can be eaten. When the olive first develops it is green, then it slowly ripens and turns light brown, pale purple, purple and finally black and shiny before it shrivels and loses its shine. For eating, olives are collected either when they are green or black. Greek Kalamata olives are black, firm and slightly sweet and are one of the most popular olives used in salads and for cooking. Another variety is the Naphlion olive which is dark green. Small green olives are often stuffed with ingredients such as anchovies, red bell peppers, or almonds.

oranges

The most popular oranges are the navel orange, which has a thick skin and is large and juicy, and the Seville orange, which has a bitter flavor and is usually preserved in sugar syrup or honey or made into a "spoon sweet." (See the introduction to Sweet Things, page 212.) These are the best oranges for making marmalade. Blood oranges are not the most popular oranges in Greece but, when in season, do

Preserved storage jars at Knossos, a Minoan palace on Crete

introduction

Crete's many coastal inlets provide natural harbors

use these red-tinged oranges in desserts such as Oranges in Caramel Sauce (see page 233) as they have the finest flavor and look very attractive. Use a lemon zester in recipes requiring the shredded zest of oranges, to help with what is usually the laborious task of cutting the zest into thin strips.

orange flower water

Distilled from orange flowers, this water is used to flavor lamb dishes, desserts, confectionery, and drinks, and is sprinkled onto sweet pastries.

oregano

Also known as wild marjoram, this grows prolifically in Greece and for that reason is their most popular herb. It is used both dried and fresh. In Greek its name, appropriately enough, means "the joy of the mountains." It has a stronger, sharper flavor than marjoram. See the separate entry for rigani.

orzo

This is very tiny pasta which looks like flat grains of wheat. It is added to soups, meat dishes, and is served as an accompaniment.

ouzo
This is the Greeks' favorite spirit. Distilled from grapes, it is a clear, anise-flavored, fiery alcoholic liquid. It can be drunk neat, on the rocks, or with water, when it becomes white and cloudy. It is served as an apéritif in small, straight-sided glasses, accompanied by mezzes.

parsley
An herb much used in Greek cookery but in its flatleaf variety as opposed to the curly form, which has a milder flavor. It is used to flavor meat stews, chicken, fish, and vegetable dishes.

phyllo pastry
This pastry, made from wheat flour and water, is rolled out into a large rectangle until it is paper thin and almost translucent. The sheets are then used four or five at a time, each one brushed with olive oil or butter, and when baked they form a flaky pastry. Phyllo pastry can be bought in packages and is suitable for freezing. It comes in different sizes; the 11½ x 19-inch/29 x 48-cm sheets are probably the most useful. When using phyllo pastry, cover the sheets with a damp dish towel until you need to use them, to keep them moist.

pine nuts
These small white kernels harvested from the pine cone are used in many Greek savory dishes. They have a sweet, nutty flavor.

pistachio nuts
These are one of the most popular nuts in Greece. They are pale green and much used in savory meat and fish dishes as well as sweet cakes and pastries. They grow on the islands off the coast of Attica, the best ones coming from Aegina.

quince
This is a popular fruit belonging to the pear and apple family. It has a pale yellow skin and scented, hard, yellow flesh that cannot be eaten raw but must be cooked. It is added to meat dishes and fruit desserts and used to make preserves and a confectionery in the form of quince paste.

retsina
A pale-colored, usually white wine, which smells and tastes of pine resin.

rígani
The collective name for the dried leaves and flowers of wild marjoram of which, in Greece, there are at least ten different varieties. It is sold, tied in bundles, in Greek markets having been picked from the hillsides. If you are unable to buy it, substitute oregano rather than marjoram as it has a closer resemblance. It is used to flavor roasts, grills, and salads.

romaine lettuce
As the name suggests, a lettuce that originated on the Greek island of Cos. It is used in salads and meat dishes, particularly with lamb and pork. (See the recipe for Pork and Cos Lettuce in Egg and Lemon Sauce on page 155.) In Greece it is usually sliced as opposed to being separated into individual leaves.

rose flower water
Distilled from roses, this water is used to flavor meat dishes, desserts such as *Rizógalo* (the Greek Rice Pudding, see page 232) and biscuits, and is also sprinkled over sweet pastries.

rosemary
This is an herb that grows wild in Greece and is used to flavor fish, meat, and chicken dishes. Branches of

rosemary are sometimes used as skewers to grill meat and impart a delicious flavor when used in this way.

roasted red bell peppers
These are available in jars from Greek shops and larger supermarkets. They have a sweet, smoky flavor and can be served as a mezze or added to savory dishes.

sage
An herb that is particularly used in sausage and pork dishes, both fresh and dried.

saffron
A spice made from the stigma of the crocus blossom, used in pilafs and fish soups.

savory
An herb considered essential for making *Loukánika* (see page 55), Greek sausages.

semolina
This is made from hard durum wheat that is ground to varying degrees of fineness. It is slightly more granular than flour and pale yellow in color. It is used to make pasta and is a traditional ingredient in some confectionery and cakes (see the recipe for Semolina and Almond Cake on page 243).

> *Thyme...is used to flavor fish and chicken dishes. It begins to flower in May, much to the delight of the bees*

sesame seeds
These small, flat white seeds are used in both savory and sweet dishes to add flavor, particularly when they are toasted, as this brings out their nutty flavor. Sesame oil is extracted from them and they are crushed for use in the making of the paste called *Tachíni*, which in turn is used to make the Chickpea and Sesame Dip known as *Húmmous kai Tachíni*. Sesame seeds are also used to make a confectionery called *Halvás*. Finely ground sesame seeds are mixed with sugar syrup or honey, sometimes almonds or pistachio nuts are added and then the mixture is pressed into a solid block. The name *Halvás* is also used for the Greek Semolina and Almond Cake (see page 243) that is often served at Easter time.

tahina
See the entry for sesame seeds.

thyme
One of the most abundant herbs that grows wild in Greece, thyme is used to flavor fish and chicken dishes. It begins to flower in May, much to the delight of the bees. (See the entry for honey.)

tomatoes
Tomatoes feature in the kitchen of most Greek cooks and are used in a great many dishes. They are stuffed, used in salads, braised vegetable dishes, fish dishes, soups, and rice pilafs. Only in some fish dishes are they combined with that other favorite Greek ingredient, lemon juice. The Greeks seldom skin, seed, and chop tomatoes but instead grate them. This is easy to do and you are simply left with the discarded skin in your hand. Canned tomatoes make a good substitute in recipes such as casseroles, braises, and baked dishes where fresh tomatoes are not essential. Add a pinch of sugar to take away any acidity. A 14-oz (400-g) can is equivalent to about 2 lb 4 oz (1 kg) fresh tomatoes.

vine leaves

Fresh vine leaves, sometimes known as grape leaves, are stuffed as in the recipe for *Dolmádes* (see page 59) and used to wrap around fish to protect the flesh during cooking and keep it moist, and give it a smoky flavor. Packages of vine leaves preserved in brine, or salted and dried, are available. Before use these should be soaked in boiling water for 20 minutes, drained and soaked for a further 20 minutes and drained again. If you are able to pick them fresh, use small leaves, tie them in bundles by their stalks and blanch in boiling salted water for 1 minute. Dry the leaves and cut out the tough stalks before using.

walnuts

These are one of Greece's favorite nuts and are used extensively in cooking. They are offered as a mezze and feature in *Baklavás* (Walnut Pastries, see page 240) and *Karitdópita* (Walnut Cake, see page 248), two of the most delicious Greek walnut desserts.

yogurt

Greek yogurt is made from sheep's or cow's milk. Commercially produced authentic Greek yogurt is natural yogurt made from a blend of cow's milk, cream, and yogurt culture using traditional Greek methods so that the end result is a strained, thick yogurt that is smooth and velvety in consistency with a rich, creamy taste. Commercially produced authentic Greek sheep's milk yogurt, which is a set yogurt, is also available, as well as Greek yogurts containing a lower percentage of fat. Yogurts described as Greek-style can be used as a substitute.

Greek yogurt can be used in a multitude of both savory and sweet dishes and a bowl of chilled yogurt is served at almost every Greek meal, as a mezze or an accompaniment to savory dishes. It is also used to tenderize meat, to make sauces, dressings, cakes, pastries, and desserts or simply served on its own with Greek honey drizzled on top, a dessert known as *yaoúrti me méli*.

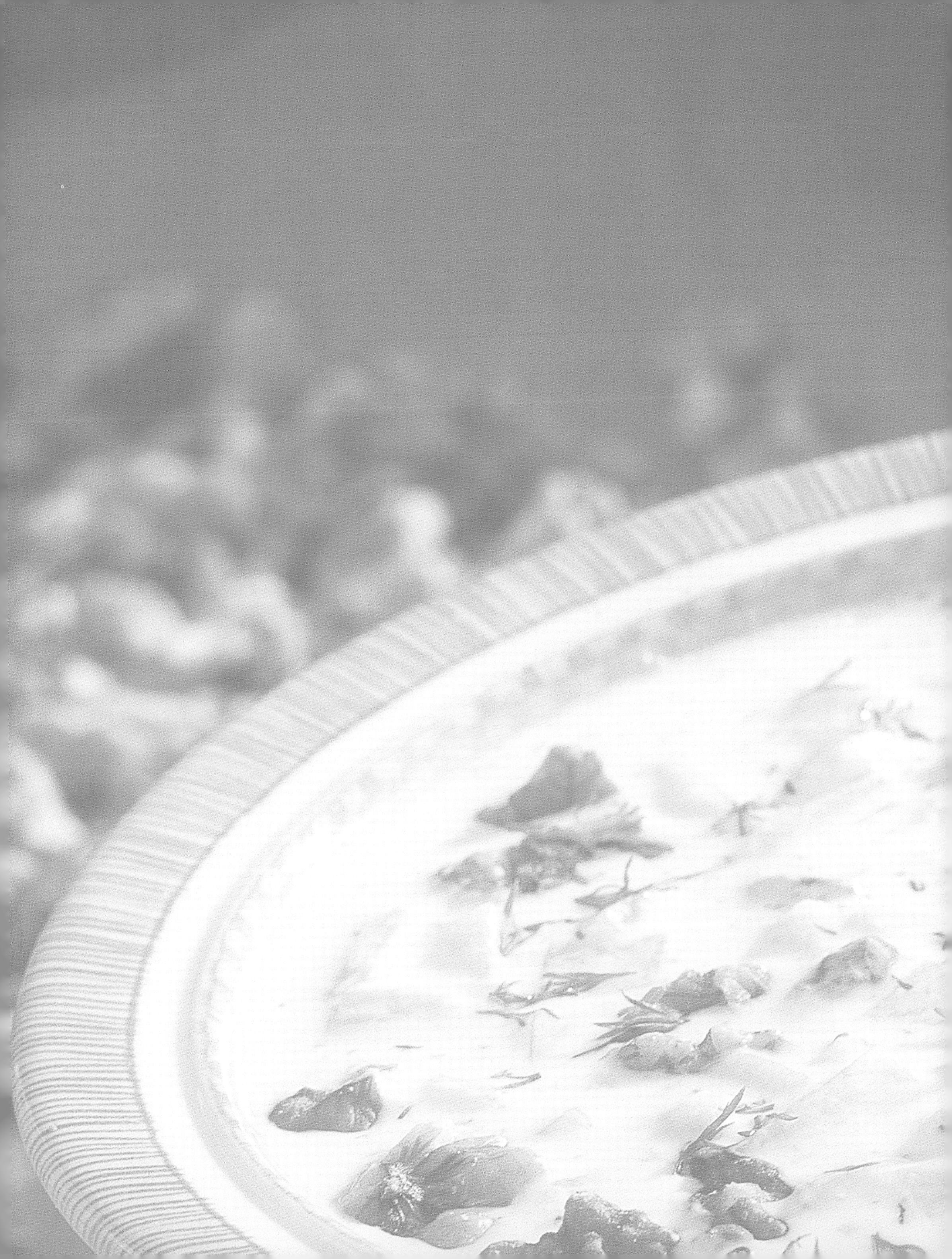

MEZZES & SOUPS

In Greece, as in many other countries, a selection of small, savory snacks or appetizers is served with a drink, whether it be a beer, an ouzo, a glass of wine, a coffee, or even a glass of water. The name for them varies in different countries, but in English-speaking countries they are known as *mezze*.

Mezzes are served either with an apéritif before a meal, in a bar or café, at a table in a *taverna*, or in the home. They are very much part of Greek social life for they are available at any time of day and offer the Greeks the opportunity to relax, have a drink, meet and chat with friends, show warmth and hospitality, and pass the time. In fact, *Pása Témpos* (see page 46) literally means "to pass the time"; in Greek cafés bowls of roasted nuts and seeds are served with drinks and are called *pása témpos*. The *pása témpos* man is the vendor of roasted nuts and seeds in the streets and markets of Greece. Mezze dishes, served on their own, also make interesting appetizers, are ideal for a light lunch, supper, or a picnic, and can even be served as a meal at a buffet party. It is a hospitable way of eating, for an unexpected guest can easily be catered for or a stranger included. You could not visit a Greek's home without being offered something to eat and this is where the mezze comes in so useful. You are expected to eat as much as you want from a mezze table and the host is expected to replenish the dishes with more or different mezzes as required.

A good mezze table will provide a variety of textures, tastes, and colors. The simplest mezze will include just a small selection of appetizers such as olives, pistachio nuts, salted almonds, pickled lemons, radishes, fried squares of feta cheese, or some roasted watermelon seeds. A more adventurous selection might include salads, stuffed vegetables, fried squid or octopus, bean dishes, dips and hot pastries. *Taramasaláta* (see page 48), the cod roe dip, *Dolmádes* (Stuffed Vine Leaves, see page 59), and *Húmmous kai Tachíni* (Chickpea and Sesame Dip, see page 51) and *Skordaliá*, Greece's famous classic Garlic Sauce (see page 64), are just a few well-known examples. *Skordaliá* has been a favorite dish since the days of the ancient Greeks and although the recipe varies with the region in Greece (some make it with ground almonds and breadcrumbs and others with ground almonds and mashed potatoes), it was originally made only with almonds. Presumably the additional ingredient has been added in more recent times to stretch the dish and keep the cost down.

A bowl of chilled Greek yogurt appears at almost every Greek meal, either served naturally or flavored with herbs and garlic. *Tzatzíki* is the very popular Cucumber and Yogurt Dip flavored with garlic and mint or dill (see page 47). It is also, incidentally, the traditional accompaniment to *Souvlákia* (Marinated Lamb and Vegetable Kabobs, see page 135). Even recipes that are considered to be main dishes, such as *Spanakópita* (Spinach and Feta Pie, see page 190) and *Souvlákia*, can be served as long as they are small.

As a guide, a traditional mezze table may contain

> *You are expected to eat as much as you want from a mezze table and the host is expected to replenish the dishes*

Detail of a Rethimnon doorway. Many Greek houses have a central, shaded courtyard inside the front door or gates, helping to keep the house cool

about 25 dishes but 12–15 dishes would provide a good selection. They may be cold or warm but all are small. Many of the recipes in this chapter could also be served as an appetizer or snack, and the recommended servings given are as if this were the case. If serving a number of mezze dishes, you may find that they serve more than the recipe suggests.

It is not common in Greece to be served a separate first or soup course, except in some restaurants. Nevertheless, soups are popular and these are served as a complete light or substantial main course. A favorite soup throughout Greece is *Soupa Avgolémono* (see page 66) which consists of chicken stock and rice thickened with the famous egg and lemon sauce. In a fish restaurant, this soup is eaten first followed by the fish itself. Fish soups, (see *Soúpa tou Psará* on page 72), also known as *Kaccaviá*, which were traditionally made in a three-legged earthenware pot called a *kaccavi* from which it derives its name (this is the fish soup that most Greeks believe originated from the Aegean Islands

these hearty, robust soups are complete meals when served with bread, olives, radishes, and cheese, and were probably originally designed to provide nourishment when times were hard

and inspired *bouillabaisse*, the classic French fish soup), and soups containing beans, such as *Fasoláda* (see page 70), generally considered to be the national soup, also figure prominently in Greek cooking. Both of these hearty, robust soups are complete meals when served with bread, olives, radishes, and cheese, and were probably originally designed to provide nourishment when times were hard. Other Greek soup specialities are *láhana*, an aniseed-flavored cabbage soup, and *magirítsa*, a traditional Easter soup eaten after the Lenten fast is broken and made with the intestines and offal of lamb, enriched with the Greek egg and lemon sauce and flavored with lots of dill. Soups are served hot and cold and *Angourósoupa* (see page 71), a chilled cucumber soup, similar to *Tzatzíki* (Cucumber and Yoghurt Dip, see page 47) is served as a mezze, but thinned with chicken stock.

Bread appears at every Greek meal, the most common types being brown, wholegrain, white, and semolina bread. Pita bread almost invariably accompanies a mezze, as it is ideal for dipping into vegetable and fish purées, and dips. Flavored breads, such as *Eliótsomo* (Olive Bread, see page 77), are also often included as a mezze, and are good for dipping.

Working donkeys remain a common sight in Greece, whether for transporting their owners or heavy loads

Overleaf Wild, unspoilt beaches can still be found in Greece

mezzes & soups

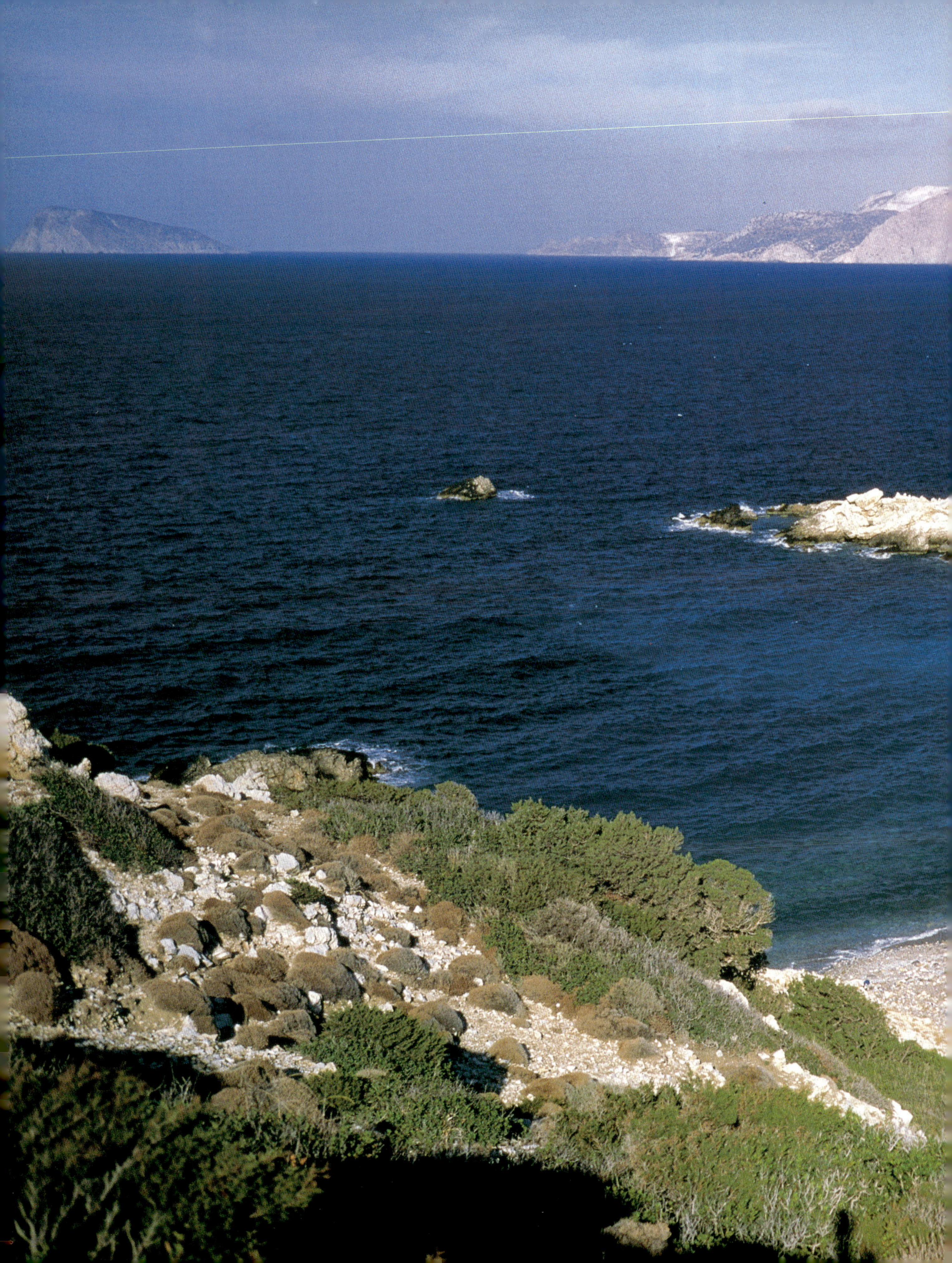

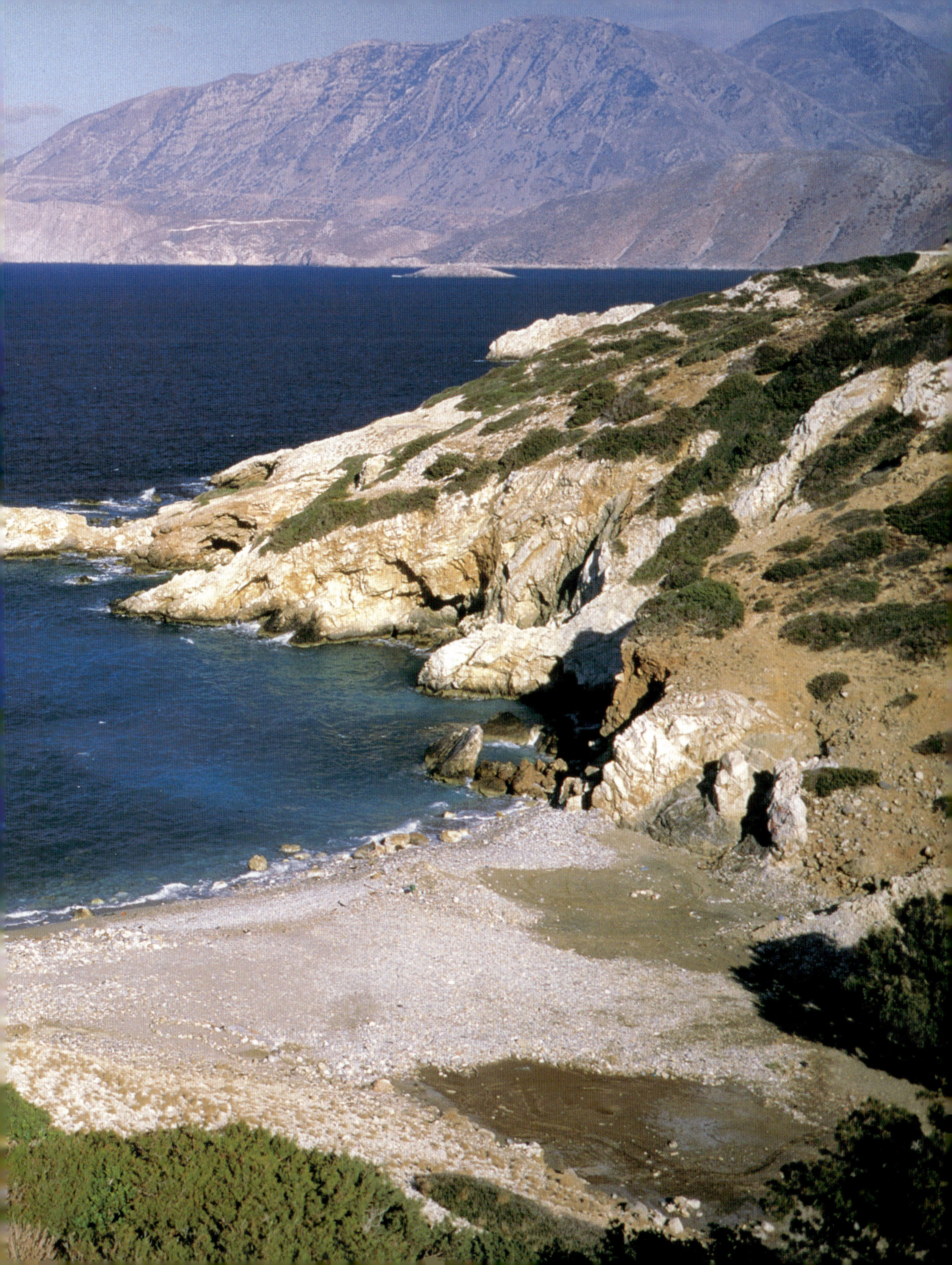

hot roasted nuts
pása témpos

In Greece you will often find bowls of hot roasted nuts, watermelon, squash, and sunflower seeds, called *pása témpos*, for sale in the streets and in cafés. *Pása témpos* can easily be made at home, using whatever nuts, herbs, and seasonings you have available.

MAKES 8 OZ/225 G

2 tbsp olive oil

1½ cups shelled pistachio nuts, almonds, or walnut halves

3 tbsp chopped fresh sage, thyme, marjoram, or oregano

1 tsp paprika or cumin

salt

1 Put the oil in a roasting pan and swirl around to cover the bottom. Add the nuts and toss to coat evenly in the oil then spread out in a single layer. Sprinkle over the herbs, paprika or cumin, and salt.

2 Bake in a preheated oven, 325°F/180°C for 20 minutes, tossing the nuts occasionally as they cook. Drain, if necessary, on paper towels and serve warm.

cucumber and yogurt dip
tzatzíki

This is not only a popular mezze dish in Greece but also the traditional accompaniment to Souvlákia, the Marinated Lamb and Vegetable Kabobs (see page 135).

SERVES 4

1 small cucumber
1¼ cups authentic Greek yogurt
1 large garlic clove, crushed
1 tbsp chopped fresh mint or dill
salt and pepper
warm pita bread, to serve

1. Peel then coarsely grate the cucumber. Put in a sieve and squeeze out as much of the water as possible. Put the cucumber into a bowl.

2. Add the yogurt, garlic, and chopped mint (reserve a little as a garnish, if desired) to the cucumber and season with pepper. Mix well together and chill in the fridge for about 2 hours before serving.

3. To serve, stir the cucumber and yogurt dip and transfer to a serving bowl. Sprinkle with salt and accompany with warmed pita bread.

smoked cod roe dip
taramasaláta

No Greek cookbook would be complete without this classic dish. It was traditionally made with salted mullet roe which is the true taramá *and from which it derives its name. Nowadays, however, it is usually made with smoked cod roe, which is more readily available. It is easily made in a food processor and is far superior to the bright pink mixture that can be bought in tubs.*

SERVES 6

8 oz/225 g smoked cod roe or fresh gray mullet roe
1 small onion, quartered
¼ cup fresh white breadcrumbs
1 large garlic clove, crushed
grated rind and juice of 1 large lemon
⅓ cup extra virgin olive oil
6 tbsp hot water
pepper

to garnish
black Greek olives
capers
chopped flat-leaf parsley

crackers, potato chips or pita bread, to serve

1 Remove the skin from the fish roe. Put the onion in a food processor and chop finely. Add the cod roe in small pieces and blend until smooth. Add the breadcrumbs, garlic, lemon rind and juice, and mix well together.

2 With the machine running, very slowly pour in the oil. When all the oil has been added, blend in the water. Season with pepper.

3 Turn the mixture into a serving bowl and chill in the fridge for at least 1 hour before serving. Serve garnished with olives, capers, and chopped parsley and accompany with crackers, chips or pita bread.

Ancient temples were built to withstand the test of time

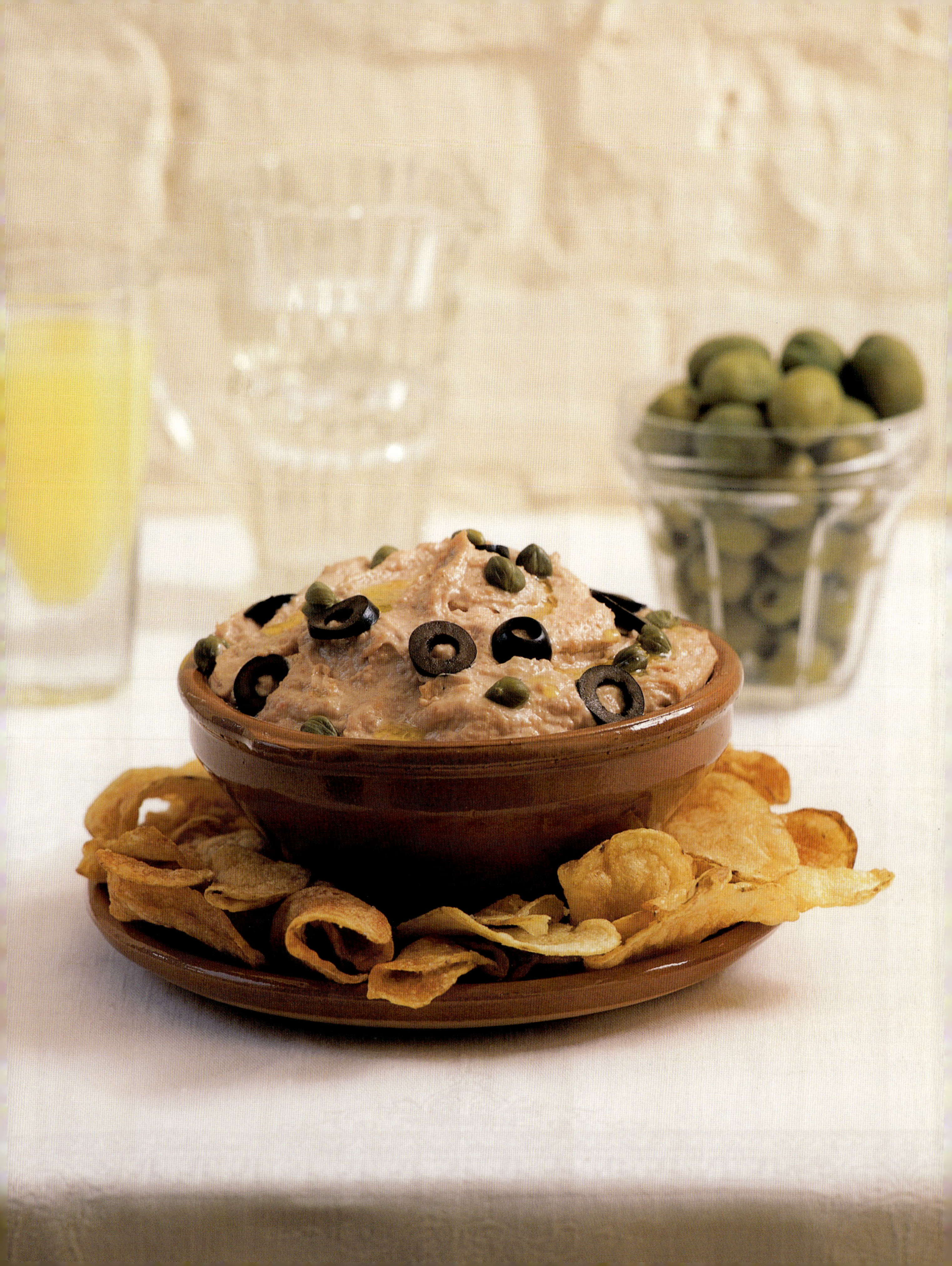

split pea dip
fáva

This is another very popular mezze dish, not dissimilar to Húmmous kai Tachíni, (see opposite) but made with yellow split peas, from which it gets its name. It is simple to make but even easier if prepared in a food processor.

SERVES 6

9 oz/250 g yellow split peas
2 small onions, 1 chopped coarsely and 1 chopped very finely
1 garlic clove, chopped coarsely
6 tbsp extra virgin olive oil
1 tbsp chopped fresh oregano
salt and pepper
warm pita bread, to serve

1 Rinse the split peas under cold running water. Put in a saucepan and add the coarsely chopped onion, the garlic, and plenty of cold water. Bring to the boil then simmer for about 45 minutes, until very tender.

2 Drain the split peas, reserving a little of the cooking liquid, and put in a food processor. Add 5 tablespoons of the olive oil and blend until smooth. If the mixture seems too dry, add enough of the reserved liquid to form a smooth, thick purée. Add the oregano and season with salt and pepper.

3 Turn the mixture into a serving bowl and sprinkle with the finely chopped onion and extra oregano if desired. Drizzle over the remaining olive oil. Serve warm or cold with pita bread.

chickpea and sesame dip
húmmous kai tachíni

This is a favorite dish found on most mezze tables. It has an earthy flavor and, although it can be bought, the flavor of the home-made variety is much better. It is improved if made with cooked dried, as opposed to canned, chickpeas. Fortunately it is simple to make, especially if prepared in a food processor.

SERVES 8

8 oz/225 g dried chickpeas, covered with water and soaked overnight
juice of 2 large lemons
²/₃ cup tahini paste
2 garlic cloves, crushed
4 tbsp extra virgin olive oil
small pinch of ground cumin
salt and pepper

to garnish
1 tsp paprika
chopped flat-leaf parsley

pita bread, to serve

1 Drain the chickpeas, put in a saucepan, and cover with cold water. Bring to the boil then simmer for about 2 hours, until very tender.

2 Drain the chickpeas, reserving a little of the liquid, and put in a food processor, reserving a few to garnish. Blend the chickpeas until smooth, gradually adding the lemon juice and enough reserved liquid to form a smooth, thick purée. Add the tahini paste, garlic, 3 tablespoons of the olive oil and the cumin and blend until smooth. Season with salt and pepper.

3 Turn the mixture into a shallow serving dish and chill in the fridge for 2-3 hours before serving. To serve, mix the reserved olive oil with the paprika and drizzle over the top of the dish. Sprinkle with the parsley and the reserved chickpeas. Accompany with warm pita bread.

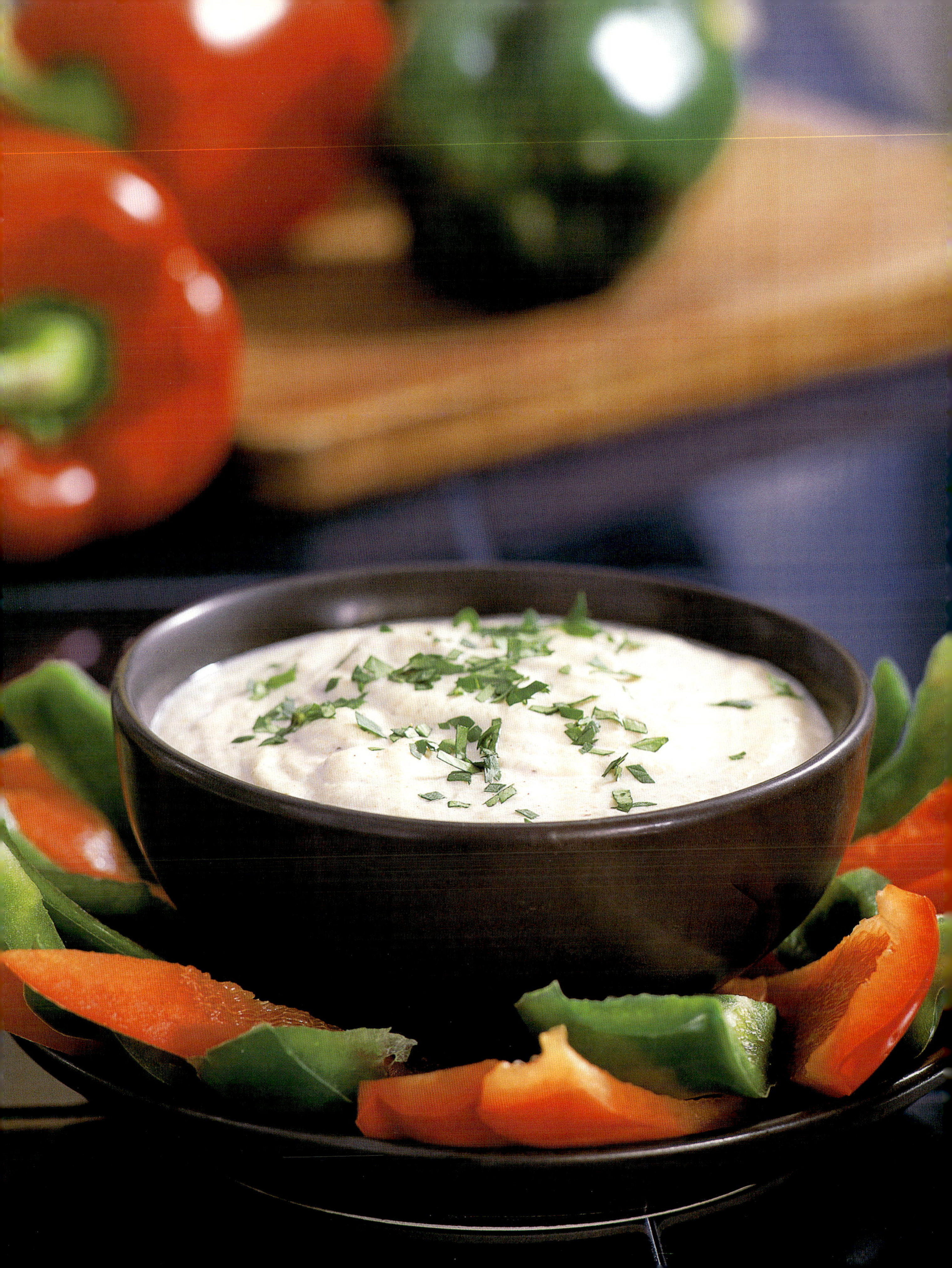

eggplant and garlic dip
melitzanosaláta

The eggplant is probably the Greeks' favorite vegetable. Apart from being a popular mezze dish, this dip also makes a good accompaniment to broiled meats.

SERVES 6

2 large eggplants
¼ cup extra virgin olive oil
juice of ½ lemon
⅔ cup authentic Greek yogurt
2 garlic cloves, crushed
pinch of ground cumin
salt and pepper
chopped fresh flat-leaf parsley, to garnish
strips of red and green bell pepper or sesame crackers, to serve

1 Prick the skins of the eggplants with a fork and put on a baking sheet. Bake in a preheated oven, 370°F/190°C, for 45 minutes, or until very soft. Leave to cool slightly then cut the eggplants in half lengthwise and scoop out the flesh.

2 Heat the oil in a large, heavy skillet, add the eggplant flesh and fry for 5 minutes. Put the eggplant mixture into a food processor, add the lemon juice, and blend until smooth. Gradually add the yogurt then the garlic and cumin. Season with salt and pepper.

3 Turn the mixture into a serving bowl and chill in the fridge for at least 1 hour. Garnish with chopped parsley and serve with raw bell pepper strips or sesame crackers.

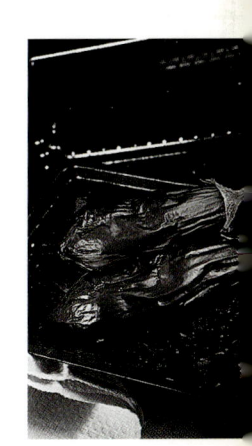

smoked red bell pepper dip
piperiá kapnistí

Jars of smoked red bell peppers can be bought in Greek food shops and larger supermarkets. They are delicious served as a mezze or can be quickly turned into a dip as shown here.

SERVES 6

4 large smoked red bell peppers and juice from the jar

3½ oz/100 g full-fat cream cheese

½ tsp lemon juice

salt and pepper

warm pita bread, to serve

1. Chop the bell peppers very finely and put in a bowl. Add the cheese, 1 tablespoon of juice from the jar of bell peppers, the lemon juice, salt and pepper and stir gently together until mixed. Chill in the fridge for at least 1 hour before serving.

2. To serve, stir the mixture and transfer to a serving bowl. Accompany with warm pita bread.

greek sausages
loukánika

These pork and beef sausages are seasoned with garlic, cinnamon, orange rind, and peppercorns, which gives them their unique flavor. They are served in Greece as a hot mezze. For ease of serving, they can be threaded onto wooden skewers, which have been soaked in water for 30 minutes, and then broiled.

MAKES ABOUT 24
12 oz/350 g minced pork
4 oz/115 g minced beef
1 garlic clove, crushed
½ tsp ground cinnamon
¼ tsp dried savory or thyme
grated rind of 1 small orange
8 black peppercorns, crushed
⅓ cup dry red wine
lemon wedges, to garnish

1 Put all the ingredients in a bowl and mix well together. Cover and let marinate in the fridge overnight or for about 12 hours.

2 Preheat the broiler. Stir the mixture and then, with damp hands, form the mixture into about 24 small sausage shapes, about 2 inches/5 cm long, and place on a broiler pan.

3 Broil the sausages for about 15 minutes, turning several times, until brown on all sides. Serve hot, with lemon wedges.

deep-fried squid
kalamarákia

This popular Greek mezze is best prepared with small squid, which are more tender than larger ones and are best stuffed and served whole.

SERVES 6
2 lb/900 g small cleaned squid
¾ cup all-purpose flour
sunflower oil, for deep-frying
salt and pepper
lemon wedges, to serve

1 Rinse and dry the squid. Slice the bodies into rings, leaving the tentacles whole. Season the flour with salt and pepper. Dip the pieces of squid in the flour, making sure they are well coated, then shake off any excess.

2 Heat the oil in a deep-fat fryer to 350°F/180°C or when a cube of bread, dropped into the fat, turns brown in 1 minute. When the oil is hot, add the squid in small batches and fry for about 1 minute, until crisp and golden. Remove from the fryer with a slotted spoon and drain on paper towels. Continue to cook the remaining squid in small batches. Sprinkle lightly with salt and serve hot, garnished with lemon wedges.

A fisherman with his nets in the sea port of Irákleio, Crete

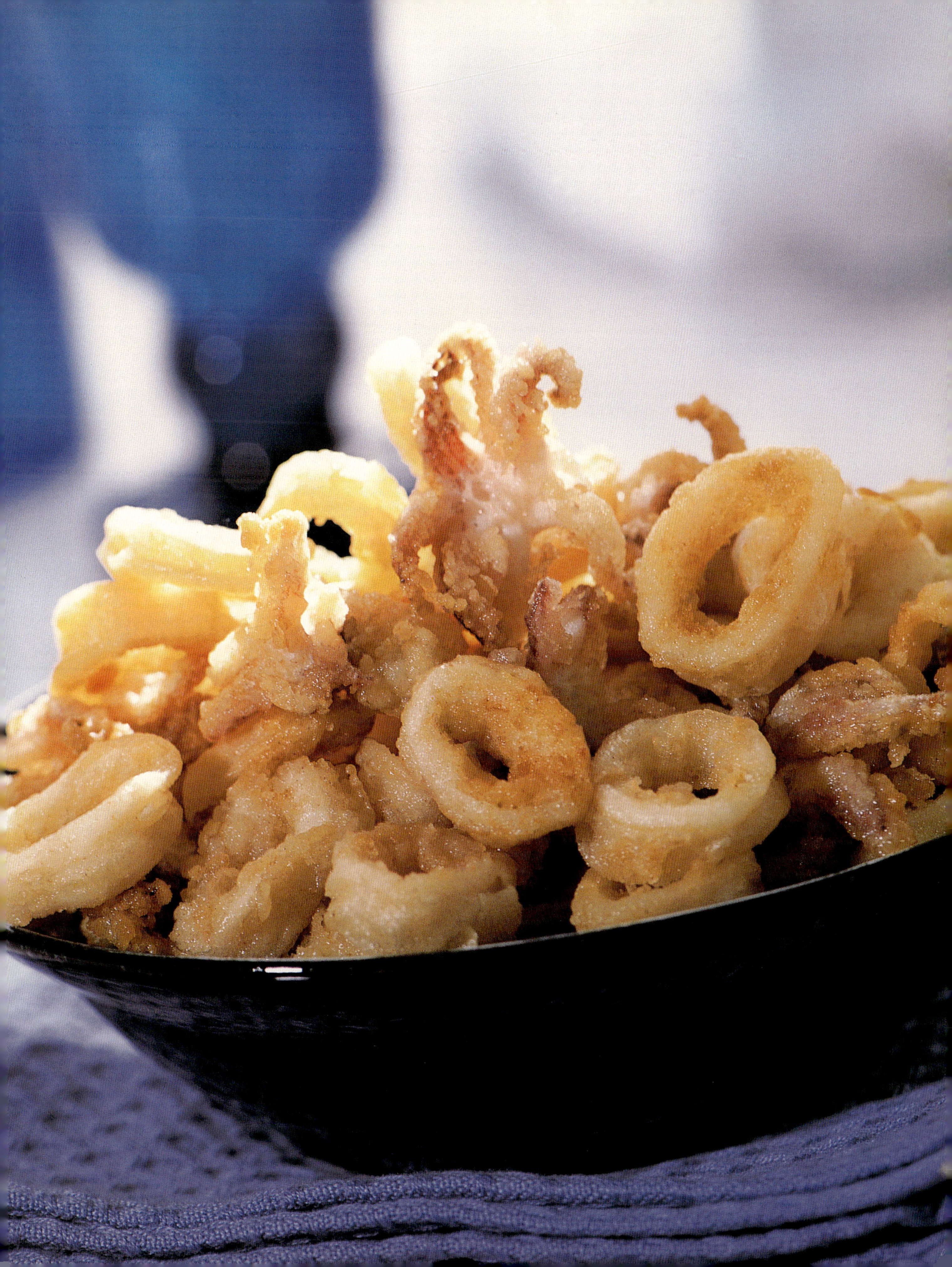

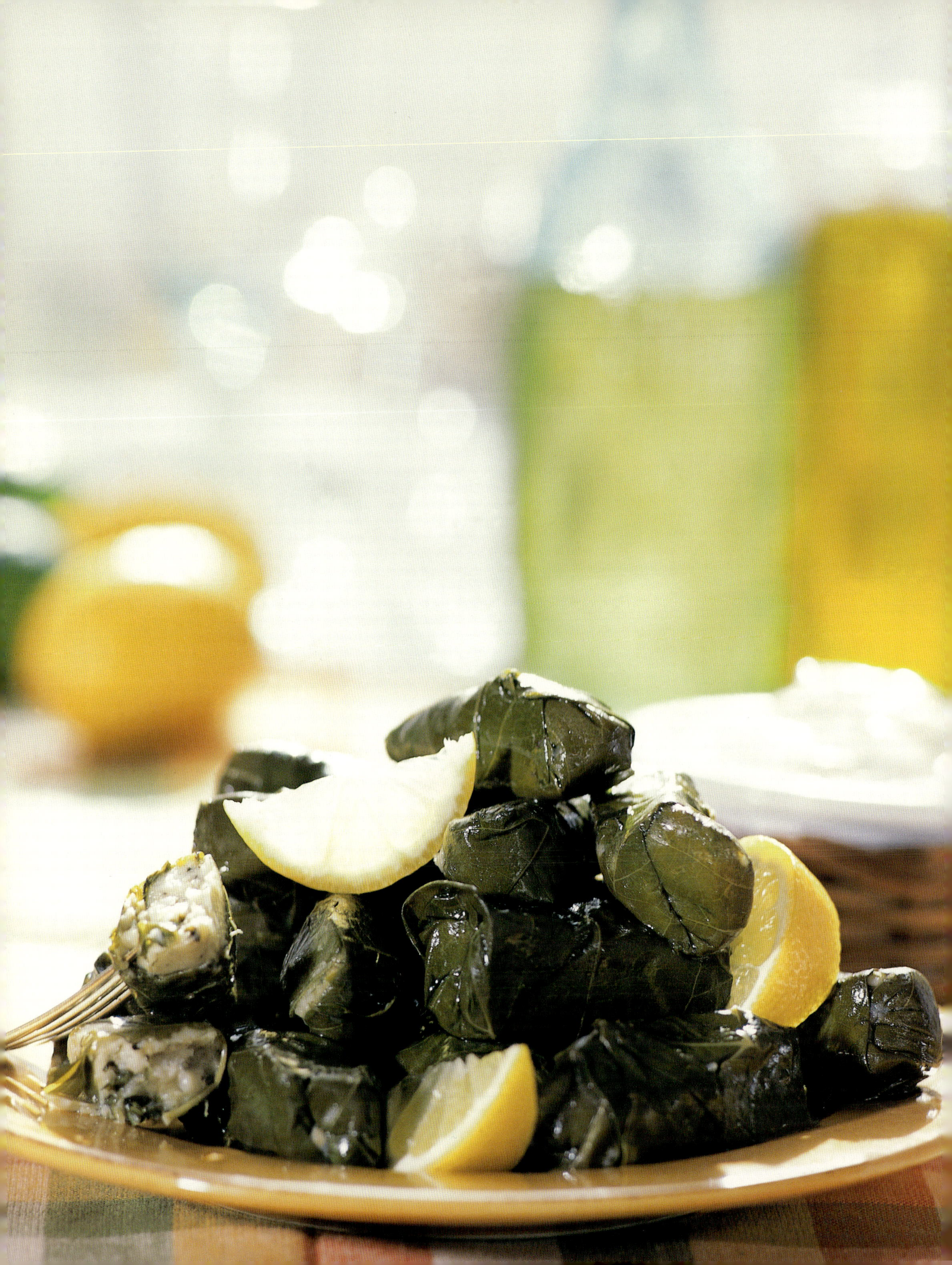

stuffed vine leaves
dolmádes

In Greece, vine leaves are picked when they are young and tender and used to wrap small packets of savory rice as well as whole fish. If you are able to pick fresh vine leaves, follow the instructions on page 113 for preparing them.

MAKES ABOUT 30

8-oz/225-g package vine leaves preserved in brine

²⁄₃ cup arborio or other short-grain rice

¾ cup olive oil

1 small onion, chopped finely

1 garlic clove, chopped finely

⅓ cup pine nuts, chopped

⅓ cup currants

3 scallions, chopped finely

1 tbsp chopped fresh mint

1 tbsp chopped fresh dill

2 tbsp chopped fresh flat-leaf parsley

juice of 1 lemon

pepper

to serve

lemon wedges

authentic Greek yogurt or Egg and Lemon Sauce (see page 155)

1. Place the vine leaves in a large bowl, pour over boiling water and leave to soak for 20 minutes. Drain, soak in cold water for 20 minutes, and then drain again.

2. Meanwhile, put the rice and a pinch of salt in a saucepan. Cover with cold water and bring to the boil, then simmer for 15-20 minutes, or as directed on the package, until tender. Drain well, put in a bowl and set aside to cool.

3. Heat 2 tablespoons of the oil in a large, heavy-bottomed skillet, add the onion and garlic and fry for 5-10 minutes until softened. Add the onions to the rice with the pine nuts, currants, scallions, mint, dill, and parsley. Season with a little salt and plenty of pepper and mix the ingredients well together.

4. Place 1 vine leaf, vein-side upwards, on a work surface. Put a little filling on the base of the leaf and fold up the bottom ends of the leaf. Fold the opposite sides of the leaf into the center then roll up the leaf around the filling. Squeeze the packet gently in your hand to seal. Continue filling and rolling the vine leaves until all the ingredients have been used up, putting any torn vine leaves in the bottom of a large flameproof casserole or Dutch oven. Put the stuffed leaves, seam-side down and in a single layer, in the casserole, packing them as close together as possible.

5. Mix the remaining oil and the lemon juice with ²⁄₃ cup water and pour into the casserole. Place a large plate over the vine leaves to keep them in place then cover the casserole with a lid. Bring to simmering point then simmer for 45 minutes.

6. Leave the vine leaves to cool in the liquid. Serve the vine leaves warm or chilled, with lemon wedges and yogurt or with Egg and Lemon Sauce.

hot cheese pastries
tirópites

These are the Greek version of the Turkish stuffed pastries known as bourekia *or* böreks. *They come in a variety of shapes, and are made with different pastry and fillings, such as minced meat, cream cheese, or spinach. In Greece these pastries are made with phyllo pastry and are traditionally filled with feta cheese.*

MAKES ABOUT 32

1 scant cup authentic Greek feta cheese
1/2 cup cottage cheese
3 tbsp chopped fresh flat-leaf parsley
2 eggs, beaten
pepper
8 sheets authentic Greek phyllo pastry
scant 1/2 cup olive oil

1. Crumble the feta cheese into a bowl. Add the cottage cheese, parsley, and eggs and beat with a fork until well blended. Season with pepper.

2. Cut the phyllo pastry, down the longest length, into 2 3/4-inch/7-cm strips. Take one strip and cover the remaining strips with a damp dish towel. Brush the strip with olive oil and put a heaping teaspoon of the cheese mixture on the bottom left-hand corner. Fold over the corner with the filling so that it meets the long side edge and forms a triangle. Continue folding the filling up and over from side to side to form a neat triangle. Place the pastry on an oiled baking sheet and brush with oil. Continue until all the pastry strips and the filling have been used.

3. Bake the pastries in a preheated oven, 375°F/190°C, for about 15 minutes until golden brown. Serve hot.

Modern urban areas sit side by side with traditional agriculture

Overleaf Greek women, dressed in traditional black, often sell handmade work outside their homes

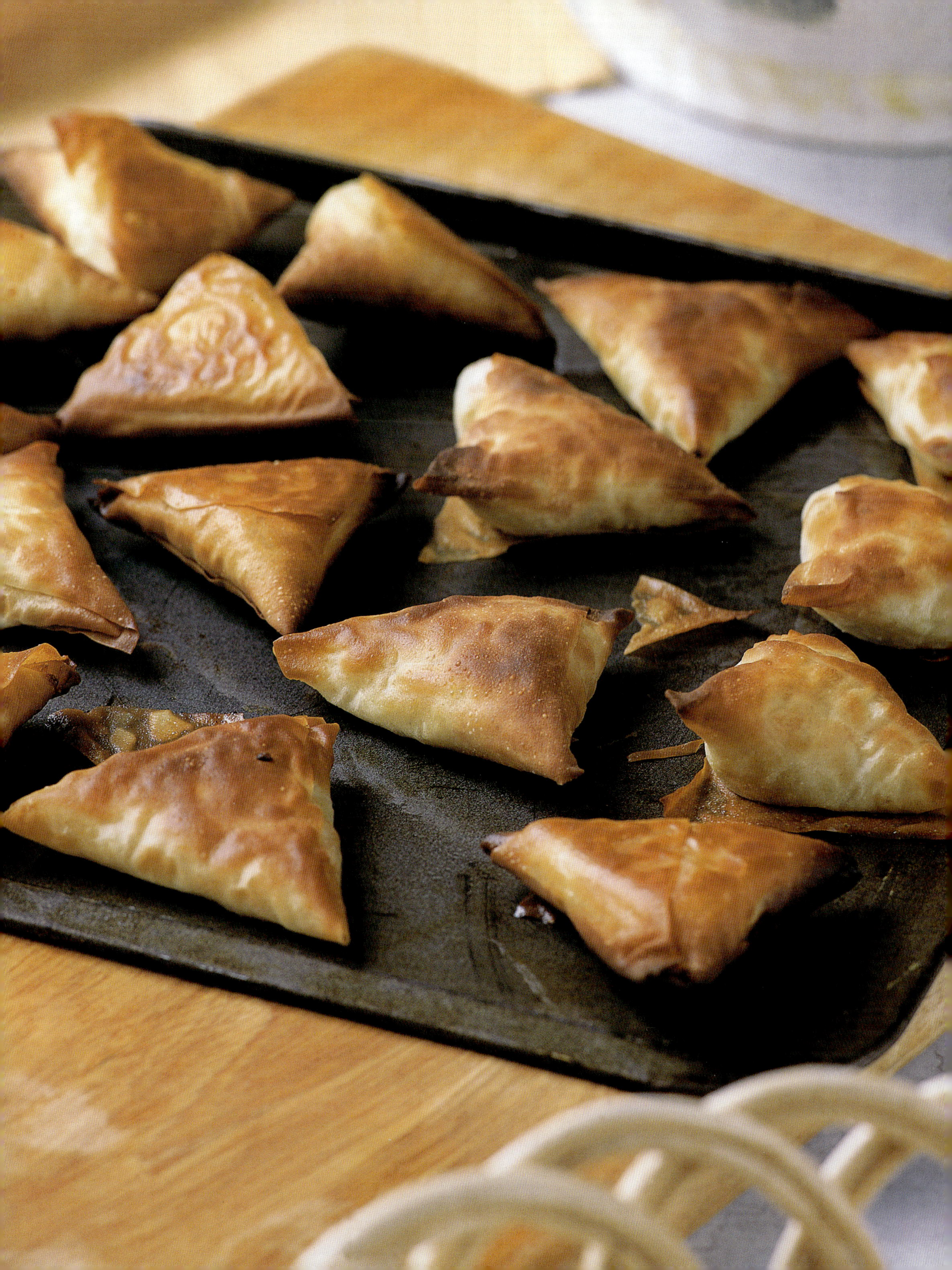

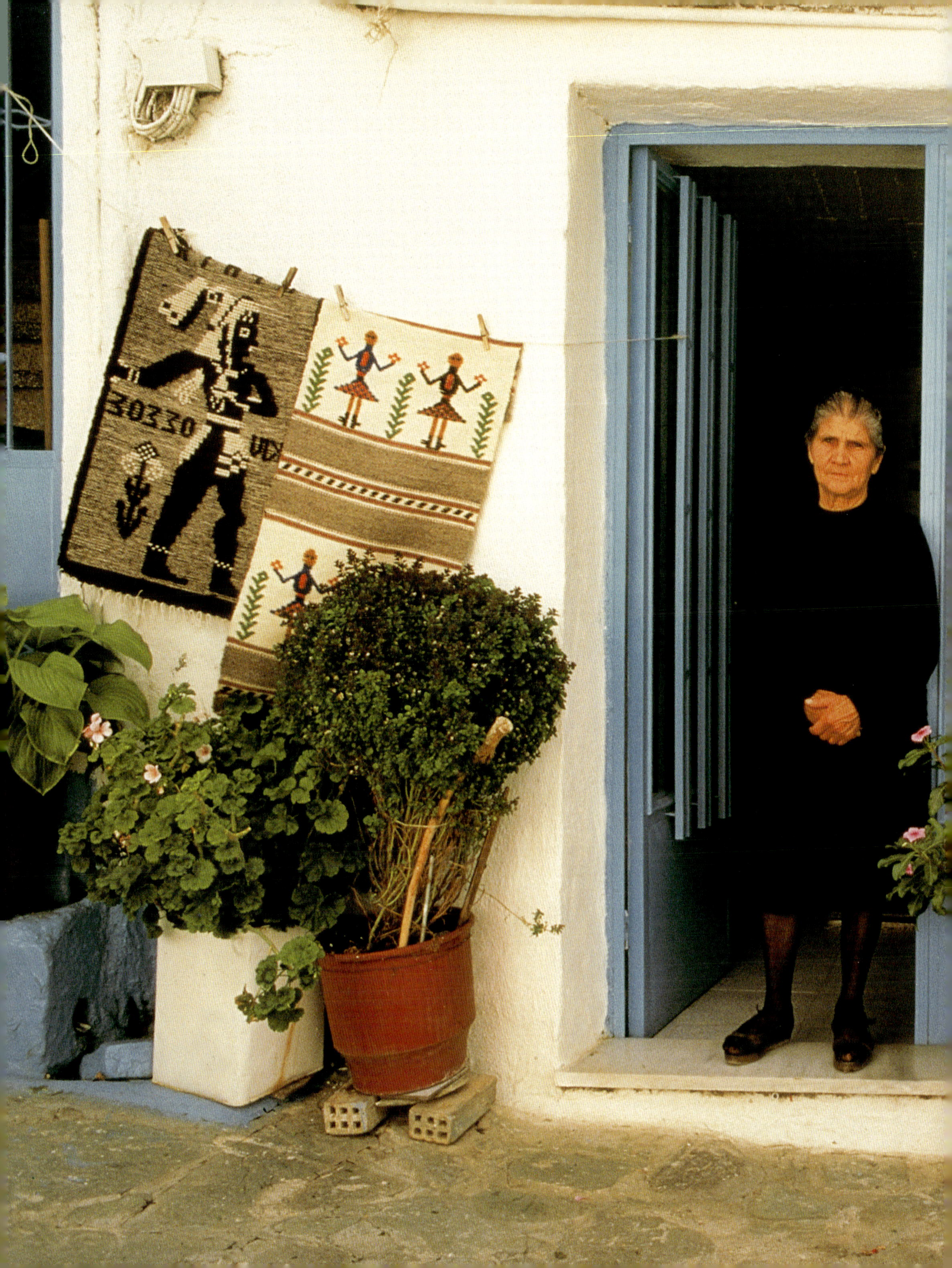

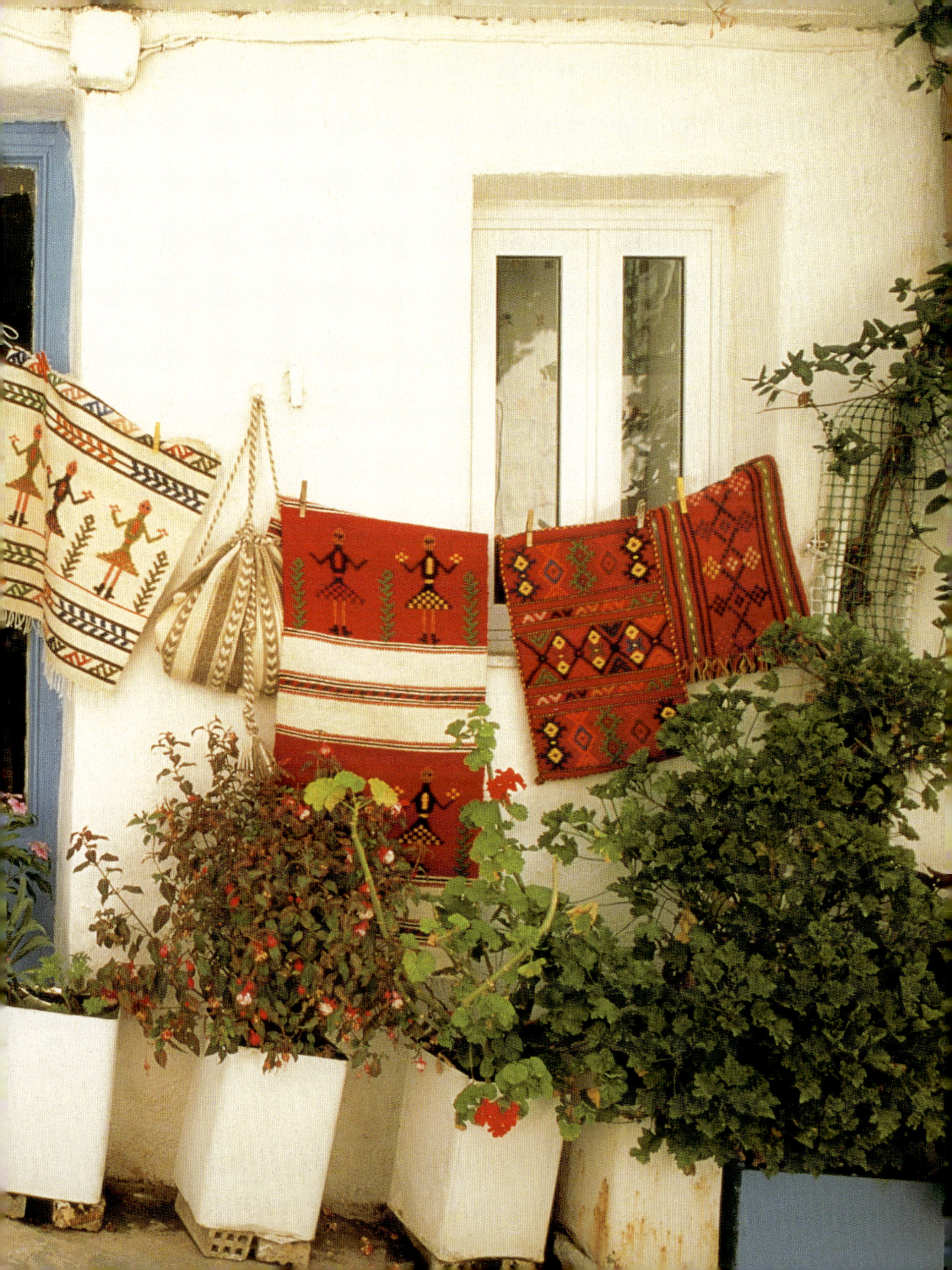

greek garlic sauce
skordaliá

Skordaliá *is Greece's classic garlic sauce. It goes very well with fried fish (see page 104), zucchini (see page 177), or boiled potatoes and beets. Alternatively it can be served as a dip with raw vegetables, as in this recipe.*

SERVES 6-8

4 oz/115 g whole blanched almonds
3 tbsp fresh white breadcrumbs
2 large garlic cloves, crushed
2 tsp lemon juice
salt and pepper
2/3 cup extra virgin olive oil
4 tbsp hot water

to serve

pita bread

raw vegetables such as bell peppers, cucumber, and carrots

1 Put the almonds in a food processor and process until finely ground. Add the breadcrumbs, garlic, lemon juice, salt, and pepper and mix well together.

2 With the machine running, very slowly pour in the oil to form a smooth, thick mixture. When all the oil has been added, blend in the water.

3 Turn the mixture into a serving bowl and chill in the fridge for at least 2 hours before serving with pita bread and raw vegetables.

yogurt and tomato soup
soúpa yaoúrti-domáta

This tastes divine yet is quick and simple to prepare. The Greeks seldom skin, seed, and chop their tomatoes—a time-consuming task. Instead they grate them, as in this recipe, and you will be amazed at just how easy this is to do. Serve the soup hot or chilled, depending on the weather.

SERVES 4

4 large tomatoes
2 tbsp olive oil
1 onion, chopped roughly
1 garlic clove, chopped
1¼ cups vegetable stock
2 oil-pack sun-dried tomatoes, chopped
1 tsp chopped fresh thyme
½ tsp ground cinnamon
1¼ cups authentic Greek yogurt
salt and pepper

1 Coarsely grate the tomatoes into a bowl, discarding their skins left in your hand. Heat the oil in a saucepan, add the onion and garlic and fry for 5 minutes until softened. Add the tomatoes and cook gently for a further 5 minutes.

2 Add the stock, sun-dried tomatoes, thyme, cinnamon, salt, and pepper, bring to the boil then simmer for 10 minutes.

3 Allow the soup to cool slightly then purée in a food processor, blender, or with a hand-held blender. Add the yogurt and mix. Season with salt and pepper.

4 If serving hot, reheat the soup gently. (Do not boil or the soup will curdle.) If serving cold, let cool and then chill in the fridge for 3–4 hours.

consommé with egg and lemon sauce
soúpa avgolémono

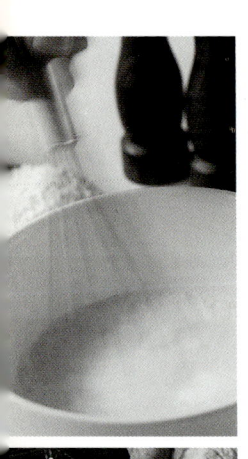

A classic Greek recipe, with a refreshing, tangy lemon flavor. Here it is made with chicken stock but you can use lamb, beef, or fish stock, and instead of the rice you can use orzo, a small form of pasta.

SERVES 4–6

6¼ cups chicken stock
¼ cup arborio or other short-grain rice
2 eggs
6 tbsp fresh lemon juice
salt and pepper

to garnish
4 thin lemon slices
finely chopped fresh flat-leaf parsley

1. Pour the stock into a large saucepan and bring to the boil. Add the rice, return to the boil, then simmer for 15-20 minutes, or according to instructions on the package, until tender.

2. Meanwhile, put the eggs and lemon juice in a bowl and whisk together until frothy.

3. When the rice is cooked, lower the heat and, whisking all the time, gradually add a ladleful of the stock to the lemon mixture. Pour the mixture into the soup and simmer, still whisking, until the soup thickens slightly. (Do not boil the mixture or it will curdle.) Season with salt and pepper.

4. Ladle the soup into individual serving bowls and garnish each with a lemon slice and chopped parsley. Serve hot.

The Greeks are justly proud of their ancient past, and active in preserving their heritage

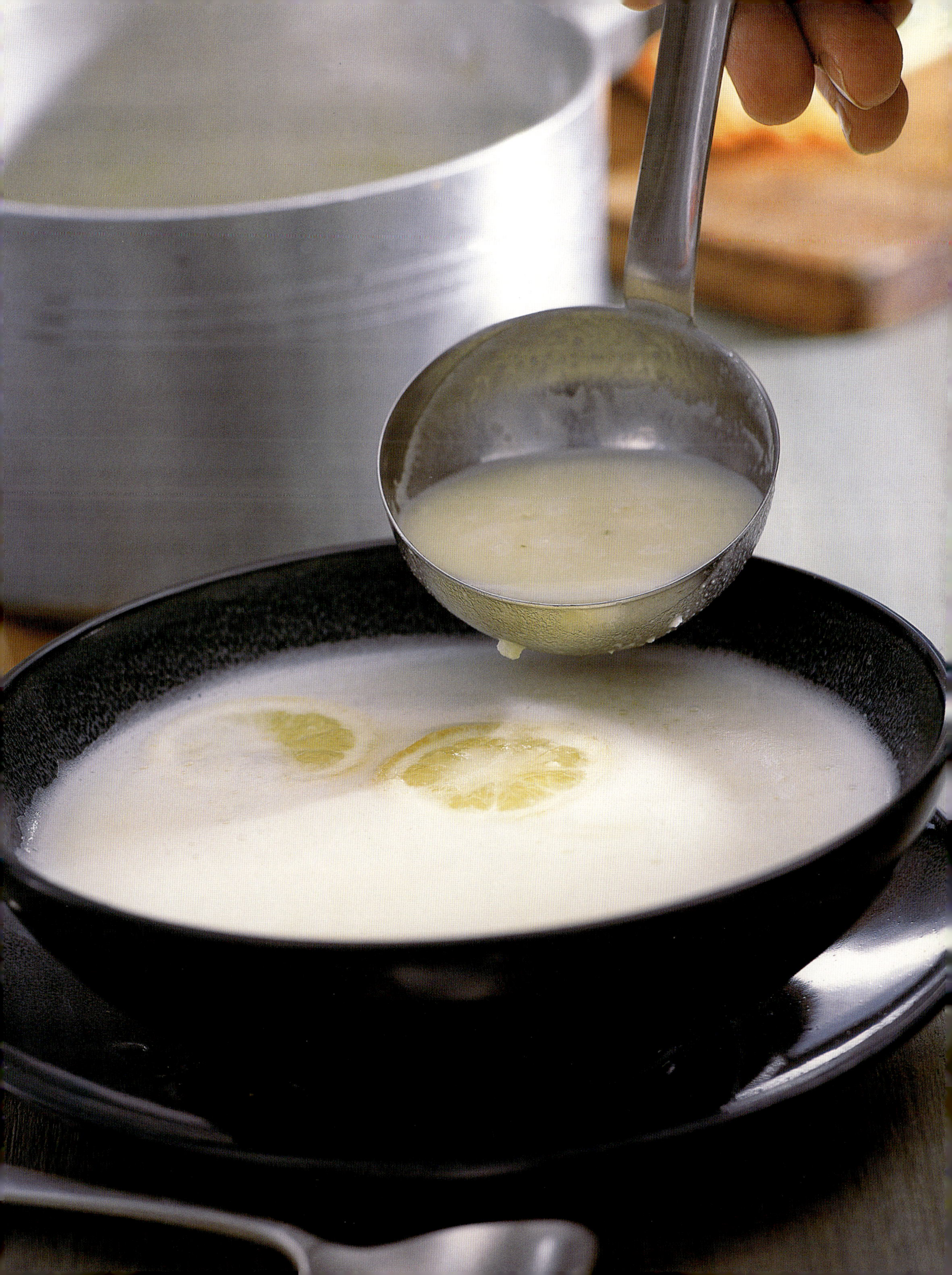

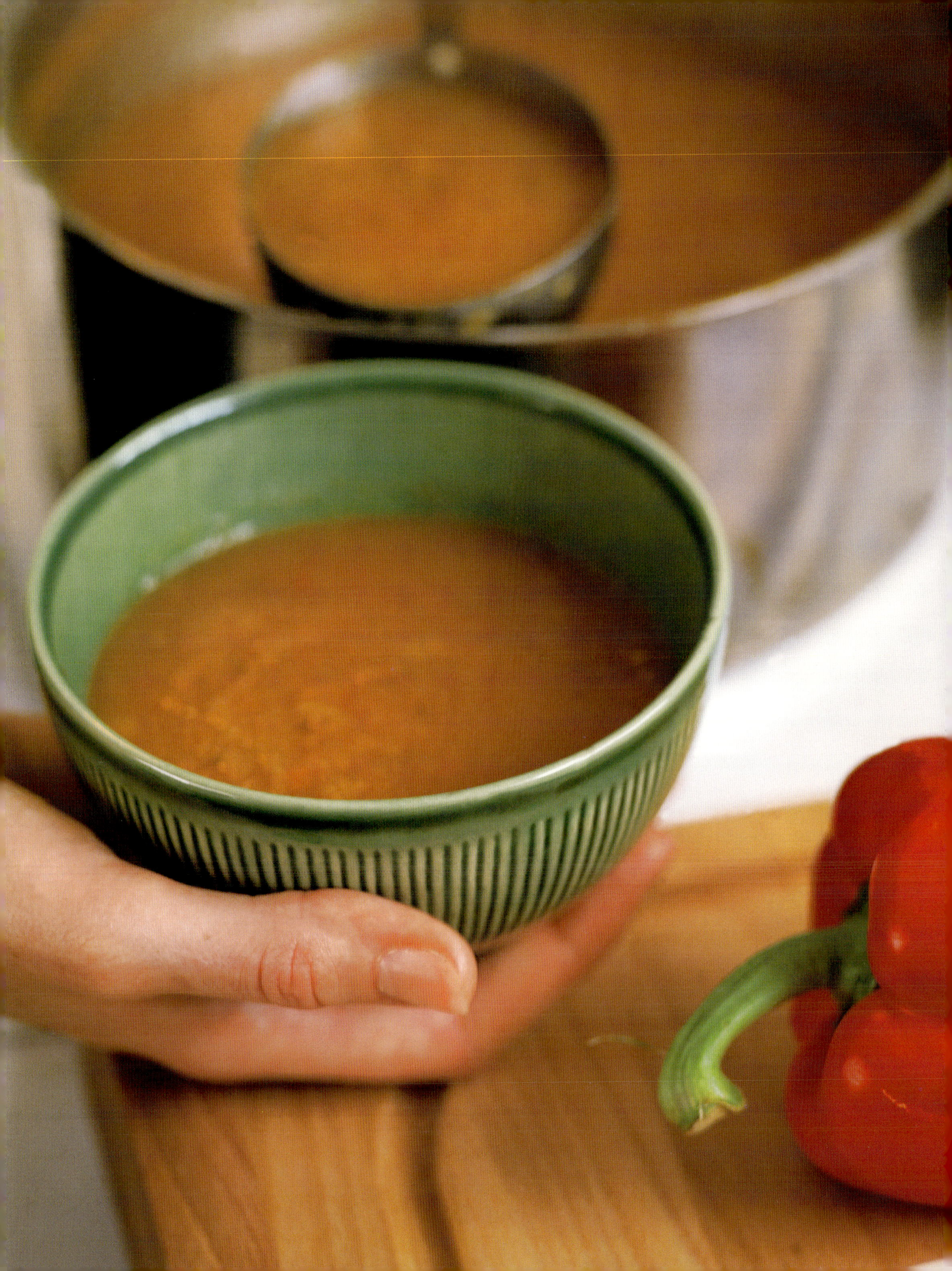

roasted vegetable soup
soúpa psitón lahanikón

Roasting vegetables really brings out their full flavor and if this soup is made the day before it is eaten, its flavor is further improved.

SERVES 6

2 eggplants

4 tomatoes

2 red bell peppers

2 onions, unpeeled

2 garlic cloves, unpeeled

4 tbsp olive oil

sprig fresh oregano

salt and pepper

7 cups chicken or vegetable stock

fresh basil leaves or chopped fresh parsley, to garnish

1 Prick the eggplants several times with a fork and put in a roasting pan. Add the tomatoes, bell peppers, unpeeled onions, and garlic. Sprinkle with 2 tablespoons of the olive oil. Roast in a preheated oven, 350°F/180°C, for 30 minutes then remove the tomatoes. Roast the eggplants, bell peppers, onions, and garlic for a further 30 minutes, until very soft and the bell pepper skins have blackened.

2 Put the cooked roasted vegetables in a bowl, cover with a damp dish towel and let cool for 3–4 hours or overnight, until cold. When cold, cut the eggplants in half, scoop out the flesh, and put in the bowl. Remove the skin from the tomatoes, cut in half, and discard the seeds and add the flesh to the bowl. Hold the bell peppers over the bowl to collect the juices and peel off the skin. Remove the stem, core, and seeds and add the flesh to the bowl. Peel the onions, cut into quarters, and add to the bowl. Squeeze the garlic cloves out of their skins into the bowl.

3 Heat the remaining olive oil in a large saucepan, add the vegetables and their juices, the leaves from the oregano, salt and pepper and cook gently for about 30 minutes, stirring frequently. Add the stock to the saucepan, bring to the boil, then simmer for 30 minutes.

4 Allow the soup to cool slightly then purée in a food processor, blender, or with a hand-held blender. If necessary, return the soup to the saucepan and reheat. Serve hot, garnished with basil leaves or chopped parsley.

bean and vegetable soup
fasoláda

This rustic soup is a national dish of Greece.

SERVES 4

8 oz/225 g dried Great Northern or cannellini beans, covered with water and soaked overnight

3¾ cups water

2 onions, chopped coarsely

2 garlic cloves, chopped

2 carrots, chopped coarsely

2 celery stalks, sliced thinly

3 tbsp olive oil

2 tsp chopped fresh thyme

1 bay leaf

pinch of sugar

14 oz/400 g canned tomatoes in juice

salt and pepper

2 oz/55 g Greek black olives, pitted and chopped

2 tbsp chopped fresh flat-leaf parsley

1. Drain the soaked beans, rinse under cold water then put in a large saucepan. Add the water, bring to the boil, and boil for 10 minutes. Reduce the heat, cover the saucepan, and simmer for 30 minutes.

2. Add the onions, garlic, carrots, celery, oil, thyme, bay leaf, sugar, and the tomatoes with their juice, breaking them up with a fork. Season with pepper. (Do not add salt at this stage as it will make the beans tough.) Return to simmering point, cover the saucepan again, and simmer for 45 minutes–1 hour, until the beans are tender.

3. Season the soup with salt and pepper and serve hot, sprinkled with the chopped olives and the parsley.

chilled cucumber soup
angourósoupa

This soup is not dissimilar to the traditional mezze dish of Tzatziki, Cucumber and Yogurt Dip (see page 47), but it is thinned with chicken stock and has the unusual addition of walnuts. It is a refreshing soup on a hot day.

SERVES 4

2 medium cucumbers
1¼ cups authentic Greek yogurt
1¼ cups chicken stock
2 tbsp walnut oil
1 large garlic clove, crushed
3 tbsp chopped fresh dill
salt and pepper
1 cup walnut pieces, chopped

1 Peel the cucumbers and chop the flesh into small dice. Beat the yogurt with the chicken stock, the walnut oil, garlic, and dill, reserving a little to garnish. Stir in the chopped cucumber and season with salt and pepper.

2 Chill the soup in the fridge for at least 4 hours. Stir in the chopped walnuts and serve garnished with the reserved chopped dill.

fishermen's soup
soúpa tou psará

SERVES 6

2 lb/900 g fillets of mixed white fish and shellfish, such as cod, flounder, halibut, monkfish, sea bass, whiting, and peeled shrimp

²/₃ cup olive oil

2 large onions, sliced

2 celery stalks, sliced thinly

2 garlic cloves, chopped

²/₃ cup white wine

4 canned tomatoes, chopped

pared rind of 1 orange

1 tsp chopped fresh thyme

2 tbsp chopped fresh parsley

2 bay leaves

salt and pepper

lemon wedges, to serve

croûtons, to garnish

Greek fishermen would make this soup with whatever fish they had caught that day and would then cook their freshly caught fish in a three-legged earthenware pot, called a kaccavi, *hence the soup is also referred to as* Kaccaviá.

1 Cut the fish into fairly large, thick, serving portions, discarding any skin. Heat the oil in a large saucepan, add the onion, celery, and garlic and fry for 5 minutes, until softened.

2 Add the fish and shrimp to the saucepan then add the wine, tomatoes, pared orange rind, thyme, parsley, bay leaves, salt and pepper, and enough cold water to cover. Bring to the boil then simmer, uncovered, for 15 minutes.

3 Serve the soup hot, with lemon wedges, and garnished with croûtons.

The Aegean Sea provides many Greek fishing families with their livelihood

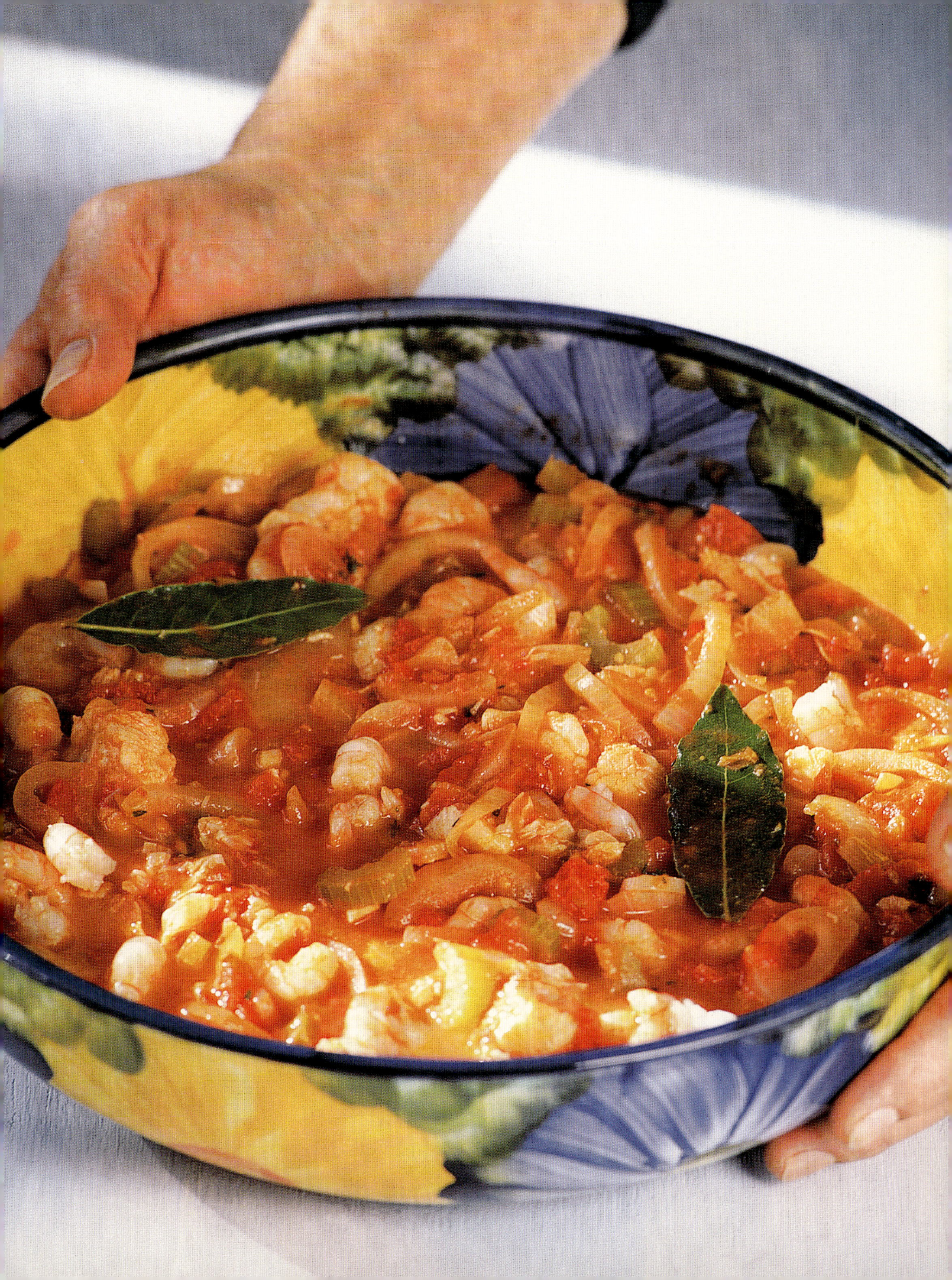

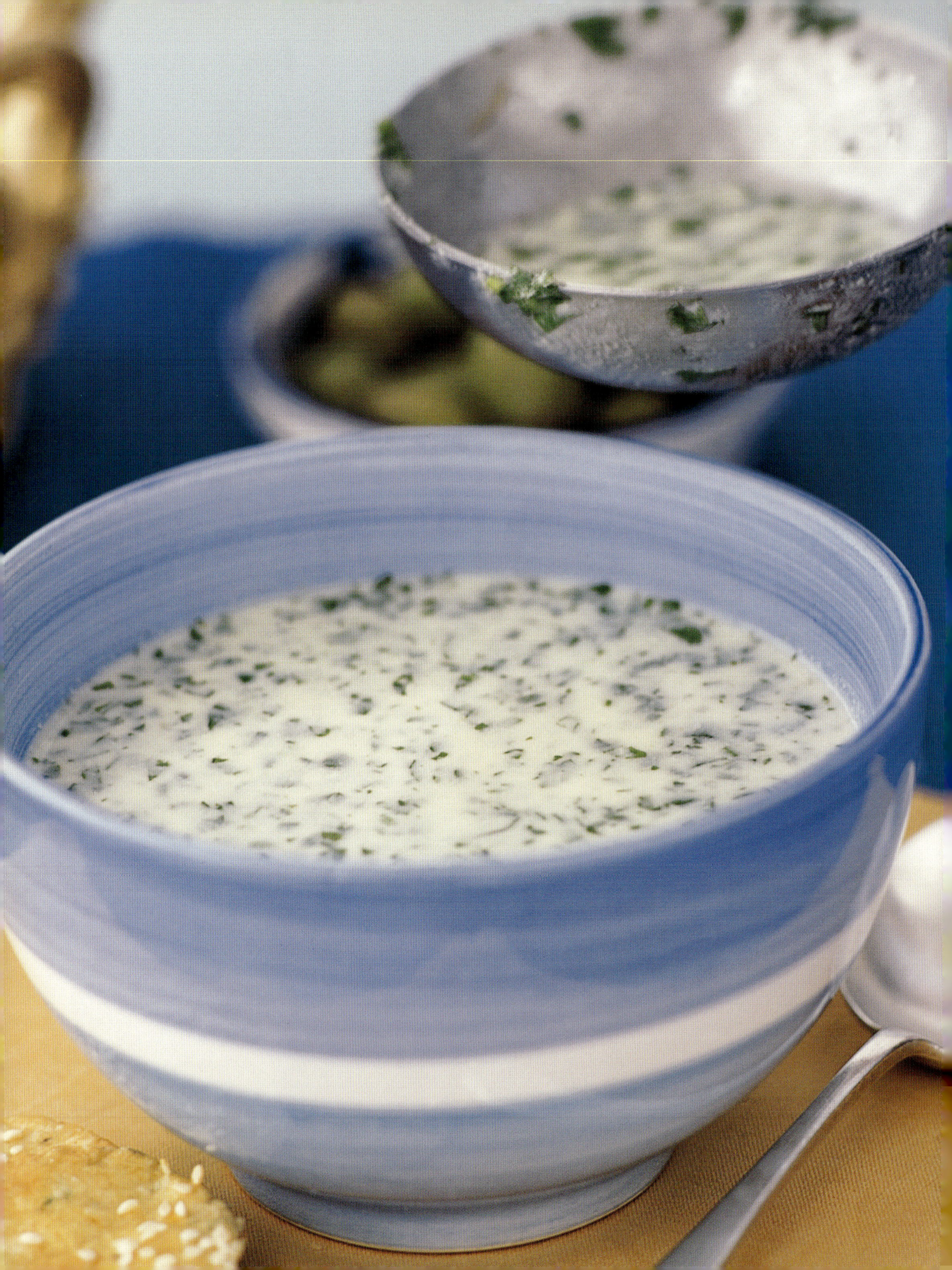

fresh herb soup
soúpa me freska mirodiká

Since herbs are used in great profusion in Greek cooking, a fresh herb soup seems a natural choice. This recipe uses cilantro but parsley could be equally successful.

SERVES 4

large bunch fresh cilantro
2½ cups chicken or vegetable stock
1 small onion, chopped coarsely
1 large garlic clove, chopped finely
finely grated rind and juice of 1 small lemon
salt and pepper
1¼ cups authentic Greek yogurt

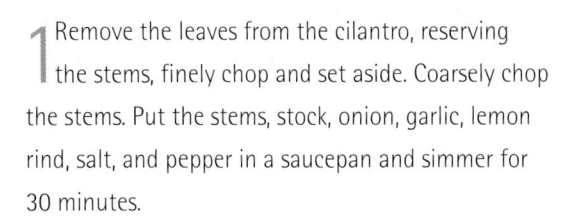

1 Remove the leaves from the cilantro, reserving the stems, finely chop and set aside. Coarsely chop the stems. Put the stems, stock, onion, garlic, lemon rind, salt, and pepper in a saucepan and simmer for 30 minutes.

2 Strain the stock and return to the rinsed saucepan. Add the lemon juice and yogurt and simmer for 2–3 minutes, until hot. (Do not boil or the soup will curdle.) Add the reserved chopped cilantro and serve hot.

*cook's tip
For freshness, buy a bunch of cilantro with its roots on. To keep it fresh, cut off the roots, place the stalks in a jug of cold water, cover with a plastic bag, and store in the refrigerator.

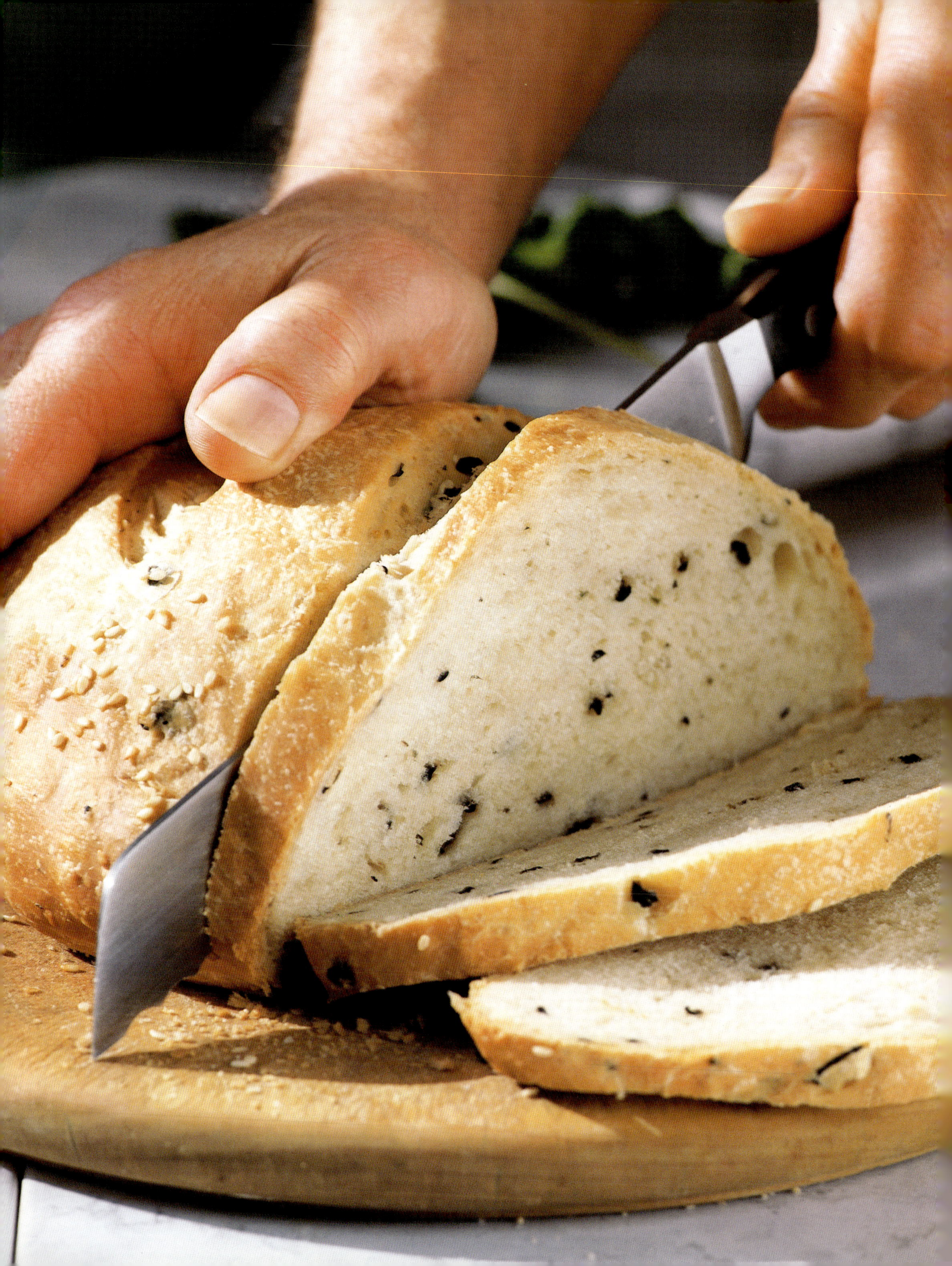

olive bread
eliótsomo

1. Put the flour, yeast, 2 teaspoons of the sesame seeds, the salt, and oregano in a large bowl and mix. Add 3 tablespoons of the olive oil and, using a wooden spoon, gradually add the water to form a firm dough.

2. Turn the dough onto a lightly floured work surface and knead for 10 minutes, until smooth. Put the dough in a clean bowl, cover with a clean, damp dish towel and let rise in a warm place for about 1 hour, until doubled in size.

3. Turn onto a lightly floured surface and knead lightly to knock out the air then knead in the olives. Divide the dough into 2 pieces and shape each piece into a smooth round. Place on a lightly oiled baking sheet, cover with a clean dish towel and set in a warm place for about 30 minutes, until doubled in size.

4. Using a sharp knife, make slashes across the top of each loaf then lightly brush with olive oil and sprinkle the remaining sesame seeds on top. Bake in a preheated oven, 425°/220°C, for 10 minutes then reduce the temperature to 375°F/190°C and bake for a further 25 minutes or until risen and brown and the bread sounds hollow when tapped on the bottom. Cool on a wire rack.

Olive trees grow in profusion in the dry, rocky terrain of Greece and olives and olive oil feature in every kind of dish. Here they are added to a bread dough which is served in small slices with mezzes. It is also an ideal bread to accompany soups. Choose either black or green olives, according to your preference.

MAKES 2 MEDIUM LOAVES

2 lb/900 g strong white bread flour

1 envelope dried yeast

3 tsp sesame seeds

1 tsp salt

½ tsp dried oregano

3 tbsp olive oil, plus extra for brushing

2½ cups warm water

8 oz/225 g Greek olives, pitted and chopped coarsely

The ancient monuments and sites of Greece attract numerous visitors

sesame crackers
almirá me sousámi

Serve these delicious crackers on their own with drinks or use as a scoop to accompany mezze dips. They are also good served with soups.

MAKES ABOUT 30

2/3 cup plus 1 tbsp all-purpose flour
3 tbsp sesame seeds
finely grated rind of 1 lemon
2 tbsp chopped fresh thyme
1/2 tsp salt
freshly ground pepper
2 tbsp butter
3–4 tbsp cold water
1 small egg white

1 Put the flour, 2 tablespoons sesame seeds, the lemon rind, thyme, salt, and pepper in a bowl. Cut the butter into small pieces and rub into the mixture until it resembles fine breadcrumbs. Gradually stir in the water until the mixture forms a firm dough.

2 Turn the mixture onto a lightly floured surface and roll out thinly. Using a 2 1/4-inch/5.5-cm round cookie cutter, cut the dough into rounds and place on baking sheets.

3 Brush the crackers with the egg white and sprinkle with the remaining sesame seeds. Bake in the oven for 20–25 minutes, until lightly browned. Cool on a wire rack. Store the crackers in an airtight tin.

Old church, Amari valley, Crete

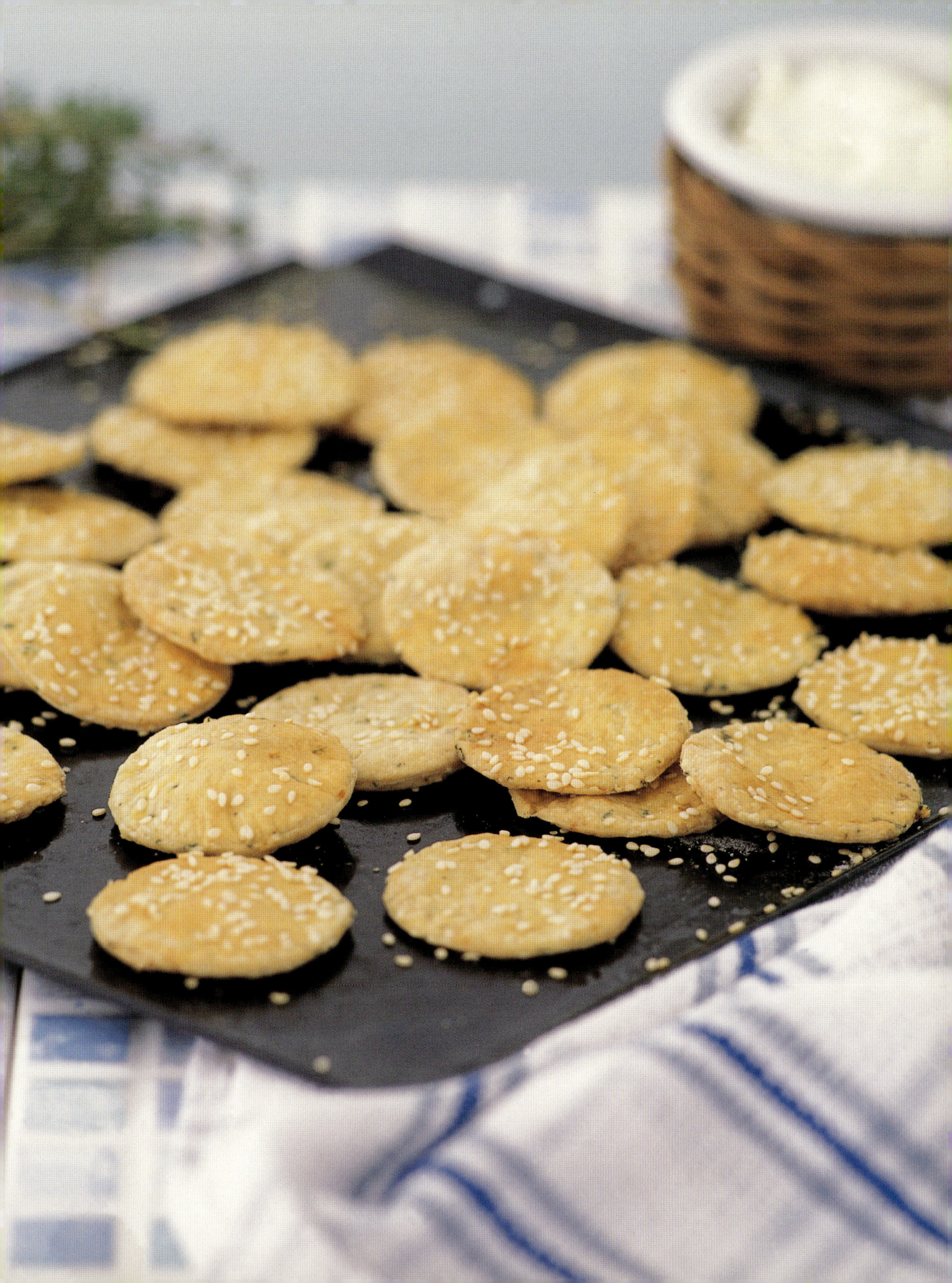

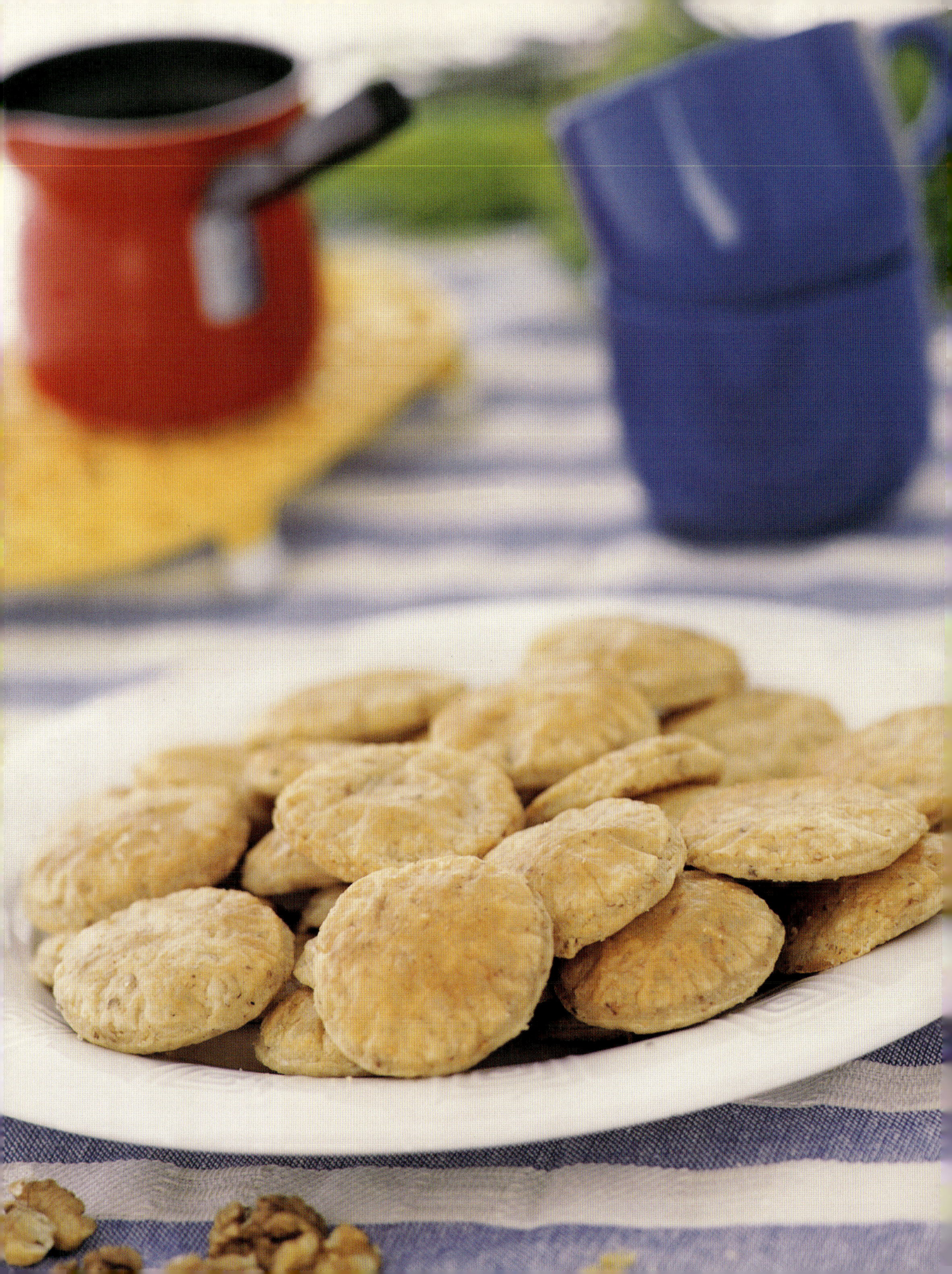

walnut cheese wafers
gufrétes me tirí kai karídia

These light, crisp wafers simply melt in the mouth and are irresistible. Serve them with a selection of mezzes.

MAKES ABOUT 38

¼ cup walnut pieces

¾ cup plus 1 tbsp all-purpose flour

salt and pepper

4 oz/115 g butter

½ cup authentic Greek Feta cheese

beaten egg, for glazing

1 Put the walnuts in a food processor and chop finely. Remove from the processor and set aside.

2 Add the flour, salt, and pepper to the processor bowl. Cut the butter into small pieces, add to the flour and mix in short bursts, until the mixture resembles fine breadcrumbs. Coarsely grate in the cheese, add the reserved walnuts and mix quickly to form a dough.

3 Turn the mixture onto a lightly floured surface and roll out thinly. Using a 2¼-inch/5.5-cm round cookie cutter, cut the dough into rounds and place on baking trays. Brush the tops with beaten egg.

4 Bake the wafers in a preheated oven, 375°F/190°C, for about 10 minutes, until golden. Cool on a wire rack. Store in an airtight tin.

variation

For the plainer cheese wafers, which really do melt in the mouth, just omit the walnuts.

A typical white-washed town nestled in an arid landscape

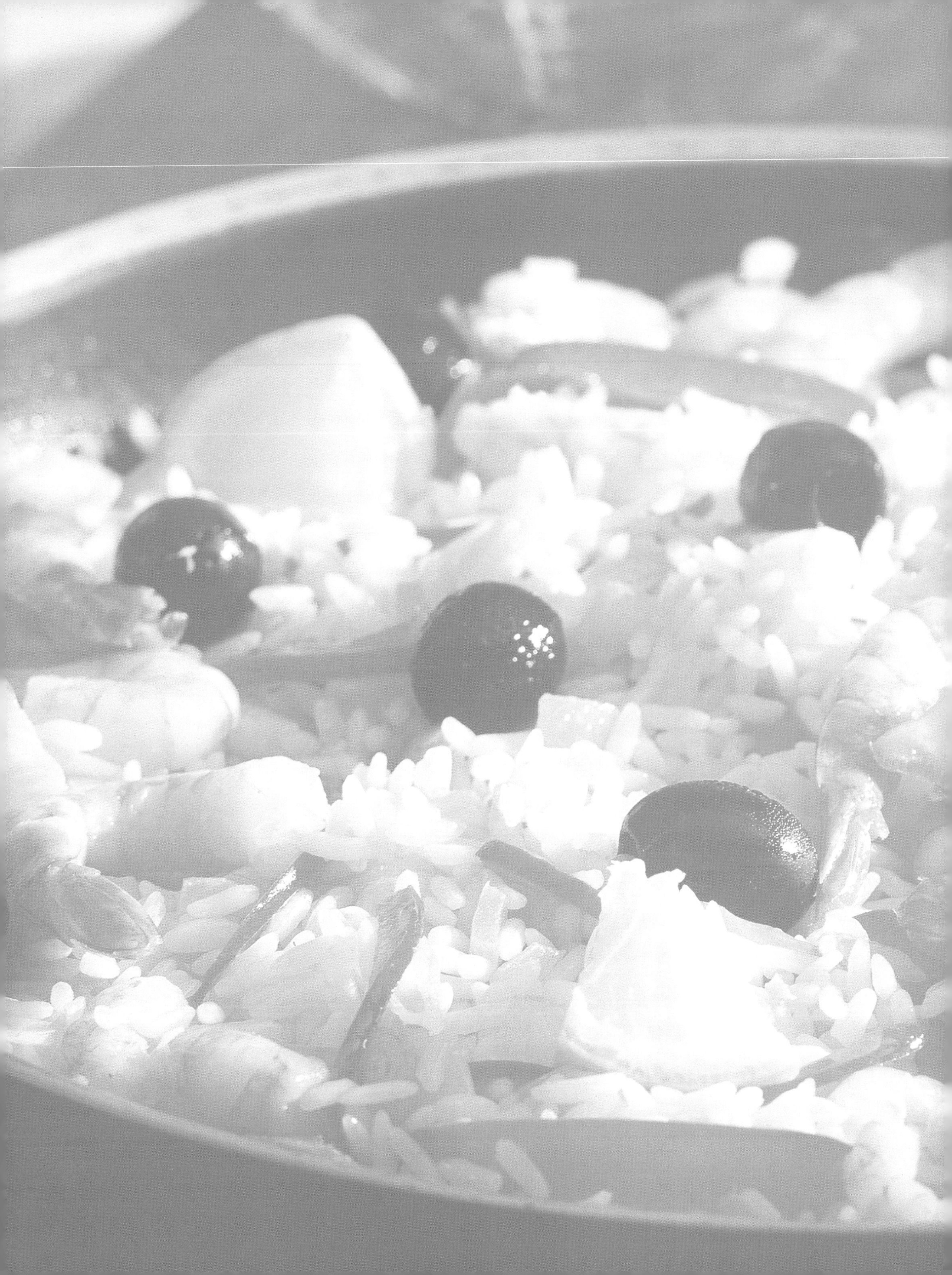

FISH DISHES

Mainland Greece lies along the Mediterranean coast and its islands give the country many more miles of coastline, so fish plays an important part in the cuisine. Fishing is a major industry: fresh fish and seafood are always available and fish products are widely consumed.

To many visitors to Greece, the picture of fishing vessels in the harbors and fishermen landing their catch on the beach is a memorable sight. However, as in other parts of the world, some species that were once caught in abundance have disappeared or are now seen more rarely. Nevertheless, fish such as sea bass, sea bream, red and gray mullet, anchovies, sardines, red snapper, halibut, trout, skate, bonito (a strongly flavored oily fish), swordfish, tuna, and eel, shellfish including lobsters, prawns, oysters, mussels, cockles, scallops, whelks, clams, sea urchins, and cephalopods including squid, octopus, and cuttlefish, are still fished in varying quantities off the shores of mainland Greece and its islands.

It is said that the oyster was first discovered by the Greeks but, oddly enough, today it is not a popular choice. On the other hand, squid, octopus, and cuttlefish are three of the most popular seafoods. These are considered to be a prize catch and are eaten enthusiastically in Greece. These cephalopods have a distinct head with a ring of tentacles around their mouth—the name cephalopod is derived from the Greek words for head and feet. Small squid can be deep-fried as in *Kalamarákia* (see page 56), medium-size ones can be stuffed and baked and large ones can be simmered in red wine for hours until tender. Octopus is popular marinated and then fried, simmered in wine, or broiled or barbecued—as in the recipe for Fresh Sardines Baked with Lemon and Oregano (see page 93). Large octopus must be tenderized and fishermen do this by pounding their catch against rocks. This is repeated by the cook who must pound it with a mallet, some say 99 times others say 40 times, before cooking. Cuttlefish is usually stuffed or cooked in a sauce with its ink sacs.

Left *Traditional fishing nets are still used by fishermen*

Opposite *A variety of fresh fish for sale in a market. Fish is a major part of the Greek staple diet*

fish dishes

Cuttlefish can also be fried in a little olive oil, spread on small pieces of bread, and served as a mezze. All three cephalopods have ink sacs and the ink is used in cooking to flavor, color, and thicken sauces. Most cuttlefish are net-caught these days and expel their ink as they are trying to escape from the net. If necessary, it is possible to buy small envelopes of both cuttlefish and squid ink from some good fishmongers.

Another seafood traditionally enjoyed by the Greeks but not necessarily to everyone's taste is sea urchins, specifically the female ones with their delicate coral. They must be pried off a rock with a fork, using gloves to protect the hands from their spike-covered shell. They are eaten raw, with lemon juice and garlic, poached or cooked in batter. Curiously, some salt cod is eaten in Greece although cod is not found in the Mediterranean (see the recipe for Fish Fritters on page 104, traditionally eaten in Greece on Twelfth Night). Most of the cod that is available in Greece comes from the Black Sea.

Although traditionally much fish is eaten in Greece because of its availability, there is another reason too. The religious festivals observed by the Greek Orthodox

the picture of fishing vessels and fishermen landing their catch on the beach is a memorable sight

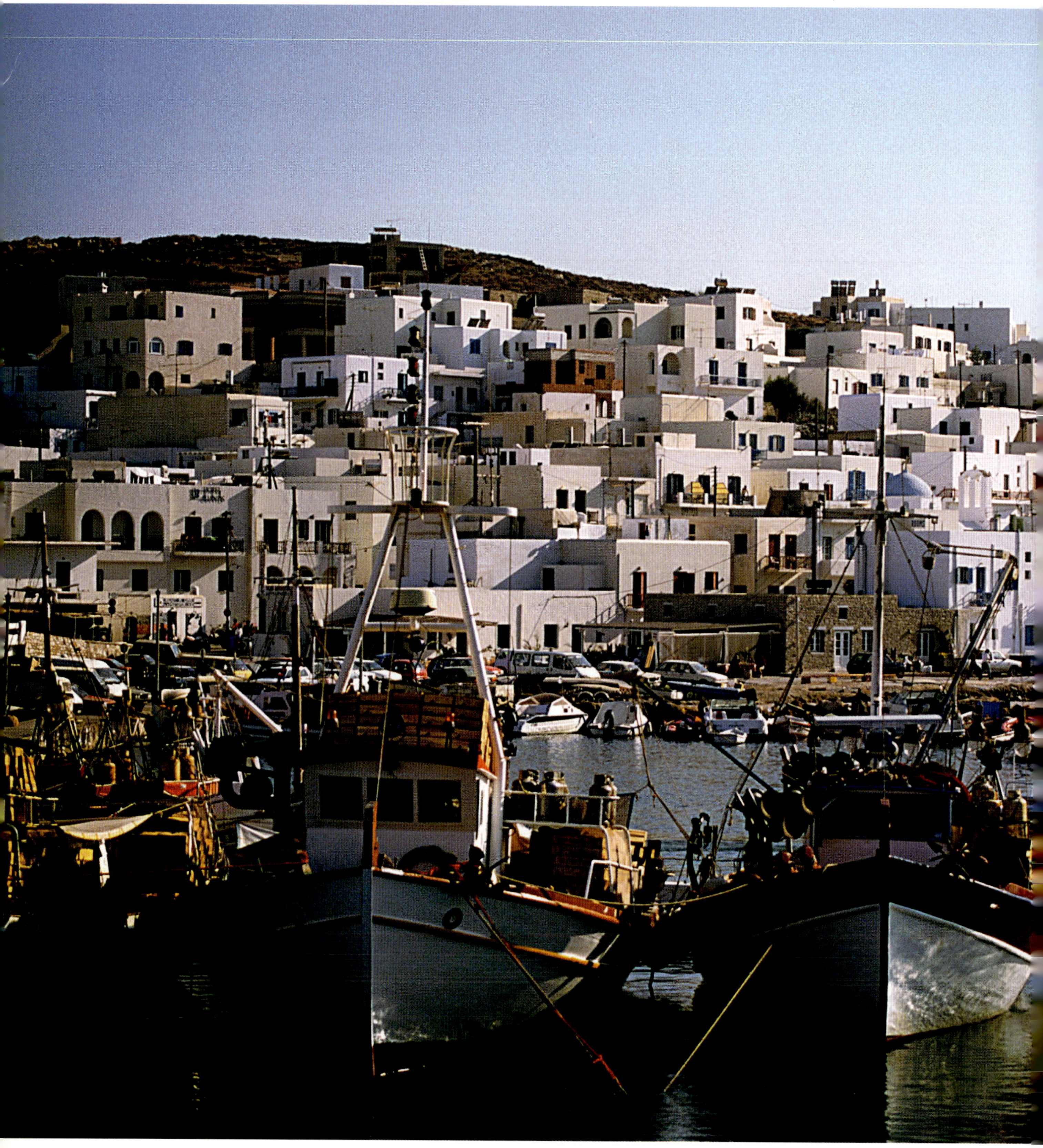

fish dishes

Church meant that meat, eggs, and dairy produce could not be eaten on certain days, and even today on the first day of Lent, in Greece known as Clean Monday, meat is not eaten and fish is the chosen dish.

In Greece, the most important consideration when serving fish is its freshness. In some fish restaurants the fish can be seen swimming in tanks and customers are invited to select the actual fish they want to eat. Shortly afterwards it is presented at table, cooked and served very simply. Apart from broiling, the most popular method of cooking fish in Greece is *plakí*, where the fish is baked or braised with vegetables. Fish is also barbecued, fried, wrapped in fresh vine leaves, marinated, served with a sauce, flavored with herbs or garlic, or simply flavored with the ubiquitous lemon. The Greeks seldom combine tomatoes with lemon juice but baked fish dishes are an exception as in the recipe for Roasted Fish from Spatsae Island (see page 96). Incidentally, this recipe also illustrates a method of baking fish in a tomato sauce with a topping of breadcrumbs or feta cheese to which the islanders have given their name. Fish in Greece is also always served with its head intact as this is considered to be the part of the fish with all the flavor. It is also usually served warm rather than hot, as with most Greek food.

Although some fish lend themselves to one particular preparation or method of cooking, or a specific flavoring, the majority of recipes can be used for a variety of different dishes and it is for this reason that many Greek recipe names are called *psári*, which simply means fish. The cook can use whatever fish is freshly landed that day. So, choose the freshest, loveliest-looking fish you can find, select a recipe, and go from there!

Left Fish and seafood in Greece are always freshly caught in their own waters and taken straight to local markets

Overleaf Crystal-clear water and a picturesque bay, Crete

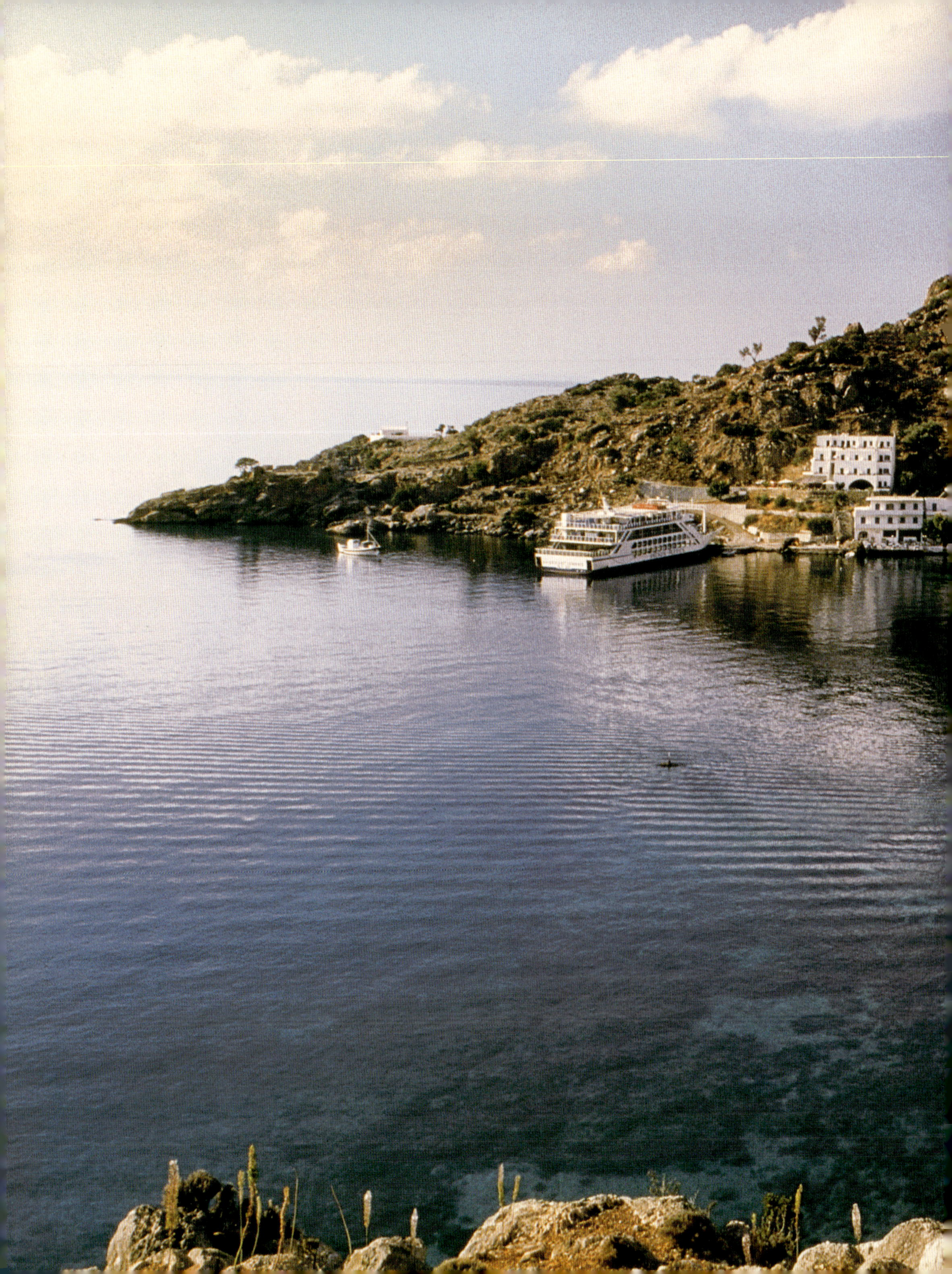

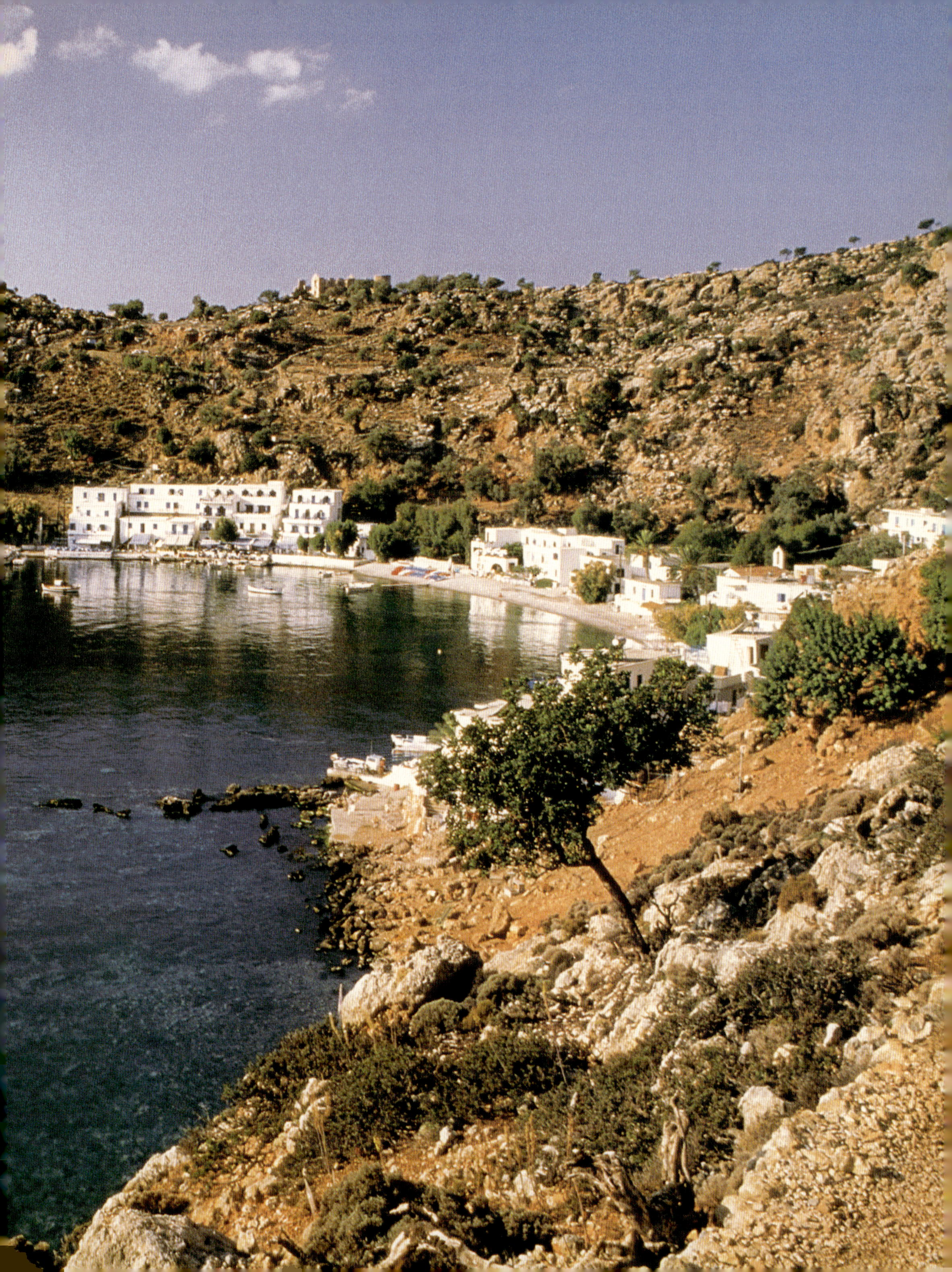

traditional greek baked fish
psári plakí

SERVES 4-6

5 tbsp olive oil

2 onions, sliced finely

2 garlic cloves, chopped finely

2 carrots, sliced thinly

2 celery stalks, sliced thinly

$^2/_3$ cup dry white wine

14 oz/400 g canned chopped tomatoes in juice

pinch of sugar

1 large lemon, sliced thinly

salt and pepper

2 tbsp chopped fresh flat-leaf parsley

1 tsp chopped fresh marjoram

2–3 lb/1–1.3 kg fat whole fish, such as sea bream, bass, tilapia, red snapper, red or gray mullet, scaled and gutted

The traditional way of baking fish in Greece is to cook it whole with tomatoes and lemons (which are eaten with the rind on), although both the Greeks and the Turks claim to have originated the method. A variety of fish can be cooked in this way so choose from the suggestions in the recipe. Serve with boiled new potatoes.

1. Heat 4 tablespoons of the oil in a large saucepan, add the onions and garlic, and fry for 5 minutes, until softened. Add the carrots and celery and fry for 5-10 minutes, until slightly softened.

2. Pour the wine into the saucepan and bring to the boil. Add the tomatoes and their juice, the sugar, lemon slices, salt, and pepper and simmer for 20 minutes. Add the parsley and marjoram.

3. Put the fish in a greased, shallow ovenproof dish. Pour the vegetables around the fish, arranging some of the lemon slices on top. Sprinkle with the remaining oil and season with salt and pepper.

4. Bake the fish, uncovered, in a preheated oven, 350°F/180°C, for 45 minutes–1 hour depending on the thickness of the fish, until tender. Serve immediately, straight from the oven.

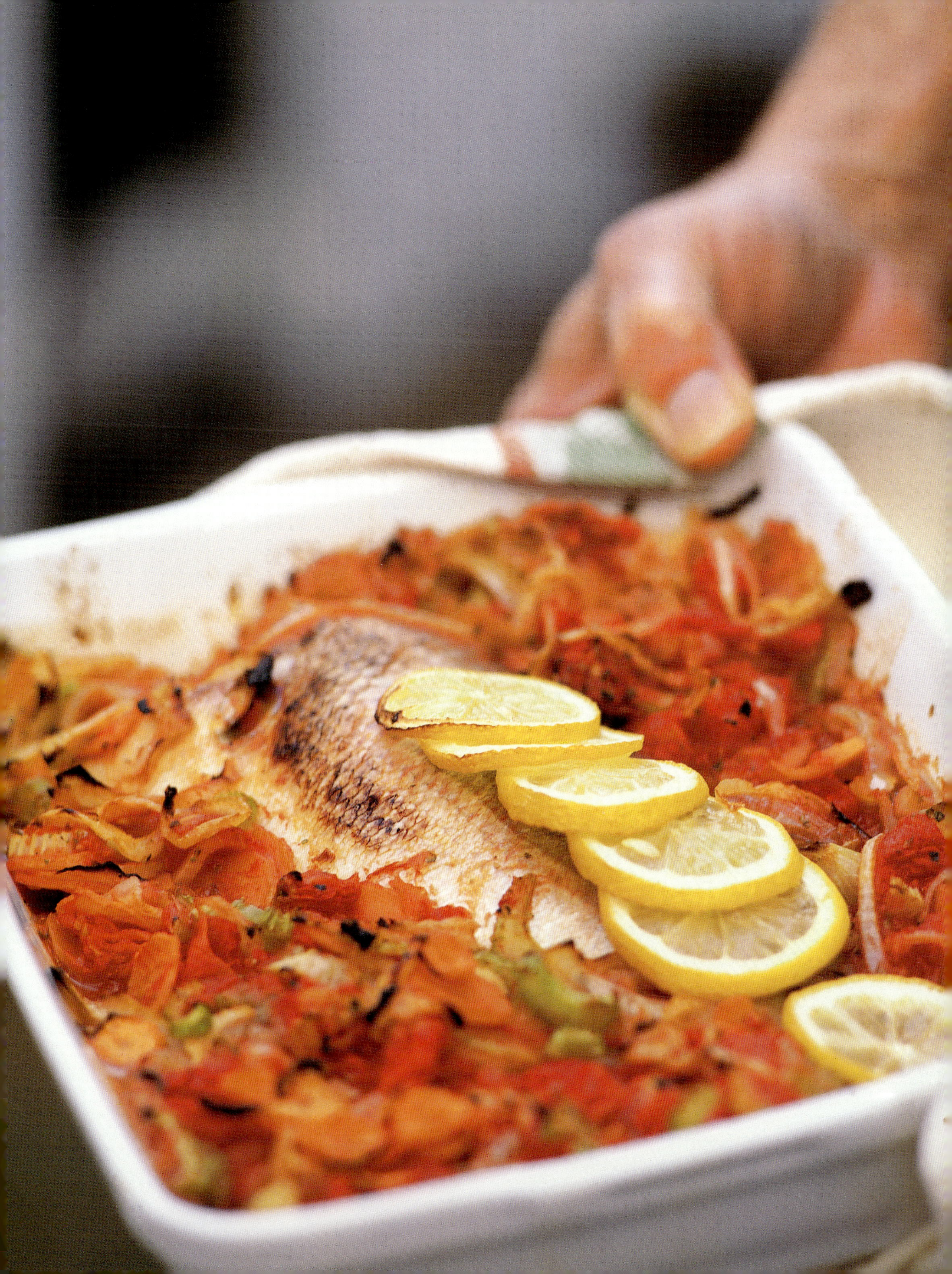

broiled red snapper with garlic
psári skordáto

Nothing could be simpler than this broiled fish dish with the true flavors of Greece. However, there are two golden rules. The first is to choose really fresh fish and the second is always to include an herb. Sprigs of the herb you choose can also be used as a brush for basting the fish and for imparting extra flavor, whether you're cooking in an oven or over a barbecue.

SERVES 4

2 tbsp lemon juice

4 tbsp olive oil

salt and pepper

4 red snapper or mullet, scaled and gutted

2 tbsp chopped fresh herbs such as oregano, marjoram, flat-leaf parsley, or thyme

to garnish

2 garlic cloves, chopped finely

2 tbsp chopped fresh flat-leaf parsley

lemon wedges

1 Preheat the broiler. Put the lemon juice, oil, salt, and pepper in a bowl and whisk together. Brush the mixture inside and on both sides of the fish and sprinkle on the chopped herb of your choice. Place on a greased broiler pan.

2 Broil the fish for about 10 minutes, basting frequently and turning once, until golden brown.

3 Meanwhile, mix together the chopped garlic and chopped parsley. Sprinkle the garlic mixture on top of the cooked fish and serve hot or cold.

fresh sardines baked with lemon and oregano
sardéles me rígani

If you wish, the sardines can be broiled, instead of baked: marinate them in the oil, lemon juice, and oregano then cook under a broiler or on a barbecue. In Greece, prepared octopus is often cooked in this way.

SERVES 4
2 lemons
12 large fresh sardines, gutted
4 tbsp olive oil
4 tbsp chopped fresh oregano
salt and pepper
lemon wedges, to garnish

1 Slice 1 of the lemons and grate and squeeze the juice from the second one.

2 Cut the heads off the sardines and place the fish in a shallow, ovenproof dish, large enough to hold them in a single layer. Place the lemon slices between the fish. Drizzle the lemon juice and oil over the fish. Sprinkle over the lemon rind and oregano and season with salt and pepper.

3 Bake in a preheated oven, 375°F/190°C, for 20–30 minutes, until the fish are tender. Serve garnished with lemon wedges.

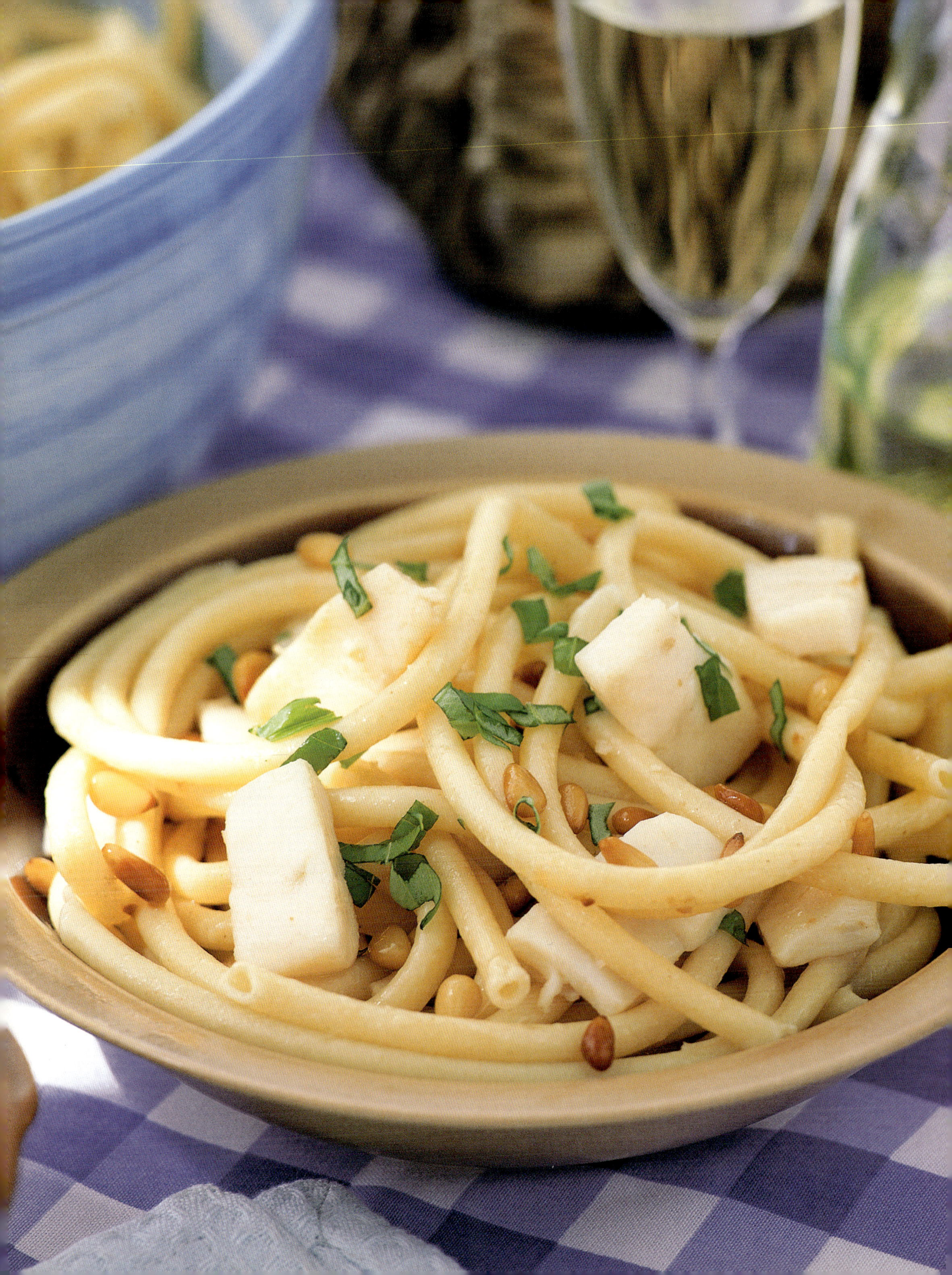

fish dishes

pasta with scallops and pine nuts
macarónia me thalasiná kai koukounária

The Greeks enjoy scallops, and none of their flavor is lost in this quick and simple dish.

SERVES 4

14 oz/400 g long, hollow Greek macaroni or other short pasta

4 tbsp olive oil

1 garlic clove, chopped finely

¼ cup pine nuts

8 large scallops, sliced

salt and pepper

2 tbsp chopped fresh basil leaves

1. Cook the macaroni in a large saucepan of boiling salted water for 10–12 minutes or as directed on the package, until tender.

2. About 5 minutes before the pasta is ready, heat the oil in a skillet. Add the garlic and fry for 1–2 minutes until softened but not browned. Add the pine nuts and cook until browned. Stir in the scallops and cook until just opaque. Season with salt and pepper.

3. When the pasta is cooked, drain and return to the saucepan. Add the scallops and the juices in the skillet to the pasta and toss together. Serve sprinkled with the chopped basil leaves.

The simplicity of a white church dome stands out against the deep blue of the sea and sky

roasted fish from spetsae island
psária spetsiótika

SERVE 4

2 tbsp olive oil

1 onion, chopped finely

2 garlic cloves, chopped finely

½ cup dry white wine

14 oz/400 g canned chopped tomatoes in juice

pinch of sugar

2 tbsp chopped fresh flat-leaf parsley

salt and pepper

4 fish fillets, each weighing about 6 oz/175 g, such as sea bass, brill, turbot, cod, monkfish, or tilapia

juice of ½ lemon

⅓ cup dry white breadcrumbs

chopped fresh flat-leaf parsley, to garnish

As the title suggests, this is a dish from the wooded island of Spetsae, one of the four Saronic islands south of Athens. It can be made with a variety of fish, steaks as well as fillets, which are covered in a tomato sauce and a golden breadcrumb topping.

1 Heat the oil in a skillet, add the onion and garlic and fry for 5 minutes, until golden. Add the wine, the tomatoes and their juice, sugar, parsley, salt, and pepper and bring to the boil then boil gently for about 30 minutes, until the sauce has thickened. If necessary, increase the heat to reduce the liquid.

2 Meanwhile, put the fish in a greased ovenproof dish. Sprinkle over the lemon juice and season with salt and pepper.

3 When the tomato sauce has thickened, spread the sauce over the fish fillets. Roast in a preheated oven, 325°F/170°C, uncovered, for 10–15 minutes, depending on the thickness of the fish.

4 Increase the oven temperature to 425°F/220°C. Sprinkle the breadcrumbs on top of the fish. Return to the oven and roast for a further 15 minutes, until the fish is tender and the top light golden brown and crisp. Serve hot, garnished with chopped parsley.

For many rural Greeks, the traditional lifestyle is unchanged

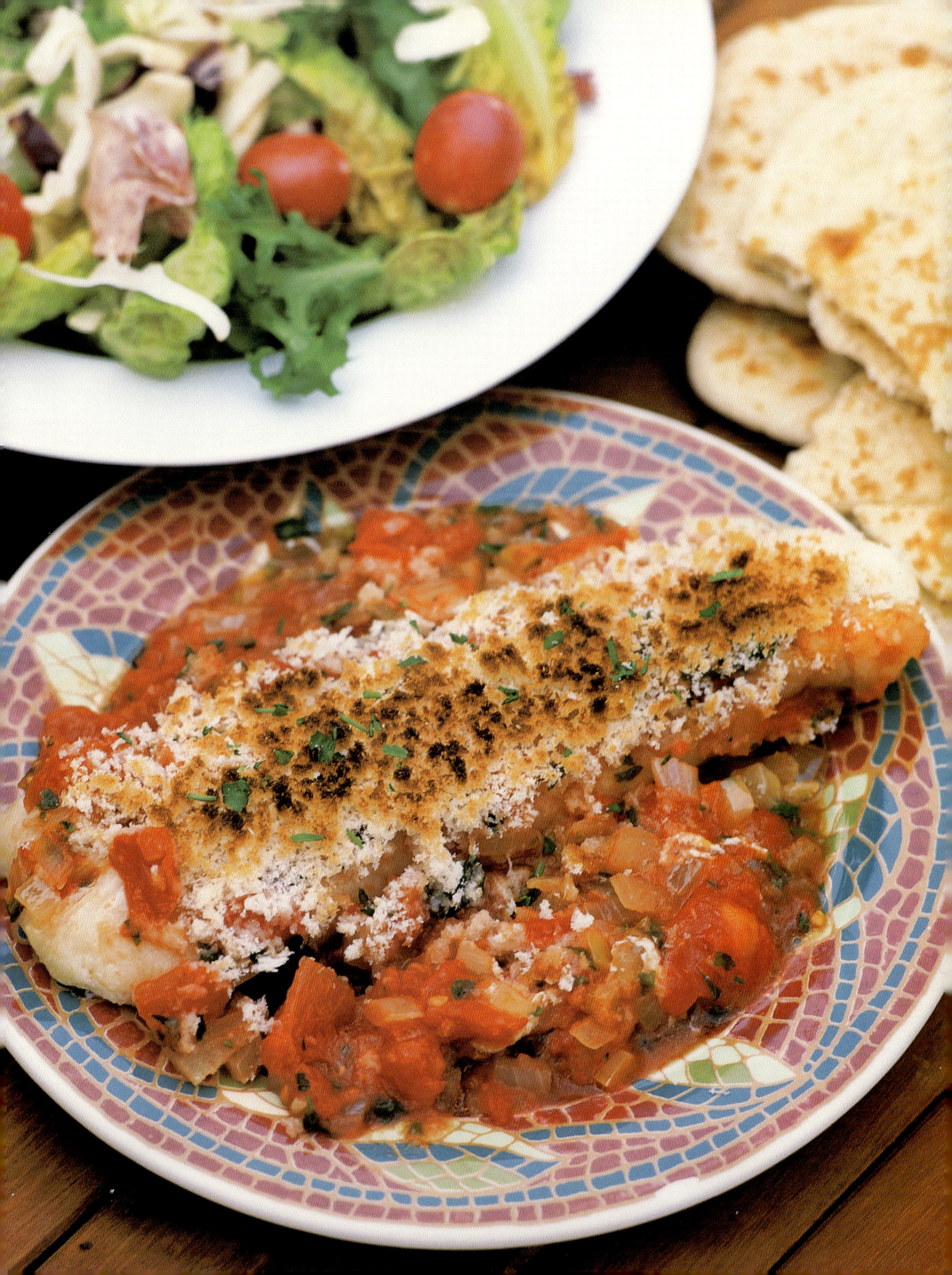

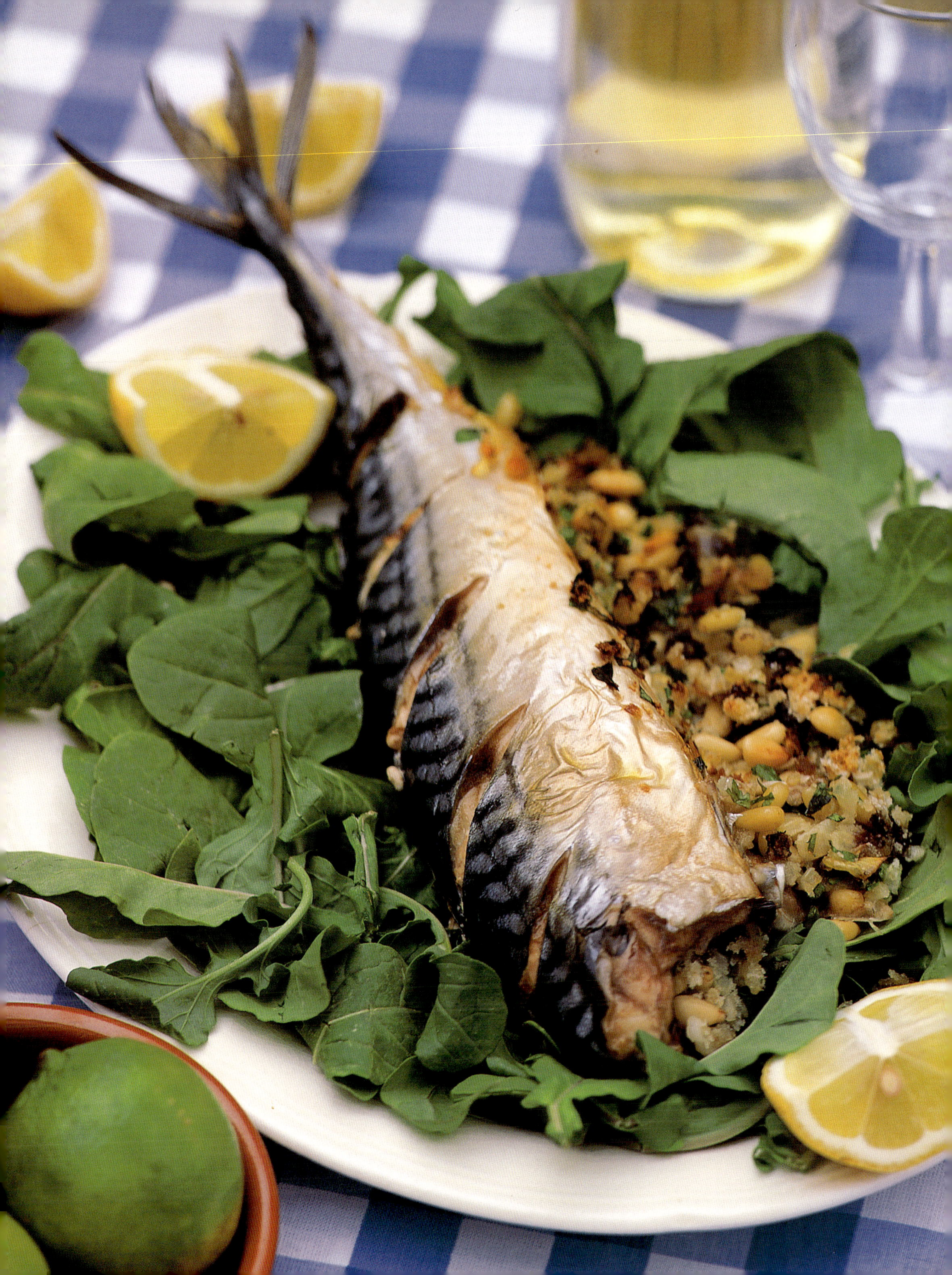

baked mackerel stuffed with raisins and pine nuts
skoubriá gemistá

Mackerel are oily fish and a stuffing, here flavored with lemon, raisins, and crunchy pine nuts, complements them very successfully. Trout can be used as an alternative.

SERVES 4

3 tbsp olive oil
1 onion, chopped finely
²/₃ cup fresh breadcrumbs
¹/₃ cup raisins, chopped
²/₃ cup pine nuts
grated rind and juice of 1 lemon
1 tbsp chopped fresh dill
2 tbsp chopped fresh flat-leaf parsley
salt and pepper
1 egg, beaten
4 mackerel, each weighing about 12 oz/350 g, gutted
lemon wedges, to garnish

1 To make the stuffing, heat 2 tablespoons of the oil in a large, heavy-bottomed skillet, add the onion and fry for 5 minutes, until softened. Remove from the heat.

2 Put the breadcrumbs, raisins, pine nuts, lemon rind, dill, parsley, salt, and pepper in a large bowl. Add the onion and egg and mix well together.

3 Press the stuffing mixture into the cavity of the fish and place in a greased, shallow ovenproof dish large enough to hold them in a single layer. Using a sharp knife, make diagonal slashes along each fish. Drizzle over the lemon juice and the remaining oil.

4 Bake the fish, uncovered, in a preheated oven, 375°F/190°C, for 30-45 minutes, basting twice during cooking, until tender. Serve hot, garnished with lemon wedges.

monkfish and shrimp kabobs
souvlákia me psári kai garídes

The firm texture of monkfish makes it perfect for kabobs. Other firm white fish, tuna, and swordfish would be ideal alternatives. Serve the kabobs with rice. The Orange and Olive Salad on page 207 is a good accompaniment.

SERVES 4

1 lb 5 oz/600 g monkfish
1 green bell pepper
1 onion
3 tbsp olive oil
3 tbsp lemon juice
2 garlic cloves, crushed
salt and pepper
16 large fresh shrimp, peeled
16 fresh bay leaves
lemon wedges, to garnish

1 Cut the monkfish into chunks measuring about 1 inch/2.5 cm. Cut the bell pepper into similar-size chunks, discarding the core and seeds. Cut the onion into 6 wedges then cut each wedge in half widthwise and separate the layers.

2 To make the marinade, put the oil, lemon juice, garlic, salt, and pepper in a bowl and whisk together. Add the monkfish, prawns, onion and bell pepper pieces and toss together until coated in the marinade. Cover and let marinate in the fridge for 2–3 hours.

3 Thread the pieces of fish, bell pepper, onion, and bay leaves onto 8 greased, flat metal kabob skewers, alternating and dividing the ingredients as evenly as possible. Place on a greased broiler pan.

4 Preheat the broiler then broil the kabobs for 10–15 minutes, turning frequently and basting with any remaining marinade, until cooked and lightly charred. Serve hot, garnished with lemon wedges.

*cook's tip
These kebobs are ideal for cooking over a barbecue and eating outdoors. Light a charcoal barbecue 45 minutes before starting to cook and 10 minutes if using a gas barbecue and start cooking when the flames die down and the coals are glowing red. Cook for the same time as in the recipe.

Overleaf Fishing boats moored in a small Greek harbor add to the traditional charm

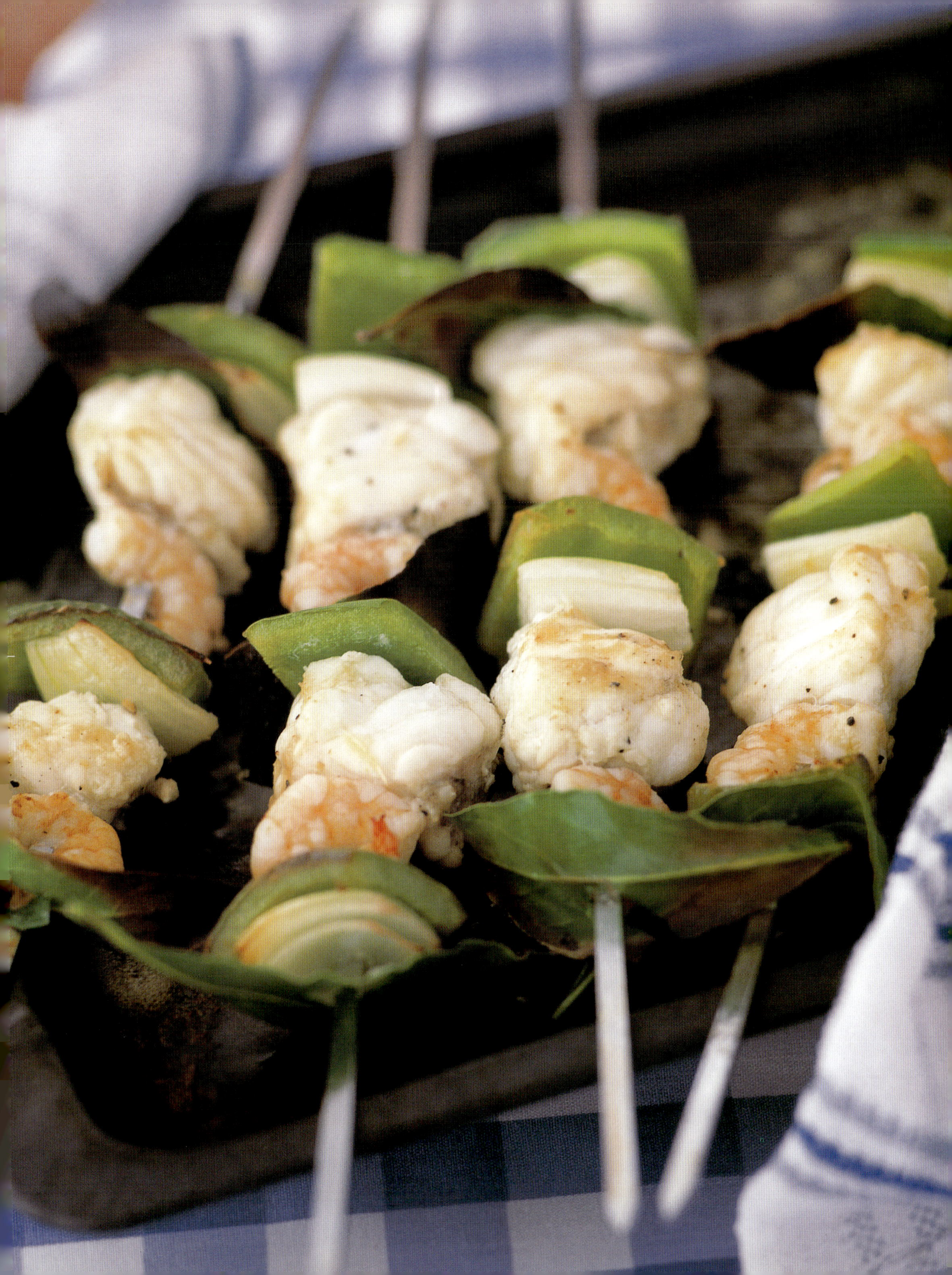

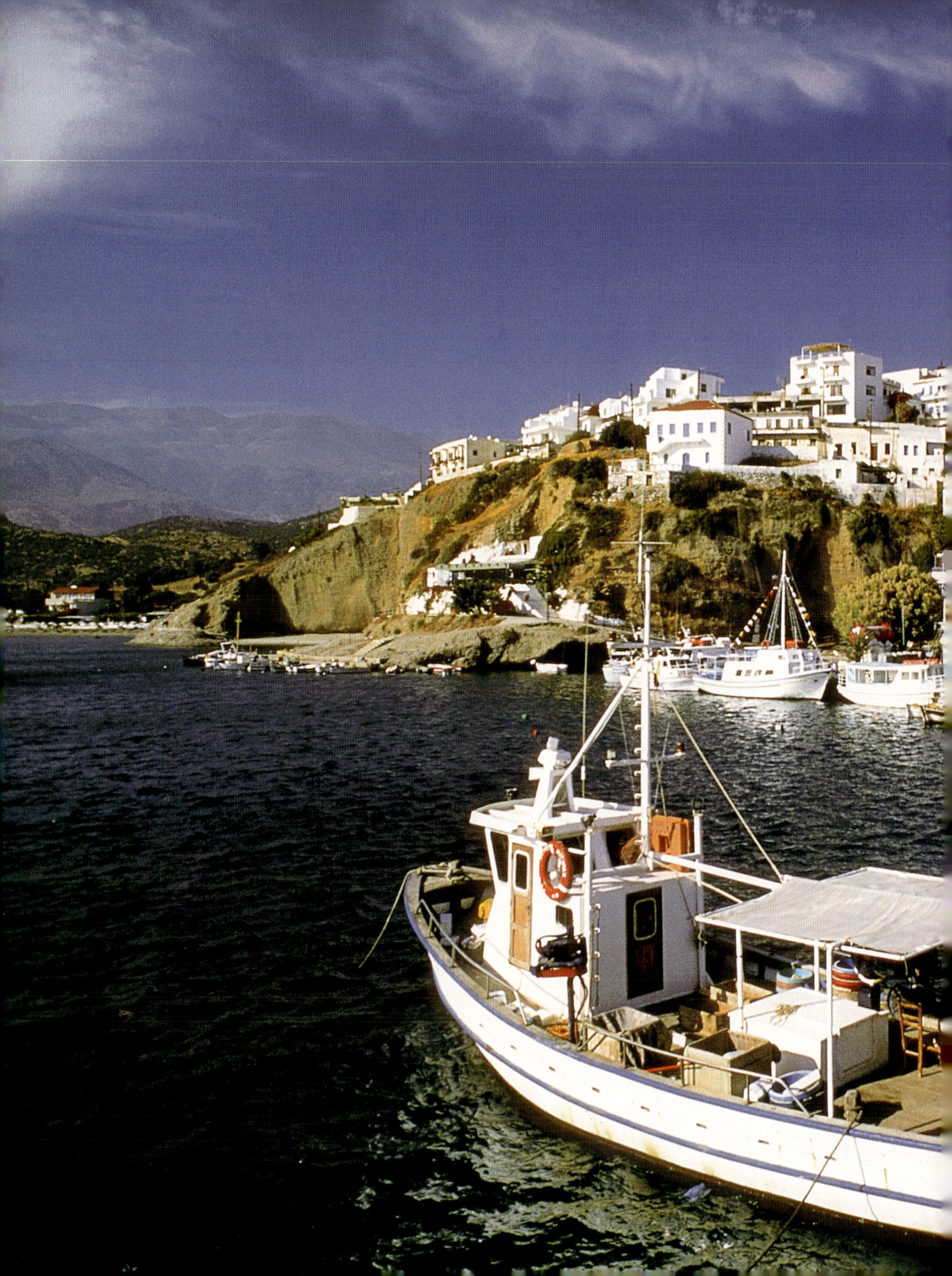

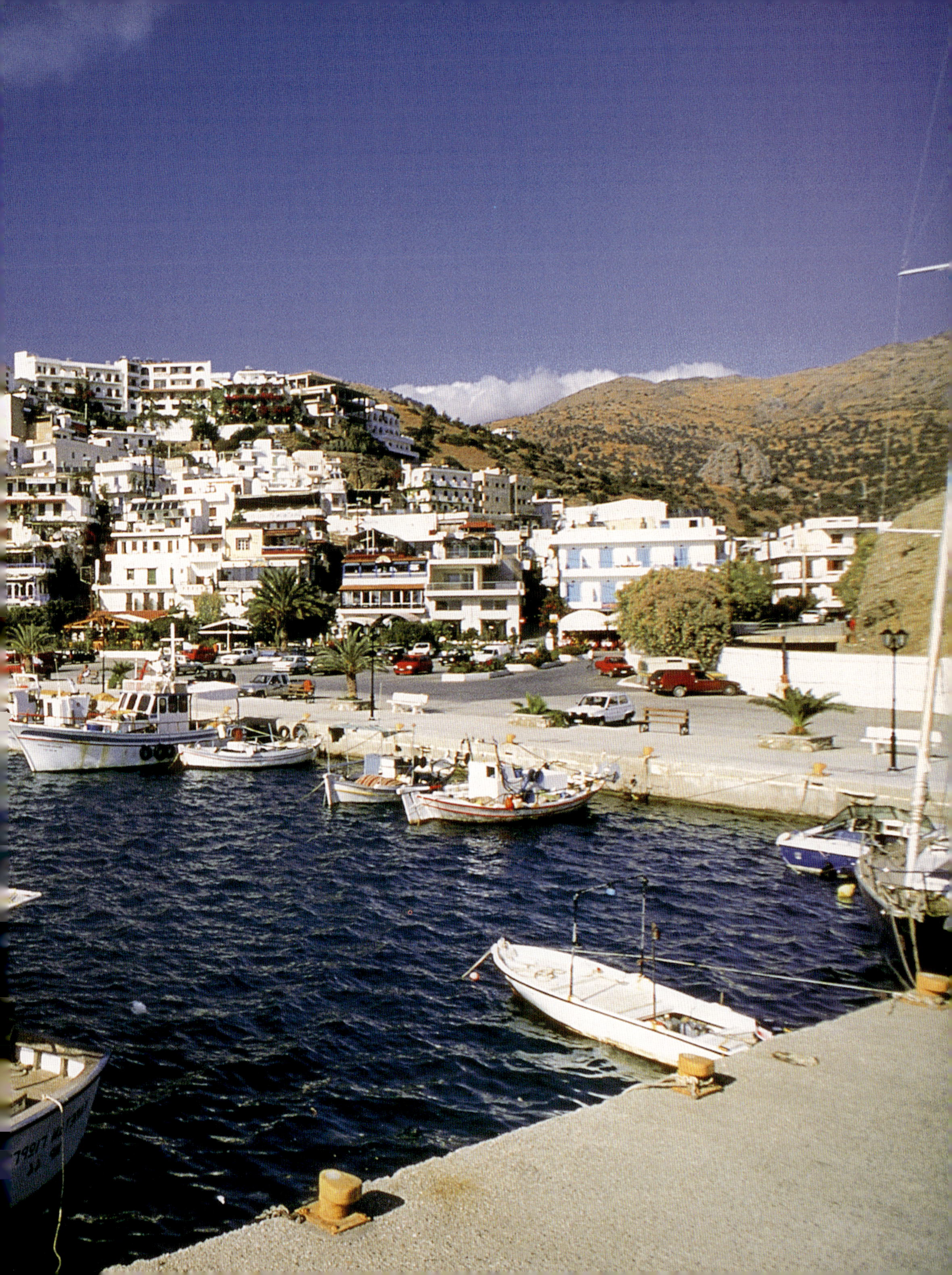

fish fritters with greek garlic sauce
psári me skordaliá

This favourite Greek dish, small pieces of fried fish traditionally served with Greek Garlic Sauce and radishes, can be made with a variety of different fish. Choose your favorite fish from the suggestions in the recipe.

SERVES 4

¾ cup plus 1 tbsp all-purpose flour, plus extra for dusting
pinch of salt
1 egg, beaten
1 tbsp olive oil
⅔ cup warm water
1½ lb/675 g white fish fillets, such as well-soaked salt cod, monkfish, or cod
sunflower oil, for deep-frying
lemon wedges, to garnish

to serve
½ recipe Greek Garlic Sauce (see page 64)
radishes

1. To make the batter, put the flour and salt in a large bowl. Make a well in the center and add the egg and oil then gradually add the water, beating all the time, to form a smooth batter.

2. Discard any skin and bones from the fish fillets and cut the flesh into chunks, measuring about 2 inches/5 cm square. Dust lightly in flour so that the batter will stick to the fish when dipped in it.

3. Heat the oil in a deep-fat fryer to 350°F/180°C or until a cube of bread, dropped into the fat, turns brown in 1 minute. When the oil is hot, dip each piece of fish in the batter to coat, add to the hot fat in small batches and fry for about 5 minutes, depending on the thickness of the fish, until crisp and golden. Remove with a slotted spoon and drain on paper towels. Continue to cook the remaining fish in small batches.

4. Serve the fish fritters hot, garnished with lemon wedges and accompanied with the Greek Garlic Sauce and a bowl of radishes.

A traditional windmill, minus its sails, silhouetted against a setting sun

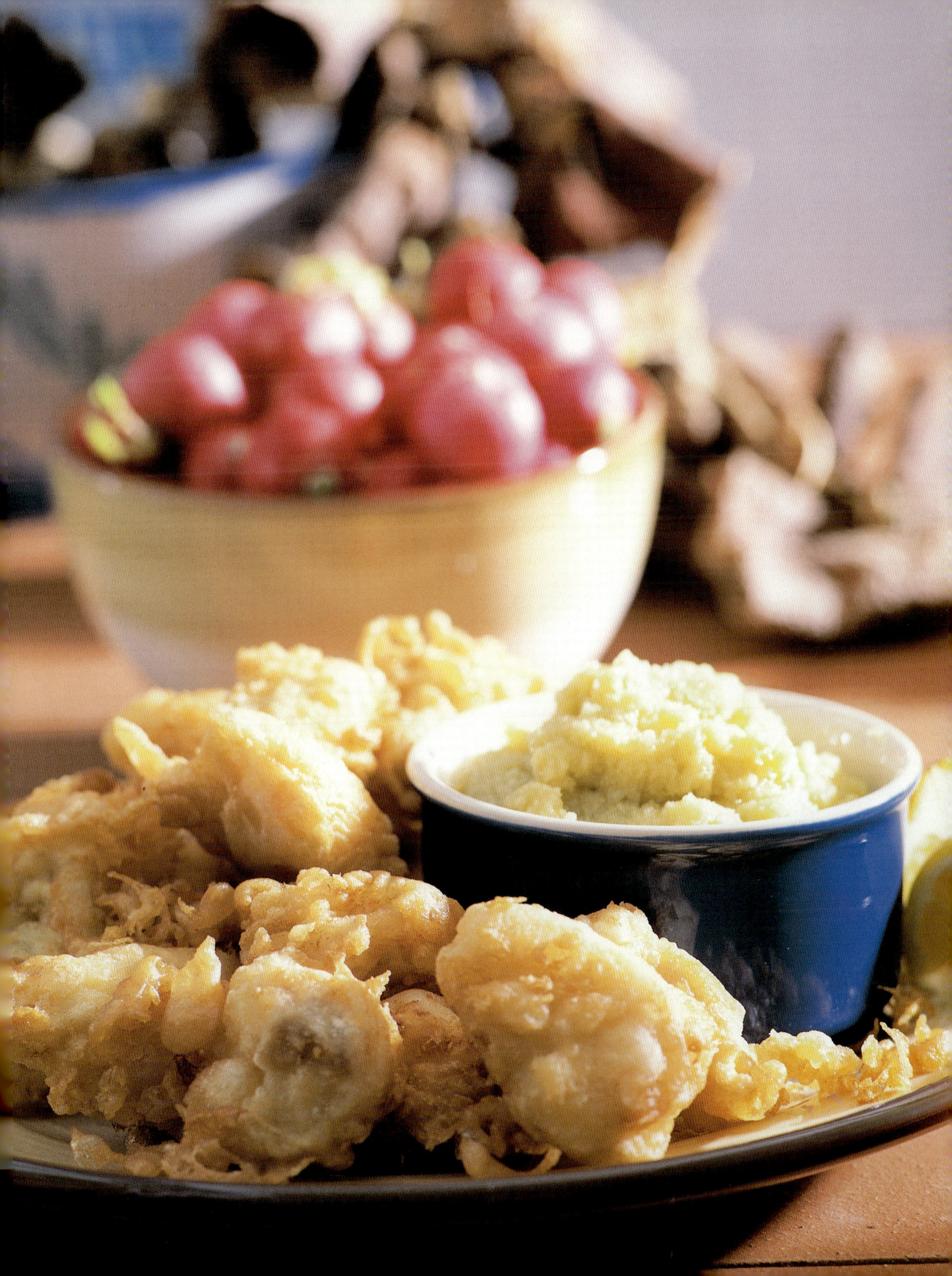

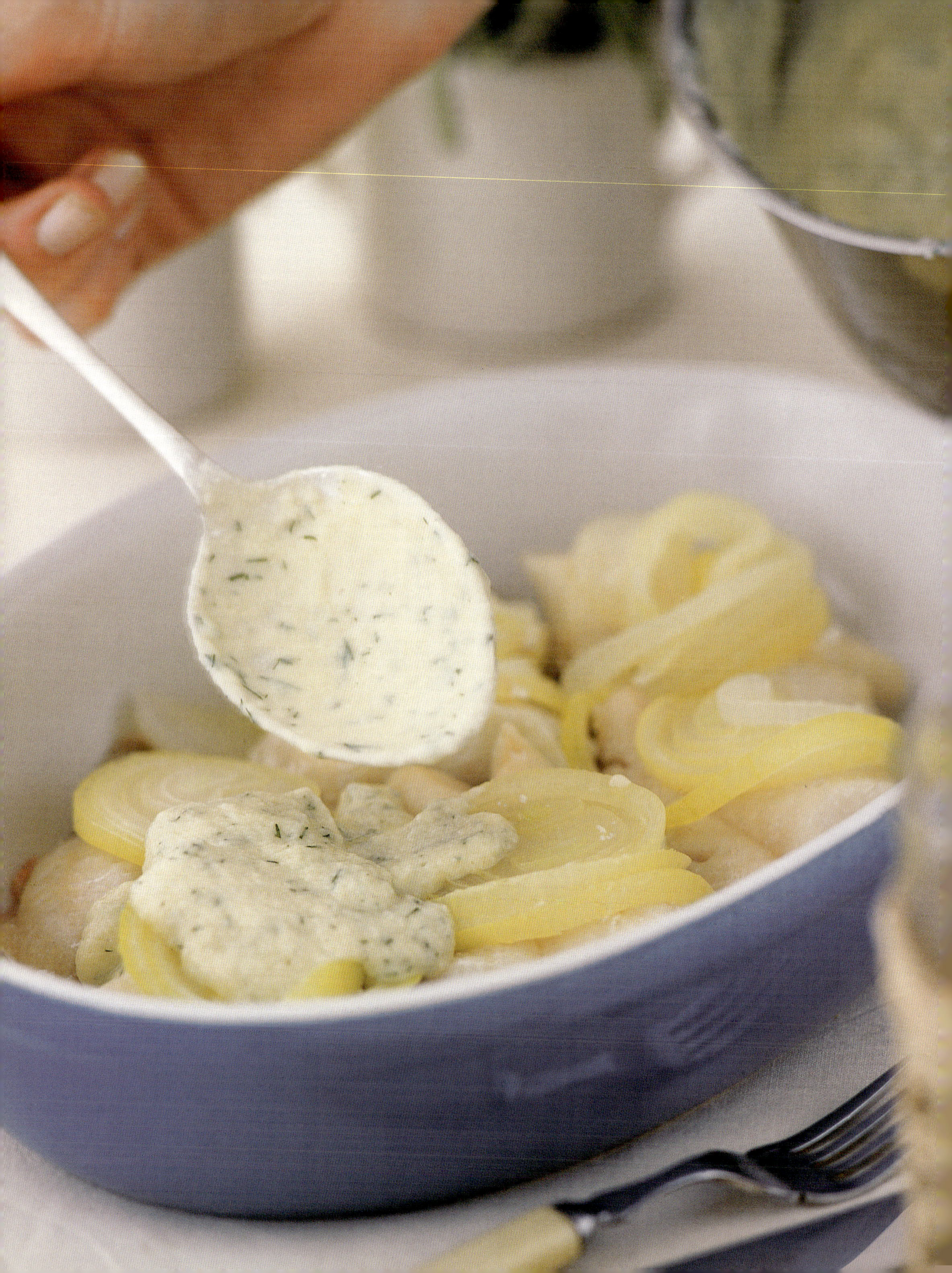

fish dishes

fish in egg and lemon sauce
psári avgolémono

A variety of fish steaks or fillets can be used for this popular recipe. Choose from monkfish, halibut, haddock, cod, trout, or salmon.

SERVES 6

6 fish steaks or fillets, each weighing about 7 oz/200g

1 onion, sliced thinly

7 tbsp fresh lemon juice

²/₃ cup water

salt and pepper

3 eggs

1 tbsp chopped fresh dill

1 Put the fish in a large, shallow saucepan and add the onion slices, lemon juice, water, salt, and pepper. Bring to the boil, cover the saucepan, and simmer for 15–20 minutes, until the fish is tender.

2 Meanwhile, put the eggs in a bowl and whisk together. When the fish is tender, remove the fish and onions from the saucepan with a slotted spoon, put on a warmed serving dish and keep warm in a low oven.

3 Strain the liquid into a measuring cup then very slowly add to the egg yolks, whisking all the time with a balloon whisk. Pour the liquid into a small saucepan and heat very gently for 2–3 minutes, whisking all the time, until the sauce thickens. (Do not boil or the sauce will curdle.)

4 Stir the dill into the sauce and season with salt and pepper. Spoon the sauce over the fish and serve hot or cold.

Much of Greece supports little pasture, hence sheep and goats are far more common than cattle

skate in mustard and caper sauce
psári me moustárda kai cápari

Both mustard and capers complement skate extremely well. Combined in a sauce, they are the perfect partners.

SERVES 4

2 skate wings

2 tbsp olive oil

1 onion, chopped finely

1 garlic clove, chopped finely

$^2/_3$ cup authentic Greek yogurt

1 tsp lemon juice

1 tbsp chopped fresh flat-leaf parsley

1 tbsp capers, chopped coarsely

1 tbsp whole-grain mustard

salt and pepper

chopped fresh flat-leaf parsley, to garnish

lemon wedges, to serve

1 Cut each skate wing in half and place in a large skillet. Cover with salted water, bring to the boil then simmer for 10–15 minutes, until tender.

2 Meanwhile, make the mustard and caper sauce. Heat the oil in a saucepan, add the onion and garlic, and cook for 5 minutes, until softened. Add the yogurt, lemon juice, parsley, and capers and cook for 1–2 minutes, until heated through. (Do not boil or the sauce will curdle.) Stir in the mustard and season with salt and pepper.

3 Drain the skate and put on 4 warmed serving plates. Pour over the mustard and caper sauce and sprinkle with chopped parsley. Serve hot, with lemon wedges.

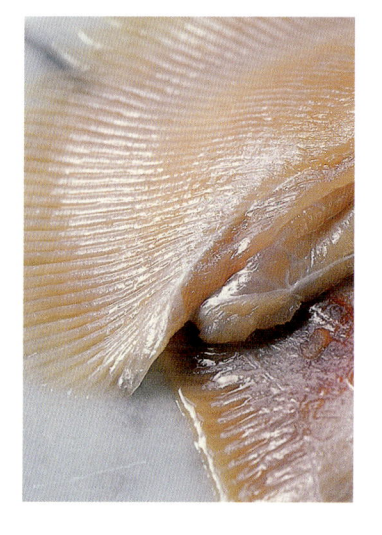

fish dishes

pan-fried fish with lemon
psári tiganitó me lemóni

You can use either tuna or swordfish steaks for this recipe, both of which benefit from being marinated before cooking to tenderize them. This dish is good served with boiled new potatoes.

SERVES 4

4 tuna or swordfish steaks, each weighing about 7 oz/200 g
salt and pepper
3 tbsp olive oil
juice of 1 lemon
lemon wedges, to garnish
Greek Garlic Sauce (see page 64), to serve (optional)

1. Put the fish steaks in a shallow dish and season with salt and pepper. Drizzle over 1 tablespoon of the oil and half the lemon juice. Cover the dish and leave to marinate in the fridge for at least 1 hour.

2. When you are ready to cook, heat the remaining oil in a skillet or rub a little over a cast-iron griddle, add the fish steaks and fry for 3-8 minutes on each side, depending on their thickness, until tender. Do not overcook the fish or it will become dry.

3. Drizzle the remaining lemon juice over the fish steaks. Serve hot, garnished with lemon wedges and accompanied with Greek Garlic Sauce, if desired.

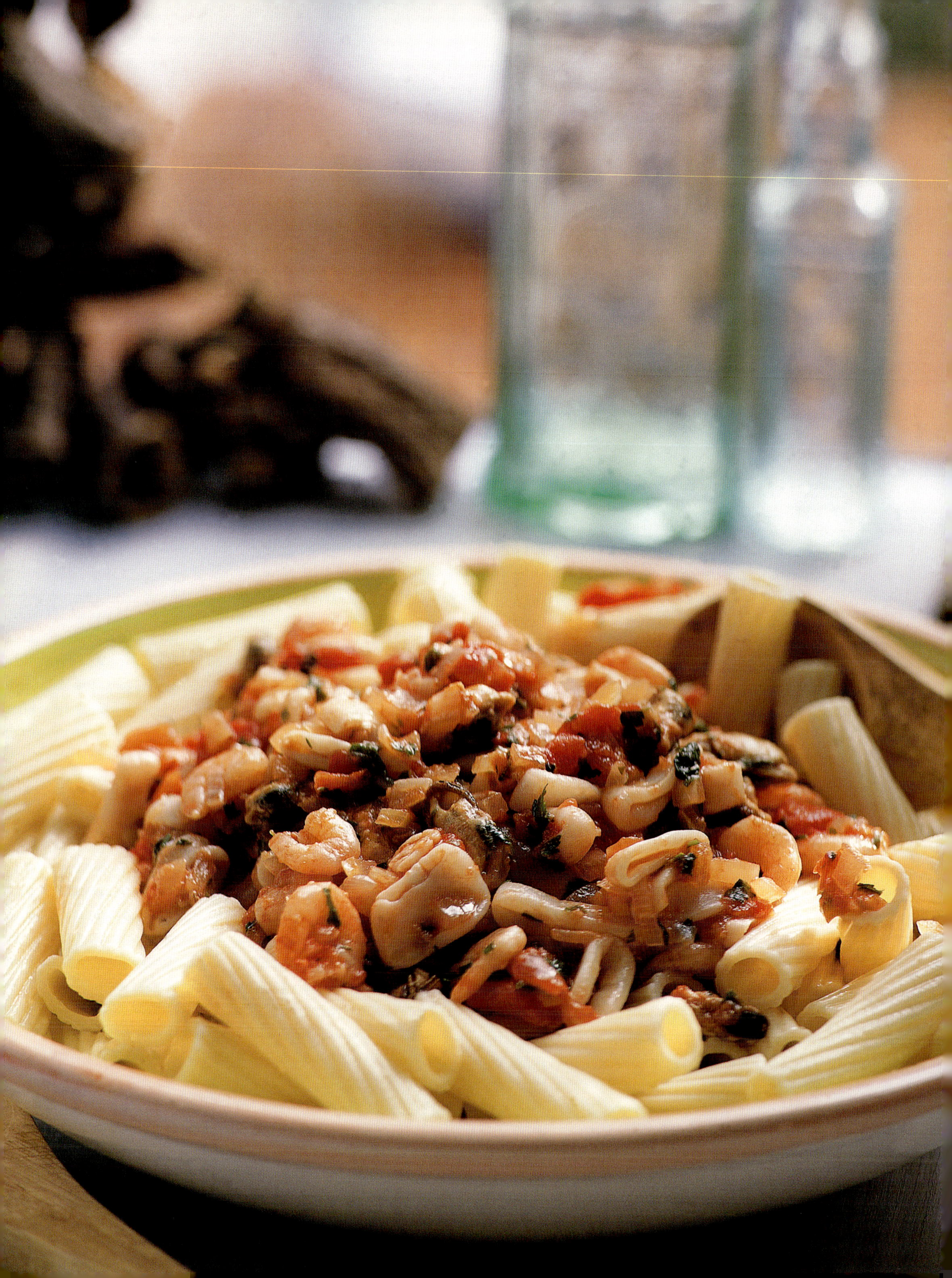

fish dishes

seafood pasta
makarónia me thalasiná

Seafood is one of the Greeks' favorite foods and in this recipe frozen seafood is combined with their favorite pasta to produce a delicious quick meal.

SERVES 4

3 tbsp olive oil

1 onion, chopped

2 garlic cloves, chopped finely

½ cup dry white wine

14 oz/400 g canned chopped tomatoes in juice

pinch of sugar

2 tbsp chopped fresh herbs such as flat-leaf parsley, oregano or marjoram

salt and pepper

14 oz/400 g long, hollow Greek macaroni or other short pasta

14 oz/400 g frozen seafood cocktail, thawed and drained

1. Heat 2 tablespoons of the oil in a large saucepan, add the onion and garlic, and fry for about 5 minutes, until softened.

2. Pour the wine into the saucepan and bring to the boil. Add the tomatoes and their juice, the sugar, chopped herbs, salt, and pepper and simmer for 15–20 minutes.

3. Meanwhile, cook the macaroni in a large saucepan of boiling salted water for 10–12 minutes or as directed on the package, until tender. Drain the pasta and return to the saucepan. Add the remaining oil and toss together.

4. Add the seafood to the tomato sauce and simmer for 3–4 minutes, until heated through. Serve the seafood on top of the pasta.

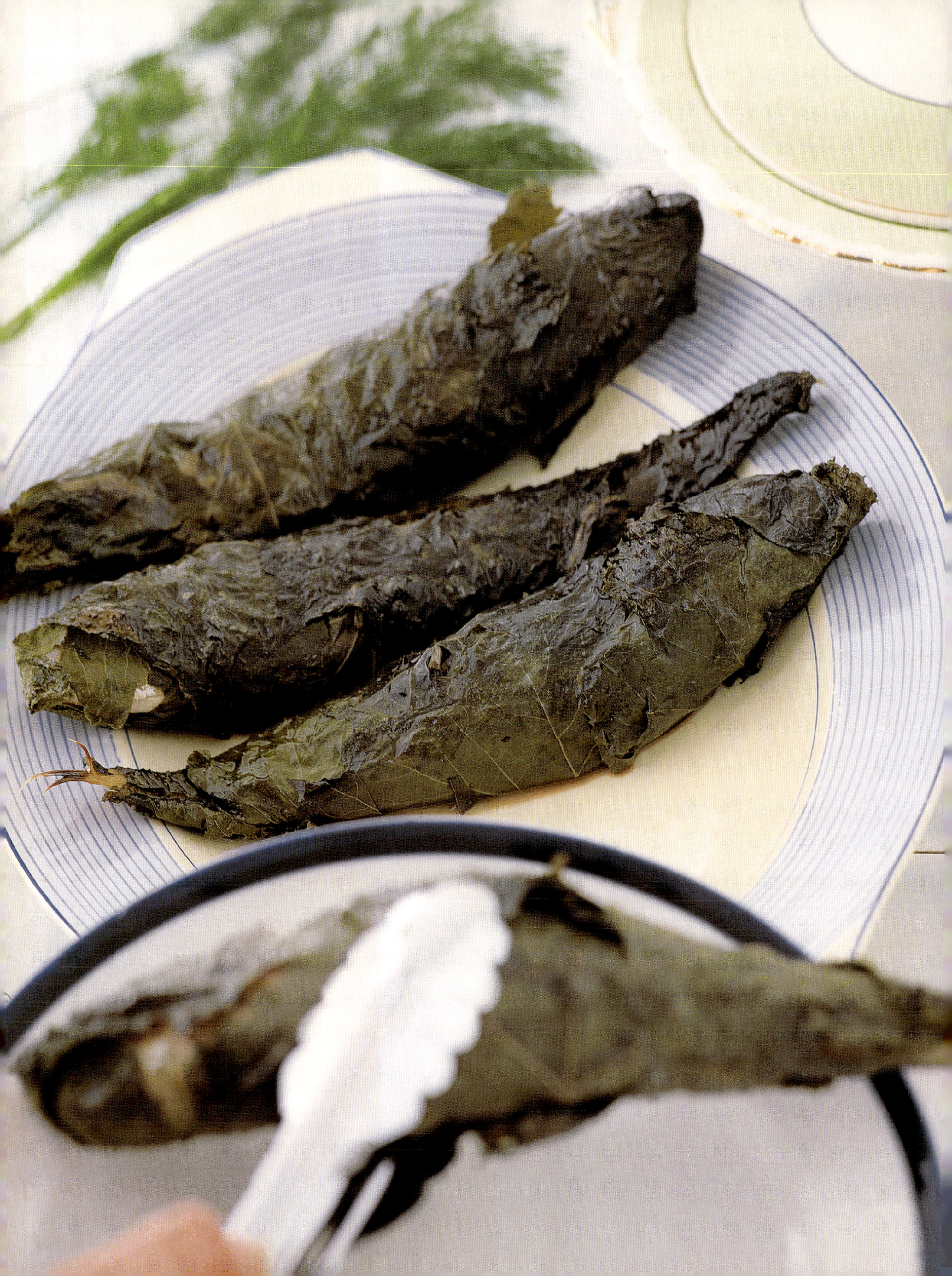

red mullet wrapped in vine leaves
barboúnia me ambelófila

Red mullet has always been a popular fish in Greece. In this recipe the fish is wrapped in vine leaves, which not only add flavor but keep it moist during cooking. The Crispy Roasted Fennel on page 179 is an ideal accompaniment.

SERVES 4

8 small fresh vine leaves or 8-oz/225-g package vine leaves preserved in brine

4 red mullet, each weighing about 7 oz/200 g, scaled and gutted

salt and pepper

1 lemon, sliced thinly and halved

small bunch fresh dill

2 tbsp olive oil

1. If using fresh vine leaves, tie them in bundles by their stalks and blanch them in boiling salted water for 1 minute. Rinse under cold running water, dry the leaves and cut out the stalks. If using preserved vine leaves, place them in a large bowl, pour over boiling water and leave to soak for 20 minutes. Drain, soak in cold water for 20 minutes, and then drain again.

2. Season the fish cavities with salt and pepper, then insert some halved lemon slices and 2–3 sprigs of fresh dill in each. Brush the fish with the olive oil and season with salt and pepper.

3. Preheat the broiler. Place 1 fish on 2 fresh, overlapping vine leaves or on 5–6 preserved vine leaves. Roll up the fish and, if using fresh vine leaves, tie with string.

4. Broil the fish for about 10 minutes, until tender. Serve hot.

An ancient church bell tower stands high above a town

shrimp pilaf
garídes piláfi

SERVES 4

3 tbsp olive oil

1 onion, chopped finely

1 red pepper, cored, deseeded and sliced thinly

1 garlic clove, crushed

1 1/3 cups long-grain white rice

3 cups fish, chicken, or vegetable stock

1 bay leaf

salt and pepper

14 oz/400 g peeled cooked shrimp, thawed and drained if frozen

to garnish

whole cooked shrimp

lemon wedges

Greek black olives

to serve

grated kefalotiri or pecorino cheese

cubes of authentic Greek feta cheese

For convenience, peeled cooked shrimp are used in this recipe. To make a mussel pilaf simply replace the shrimp with cooked mussels.

1 Heat the oil in a large, lidded skillet, add the onion, red bell pepper, and garlic, and fry for 5 minutes, until softened. Add the rice and cook for 2–3 minutes, stirring all the time, until the grains look transparent.

2 Add the stock, bay leaf, salt, and pepper. Bring to the boil, cover the skillet with a tightly fitting lid and simmer for about 15 minutes, until the rice is tender and the liquid has been absorbed. Do not stir during cooking. When cooked, very gently stir in the shrimp.

3 Remove the lid, cover the skillet with a clean dish towel, replace the lid, and let stand in a warm place for 10 minutes to dry out. Stir with a fork to separate the grains and serve garnished with whole shrimp, lemon wedges, and black olives. Accompany with kefalotiri or pecorino cheese for sprinkling on top and a bowl of feta cubes.

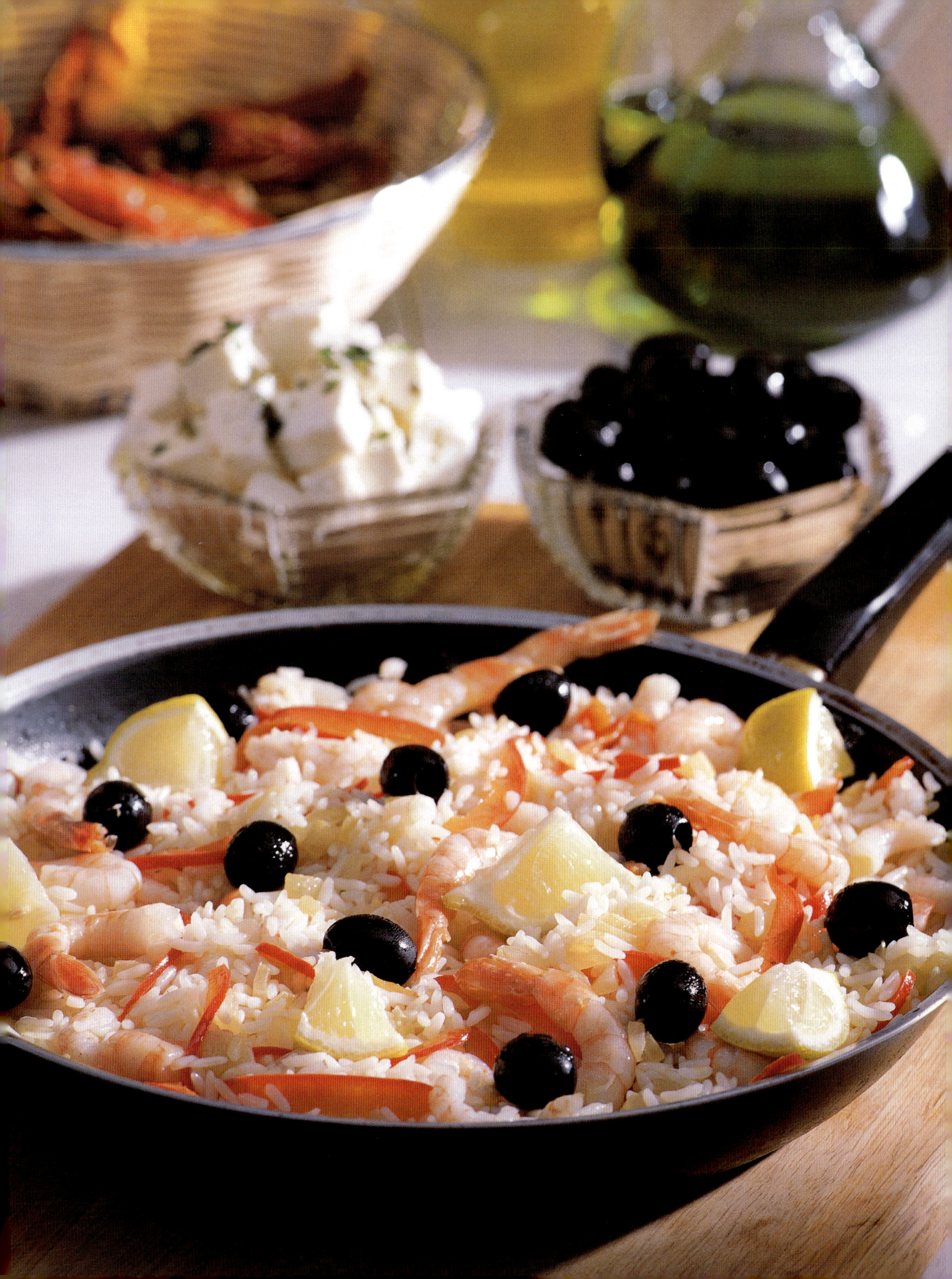

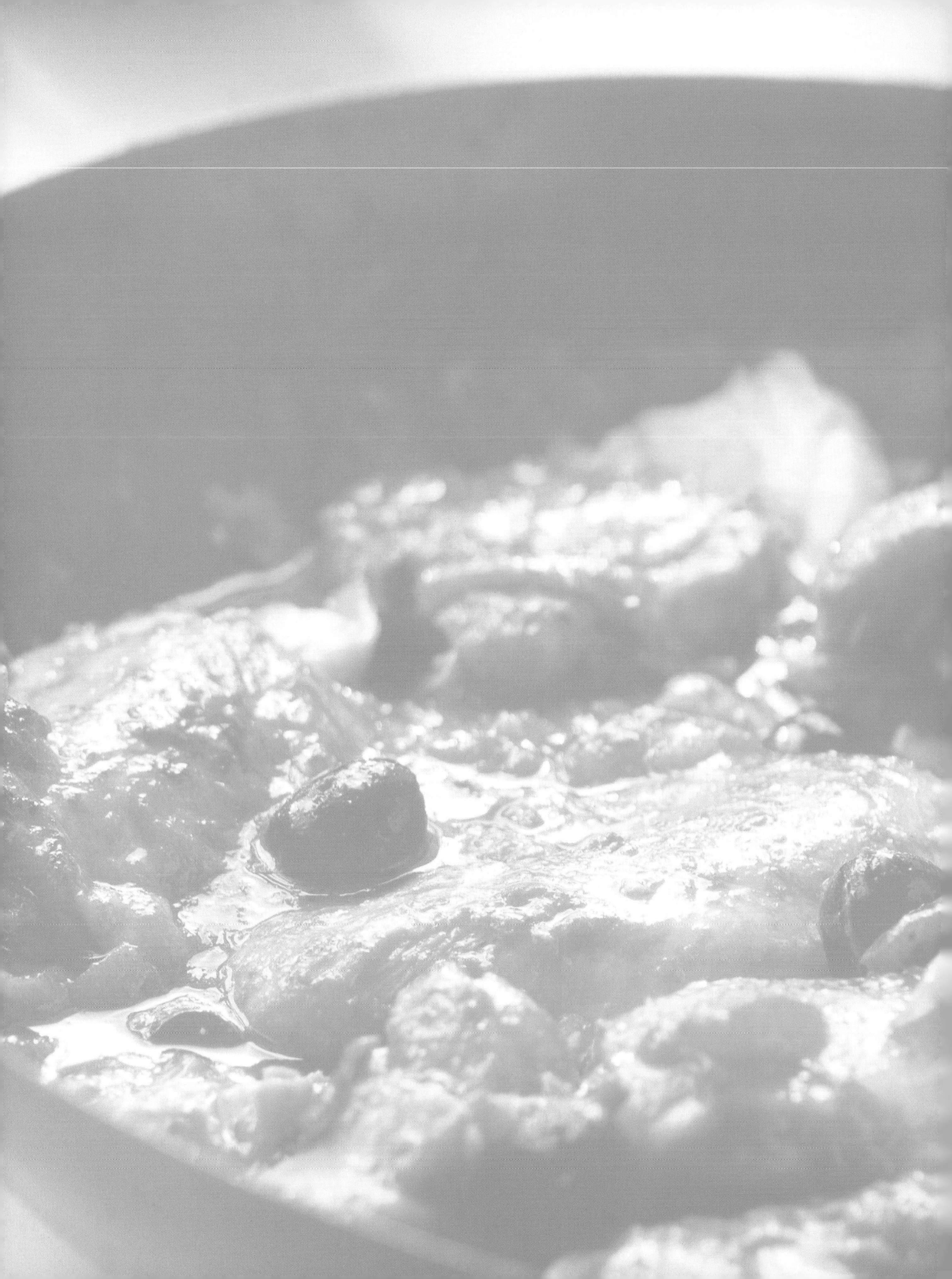

MEAT & POULTRY DISHES

Greece is not a country with an abundance of grazing pastureland. This has meant that it is difficult for the Greeks to produce large quantities of meat for their table, and what meat is available is expensive. It is for this reason that the Greeks have never been great meat-eaters.

Meat and poultry have always been reserved for festive occasions and these go well together with the feast and fast days laid down by the Greek Orthodox Church that many of its followers still observe. The Greeks have always had to use only small amounts of meat in their cooking, which has had the beneficial effect of producing some beautifully creative dishes. *Moussaká* (see page 130) and *Pastítsio* (see page 144), Greece's most famous meat dishes, where lamb is layered with eggplant or pasta and a sauce, are two very good examples.

Cattle farming is mainly restricted to the north and this is usually for beef production rather than for dairy produce. Due to the lack of lush grazing land the cattle are often slaughtered young and so produce veal. Beef and veal are usually cooked in casseroles with wine and herbs or spices, as are rabbit, hare, and other game. This is illustrated in the recipe for *Stifádo* on page 149. Dairy cattle are generally kept inside because of the poor grazing land and high temperatures in the summer and the milk production is used for the domestic market, commercially made yogurt, and some cheeses.

Beef and veal are usually cooked in casseroles with wine and herbs or spices, as are rabbit, game, and hare

Pigs are bred successfully and produce pork that is enjoyed in a variety of dishes. In the past, many rural families kept a pig and, when slaughtered, the meat was often preserved to make dry sausages and cured hams. Preserved meats are still popular in Greece today. *Pihtí* is pork or veal souse or col cut that is flavored with orange and served as a main dish with an oil and vinegar dressing. *Pastourmá* is pork or veal that is marinated in spices and garlic and then dried. It has a strong flavor and is served as a mezze. Its flavor is not dissimilar to Greece's fresh, spicy sausages, known as *Loukánika*. Made from fresh pork and beef, these are often served as a mezze and you will find the recipe for them on page 55. To serve them as a lunch or supper dish, simply make them larger and accompany them with potatoes or a pilaf. They are delicious and their flavor unforgettable.

Traditionally every Greek family kept chickens, and today they can be seen in villages, pecking along dusty roadsides. Chickens are now bred commercially and although the birds may appear scrawny, they are often free-range and corn-fed, and their flesh has an excellent flavor, unlike so many of the commercially produced chickens in the rest of Europe. Of all the poultry that is eaten in Greece, including turkey,

Ruins of ancient civilizations dot the landscape of Greece

Overleaf Many Greek towns have attractive old centers

meat & poultry dishes

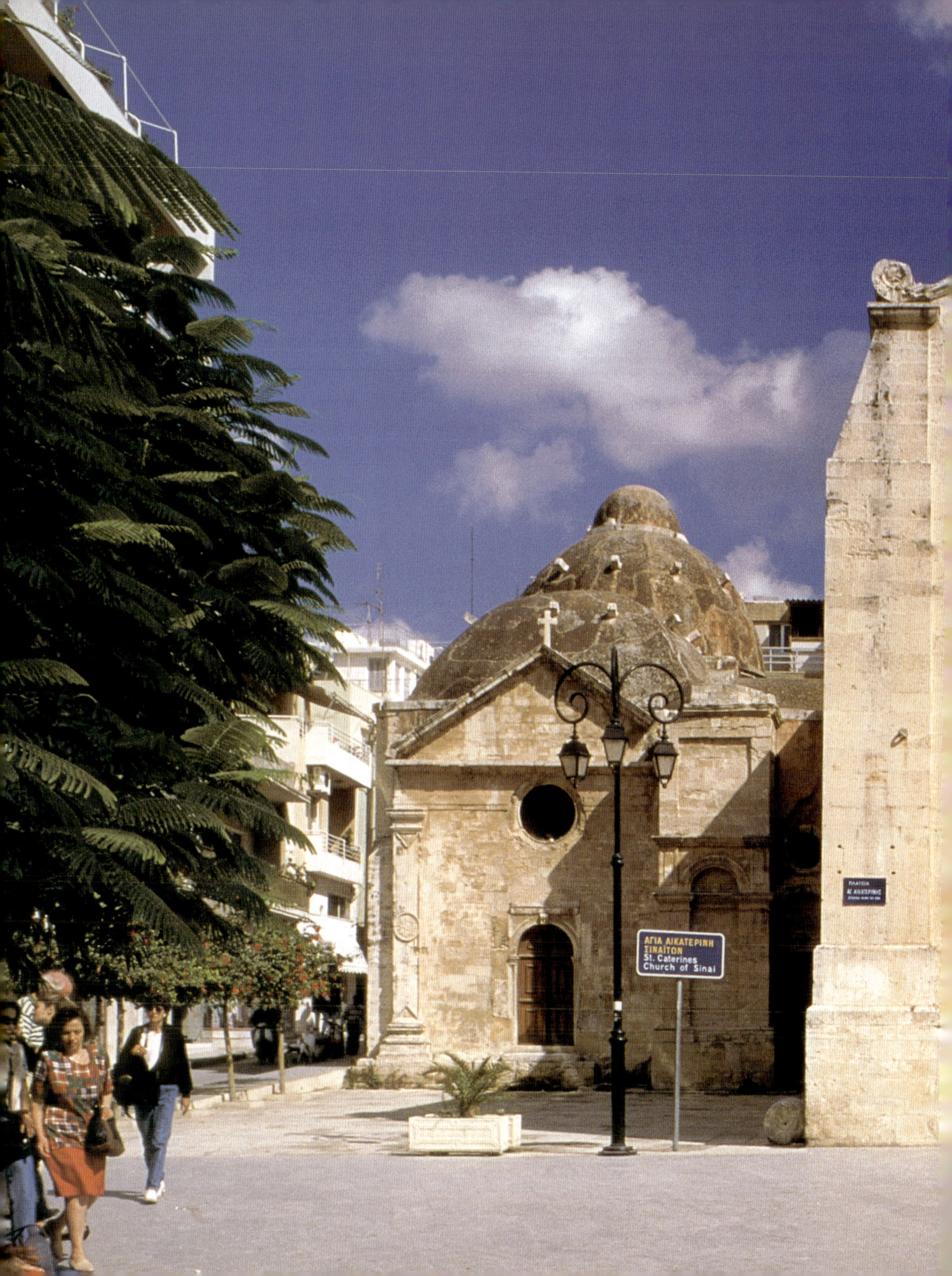
ΑΓΙΑ ΑΙΚΑΤΕΡΙΝΗ
ΣΙΝΑΙΤΟΝ
St. Caterines
Church of Sinai

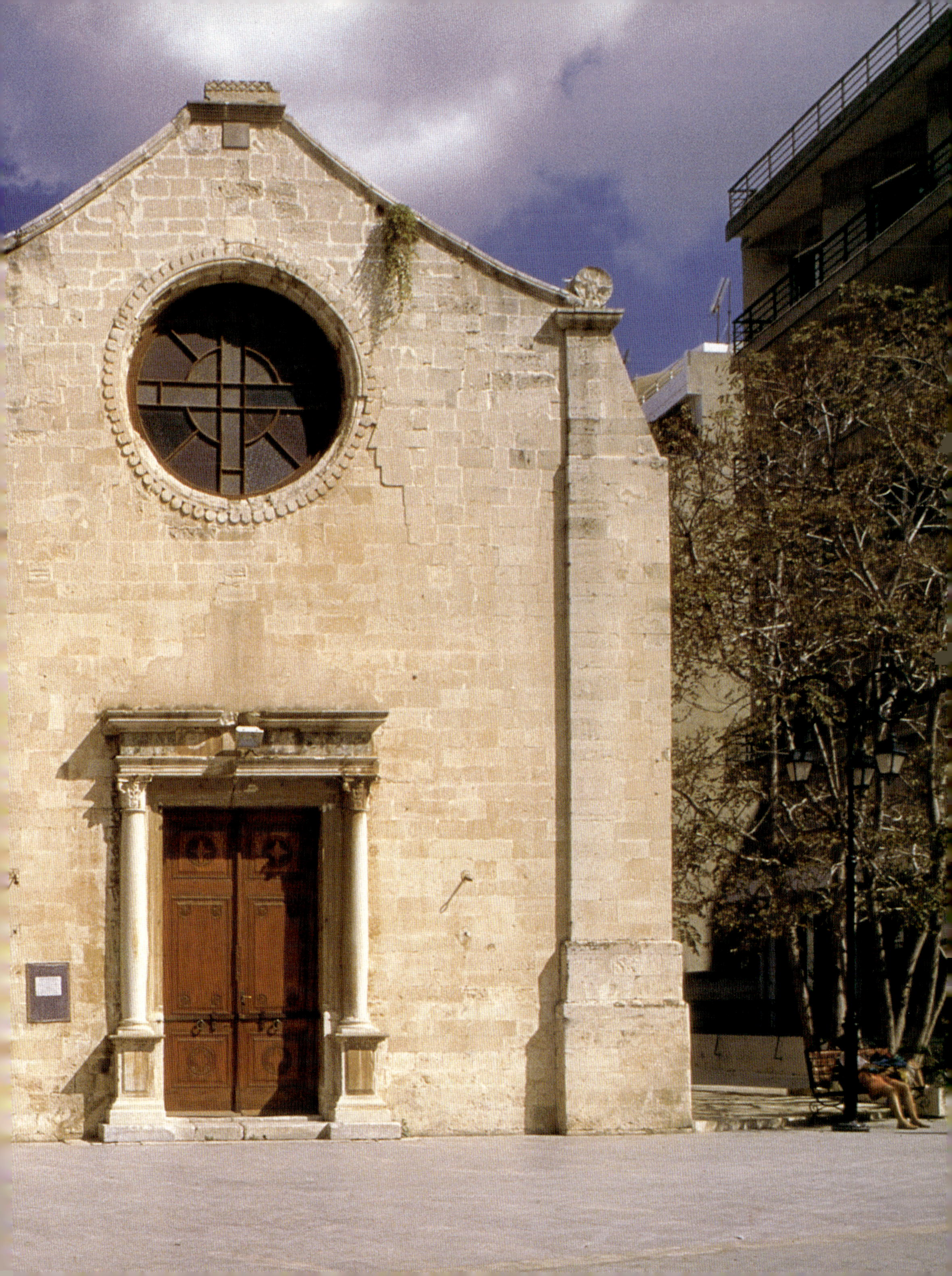

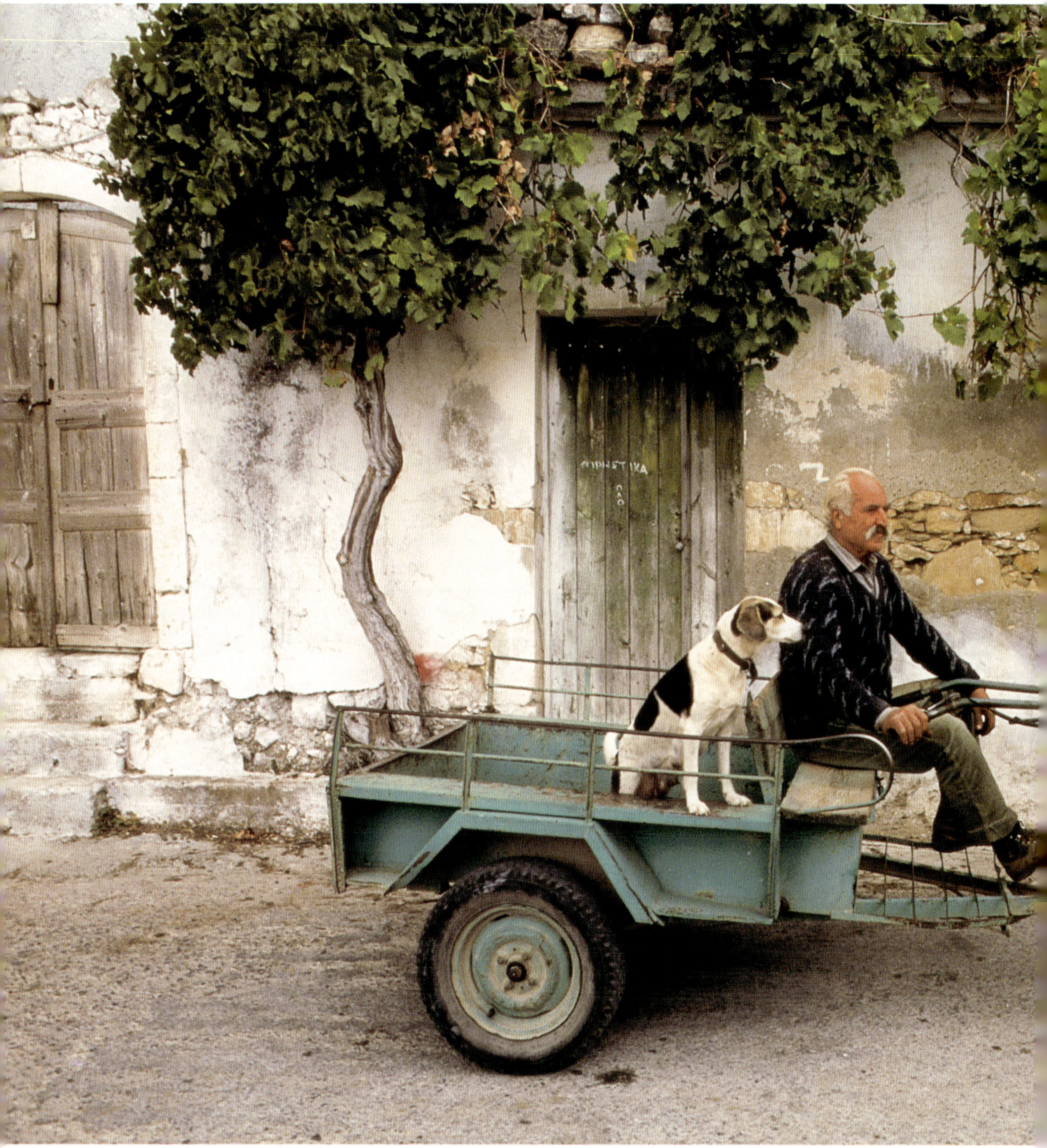

Unlike other animals, sheep and goats munch happily on the lightly grassed hillsides

duck, and goose, chicken is the most popular and it is cooked in a variety of ways. The most popular way is spit-roasting or roasting as in Roast Chicken with Oregano (see page 165), served with a number of sauces, as in the recipe for Chicken Kabobs with Yogurt Sauce on page 160 and the recipe for Chicken with Walnut Sauce on page 164, and used in pilafs, stews, and pies.

Unlike other animals, sheep and goats munch happily on the lightly grassed hillsides, and lamb, followed by kid, is the most prevalent and popular meat eaten in Greece. Offal is also much appreciated, especially lamb's offal. Lamb has always played an important part in the Greek diet. It is broiled, stewed, served in *avgolémono*, the Greek egg and lemon sauce, in oven-baked dishes, and as meatballs. Broiled lamb is particularly popular in Greece, originating from the days when cooking had to done over an open fire. *Souvlákia* (see page 135) is one of the best-known dishes. Cubes of meat are marinated, threaded onto skewers, and then grilled over a barbecue. *Souvlákia* comes from the Greek word *souvlá*, for spit or skewer, and all over Greece there are street vendors and stalls, open all hours of the day, selling *Souvlákia* wrapped in pita bread. Lamb also appears frequently in minced meat dishes, going back to the days when meat had to be minced to help tenderize it.

At Easter time, the most important festival in the Greek Orthodox Church, lamb or kid is the traditional

A farmer with his dog set off to work the fields in a rudimentary tractor. Much of farming in Greece is still small scale and labor intensive

> *tradition continues and much meat in Greece today is still cooked over a barbecue*

festive dish that ends the Lenten fast. Not so long ago this was cooked on a communal spit and even though modern kitchens in urban homes have largely replaced this custom, the new, young spring lamb or kid is eaten and much looked forward to. In villages, especially on the islands, the tradition continues and much meat in Greece today is still cooked over a barbecue. At Christmas and on New Year's Day, turkey is the traditional meat now eaten, having replaced capon. It is always stuffed and the Greeks have many interesting varieties of stuffing. Typically, the base is rice, with a mixture of onions, herbs, minced lamb, apple, pine nuts, almonds, raisins, feta cheese, chestnuts, or black olives.

The meat and poultry of Greece go particularly well with Greece's other favorite ingredients—lemon, oregano, garlic, and olive oil, as in the recipe for Roast Lamb with Orzo (see page 138). It is a point that is well illustrated in the other recipes in this chapter.

The spectacular, barren landscape of the Agia Galini, Crete

meat & poultry dishes

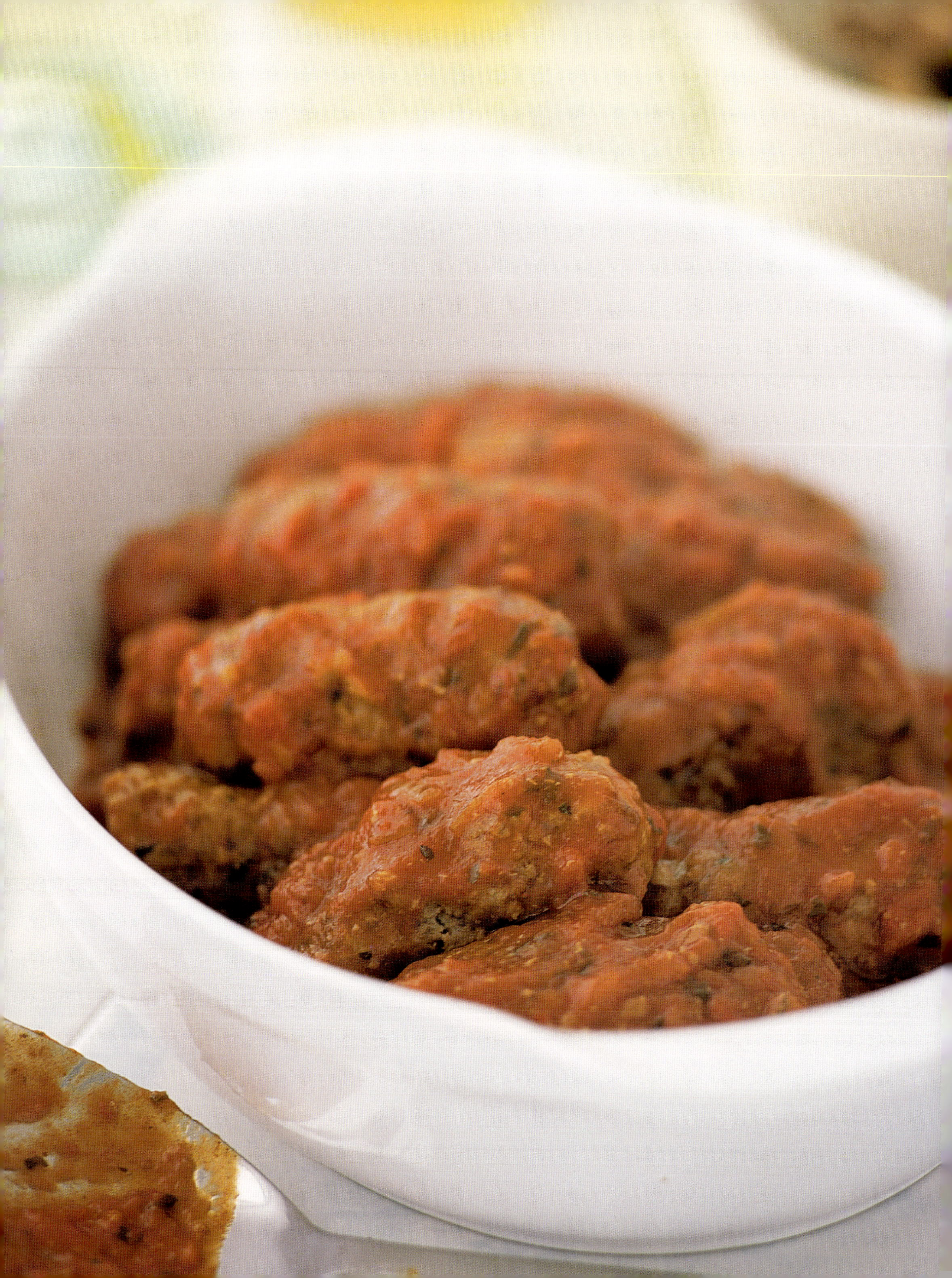

smyrna sausages in tomato sauce
soudzoukákia

These cumin-flavored sausages owe their popularity to the Greeks who once lived in Smyrna, which is now Izmir, in Turkey. A handful of green olives can be added to the sauce if desired. Serve the sausages with rice or pasta.

SERVES 4

1 lb 2 oz/500 g lean, finely minced lamb

1 cup fresh breadcrumbs

1 onion, chopped very finely

1 garlic clove, crushed

3 tbsp finely chopped fresh flat-leaf parsley

1 tsp ground cumin

pinch of ground cinnamon

salt and pepper

1 egg, beaten

2 tbsp olive oil

for the tomato sauce

1 lb 12 oz/800 g canned chopped tomatoes in juice

¼ tsp sugar

¼ cup olive oil

1 garlic clove, crushed

¼ tsp ground cumin

1 tbsp chopped fresh flat-leaf parsley

1 bay leaf

salt and pepper

1. To make the sausages, put the minced lamb, breadcrumbs, onion, garlic, parsley, cumin, cinnamon, salt, and pepper in a bowl and mix together.

2. Stir in the beaten egg then knead the mixture for about 5 minutes, until the mixture forms a paste. Let chill in the fridge for about 1 hour.

3. Meanwhile, prepare the tomato sauce. Put all the ingredients in a large saucepan (it needs to be large enough to hold the sausages in a single layer). Bring to the boil then simmer for about 30 minutes.

4. With dampened hands, form the lamb mixture into 12 equal-size sausage shapes, each about 3½ inches/9 cm long. Heat the oil in a large skillet, add the sausages, and fry for 15 minutes, until browned on all sides.

5. Using a slotted spoon, transfer the sausages to the saucepan containing the tomato sauce and simmer for 10–15 minutes. Serve hot.

grecian meatballs
keftédes

This is what the Greeks eat on festive occasions. You can use other minced meat, such as beef, pork, or veal, or even a mixture, but lamb is the meat usually used. Serve these meatballs as a light meal, with rice, or warm pita bread, accompanied with a salad.

1 Put the minced lamb in a bowl. Grate in the onion, then add the garlic, breadcrumbs, mint, and parsley. Season well with salt and pepper. Mix the ingredients well then add the beaten egg and mix to bind the mixture together. Alternatively, the ingredients can be mixed in a food processor.

2 With damp hands, form the mixture into 16 small balls and thread onto 4 flat metal skewers. Lightly oil a broiler pan and brush the meatballs with oil.

3 Preheat the broiler and cook the meatballs under a medium heat for 10 minutes, turning frequently, and brushing with more oil if necessary, until browned. Serve the meatballs with rice or tucked into warm pita bread.

SERVES 4

1 lb/450 g lean, finely minced lamb

1 medium onion

1 garlic clove, crushed

½ cup fresh white or brown breadcrumbs

1 tbsp chopped fresh mint

1 tbsp chopped fresh parsley

salt and pepper

1 egg, beaten

olive oil, for brushing

lamb with zucchini and tomatoes
arní me kolokíthia

Tender lamb simmered in a tomato sauce with zucchini. Add the ouzo for a special occasion.

SERVES 4

4–8 lamb chops

pepper

2 tbsp olive oil

1 onion, chopped finely

1 garlic clove, chopped finely

4 tbsp ouzo (optional)

14 oz/400 g canned tomatoes in juice

pinch of sugar

9 oz/250 g zucchini, sliced

2 tbsp chopped fresh thyme

salt

1. Season the lamb chops with pepper. Heat the oil in a large, flameproof casserole or Dutch oven, add the onion and garlic and fry for 5 minutes, until softened. Add the lamb chops and fry until browned on both sides.

2. Stir the ouzo into the saucepan, if using, then add the tomatoes with their juice, the sugar, zucchini, thyme, and salt. Bring to the boil and then simmer for 30–45 minutes, stirring occasionally and turning the chops once during cooking, until the lamb and zucchini are tender. If necessary, add a little water during cooking if the sauce becomes too thick. Serve hot.

lamb and eggplant moussaka
moussaká

This is Greece's best-known dish. Prepare it 1 or even 2 days before you want to serve it as it is very good reheated. It only needs bread and a fresh green salad to accompany it.

SERVES 6–8

3 large eggplants

salt

2 tbsp olive oil, plus extra for shallow-frying

1 large onion, chopped coarsely

1 large garlic clove, chopped finely

2 lb 4 oz/1 kg lean minced lamb

$1/3$ cup dry red wine

2 tbsp tomato purée

sugar

$1/4$ tsp ground cinnamon

1 tbsp chopped fresh oregano or 1 tsp dried oregano

1 bay leaf

pepper

6 tbsp butter

scant $1/3$ cup all-purpose flour

$2^{1}/_{2}$ cups milk

1 egg, beaten

$1/3$ cup kefalotiri or pecorino cheese, grated

1. Thinly slice the eggplants, put in a colander, standing over a large plate, and sprinkle each layer with salt. Cover with a plate and place a heavy weight on top. Let stand for 30 minutes.

2. Meanwhile, heat 2 tablespoons of the olive oil in a large saucepan. Add the onion and garlic and fry for 5 minutes, until softened. Add the lamb and fry for 5 minutes, until browned, stirring frequently and breaking up the meat.

3. Add the wine, tomato purée, sugar, cinnamon, oregano, bay leaf, salt, and pepper. Bring to the boil then simmer, uncovered, for 20 minutes, stirring occasionally.

4. Rinse the eggplant slices under cold running water, then pat dry with paper towels. Pour enough oil into a large skillet to cover the bottom, heat, then add a layer of eggplant slices and fry on both sides until lightly browned. Remove from the skillet and drain on paper towels. Continue until all the eggplant slices have been fried, adding more oil as necessary. Alternatively, cook the eggplant slices on a hot griddle, brushed with oil, until golden brown.

5. To make the sauce for the topping, put the butter, flour, and milk in a saucepan and heat gently, whisking vigorously all the time with a balloon whisk, until the sauce thickens, boils, and is smooth. Simmer for 1–2 minutes. Remove the saucepan from the heat and allow to cool slightly. Season the sauce with salt and pepper and then whisk in the egg.

6. Arrange a layer of eggplant in the bottom of a large, ovenproof dish then spoon over a layer of meat. Repeat, making alternate layers until all the meat and eggplant have been used. Pour over the sauce then sprinkle the grated cheese over the top.

7. Bake the moussaka in a preheated oven, 350°F/180°C, for 50–60 minutes, until golden brown. Serve hot or warm.

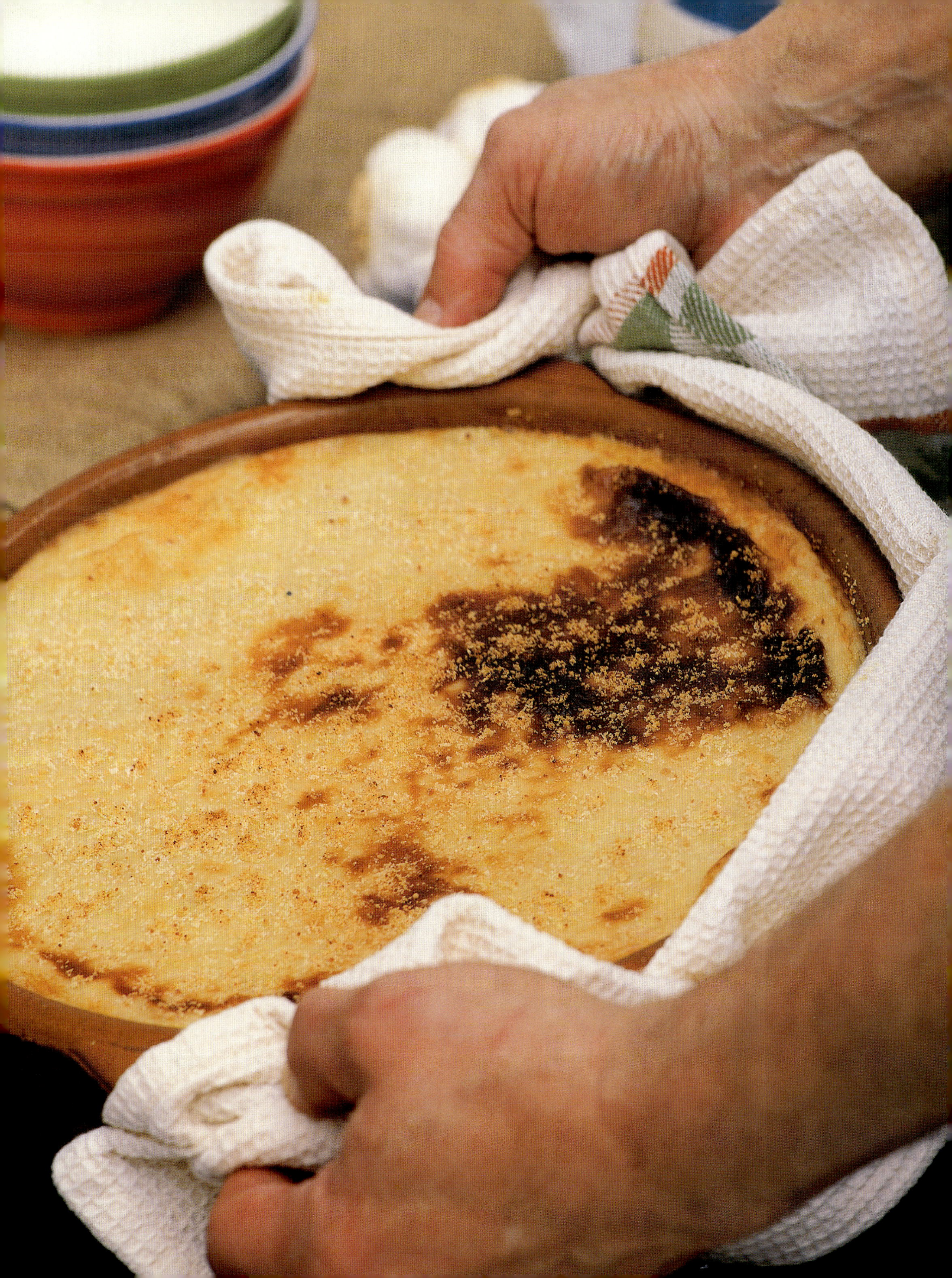

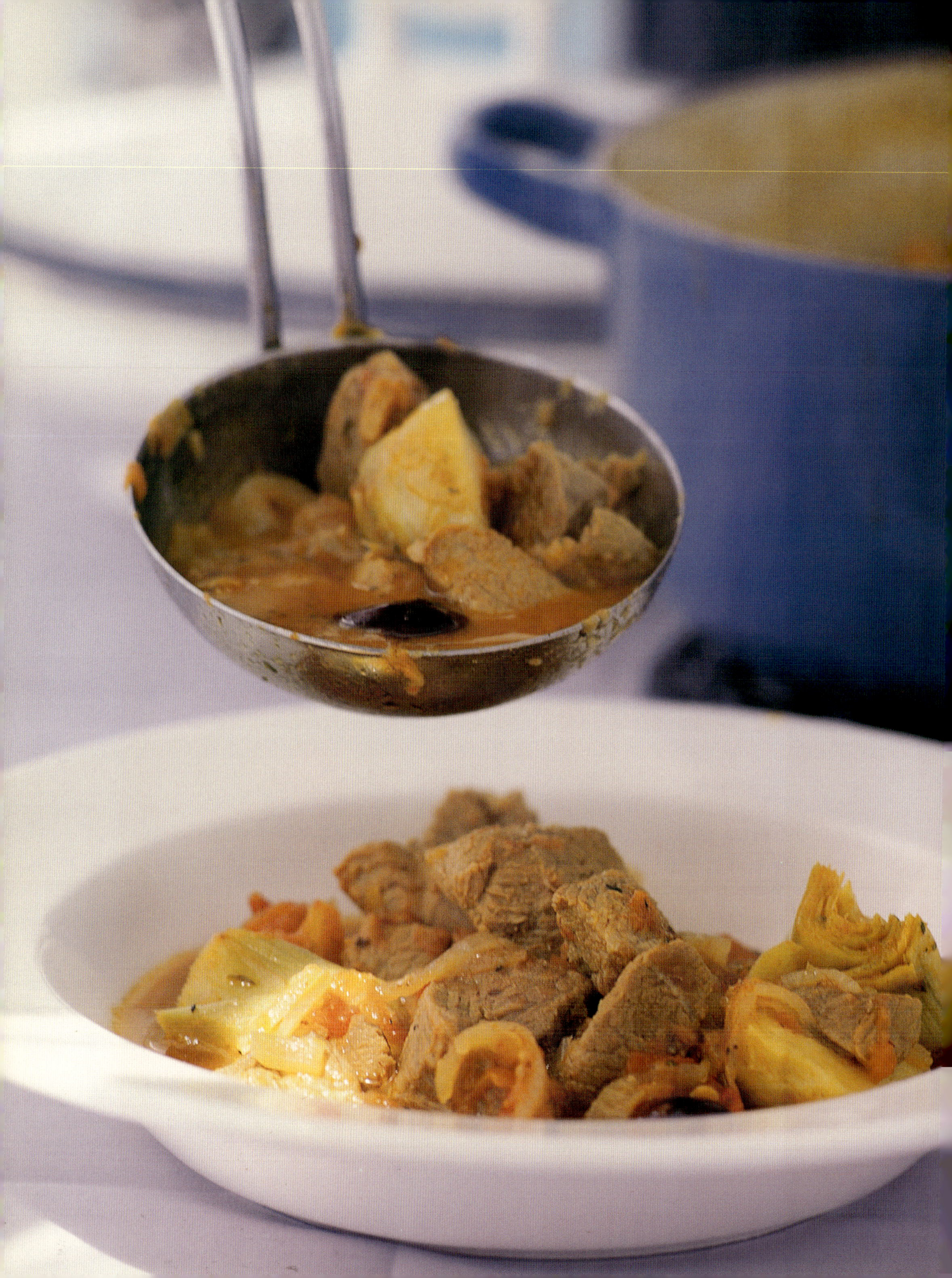

lamb with tomatoes, artichokes, and olives
arní me domátes, angináres, kai eliés

In this casserole, rich in Greek flavors, the lamb is marinated in yogurt and spices then simmered with fresh tomatoes, wine, and oregano. Artichokes and olives are added as a final touch. Serve with a rice pilaf sprinkled with toasted slivered almonds.

SERVES 4

4 tbsp authentic Greek yogurt

grated rind of 1 lemon

2 garlic cloves, crushed

3 tbsp olive oil

1 tsp ground cumin

salt and pepper

1 lb 10 oz/700 g lean boneless lamb, cubed

1 onion, sliced thinly

²/₃ cup dry white wine

1 lb/450 g tomatoes, chopped coarsely

1 tbsp tomato purée

pinch of sugar

2 tbsp chopped fresh oregano or 1 tsp dried

2 bay leaves

½ cup Kalamáta olives

14 oz/400 g canned artichoke hearts, drained and halved

1. Put the yogurt, lemon rind, garlic, 1 tablespoon of the olive oil, cumin, salt, and pepper in a large bowl and mix together. Add the lamb and toss together until coated in the mixture. Cover and let marinate for at least 1 hour.

2. Heat 1 tablespoon of the olive oil in a large flameproof casserole or Dutch oven. Add the lamb in batches and fry for about 5 minutes, stirring frequently, until browned on all sides. Using a slotted spoon, remove the meat from the casserole. Add the remaining tablespoon of oil to the casserole with the onion and fry for 5 minutes, until softened.

3. Pour the wine into the casserole, stirring in any glazed bits from the bottom, and bring to the boil. Reduce the heat and return the meat to the casserole then stir in the tomatoes, tomato purée, sugar, oregano, and bay leaves.

4. Cover the casserole with a lid and simmer for about 1½ hours, until the lamb is tender. Stir in the olives and artichokes and simmer for a further 10 minutes. Serve hot.

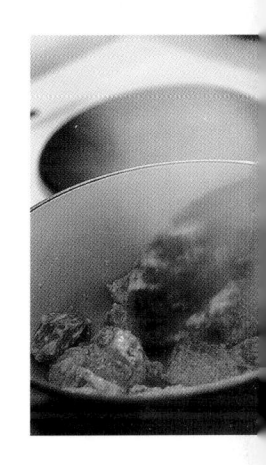

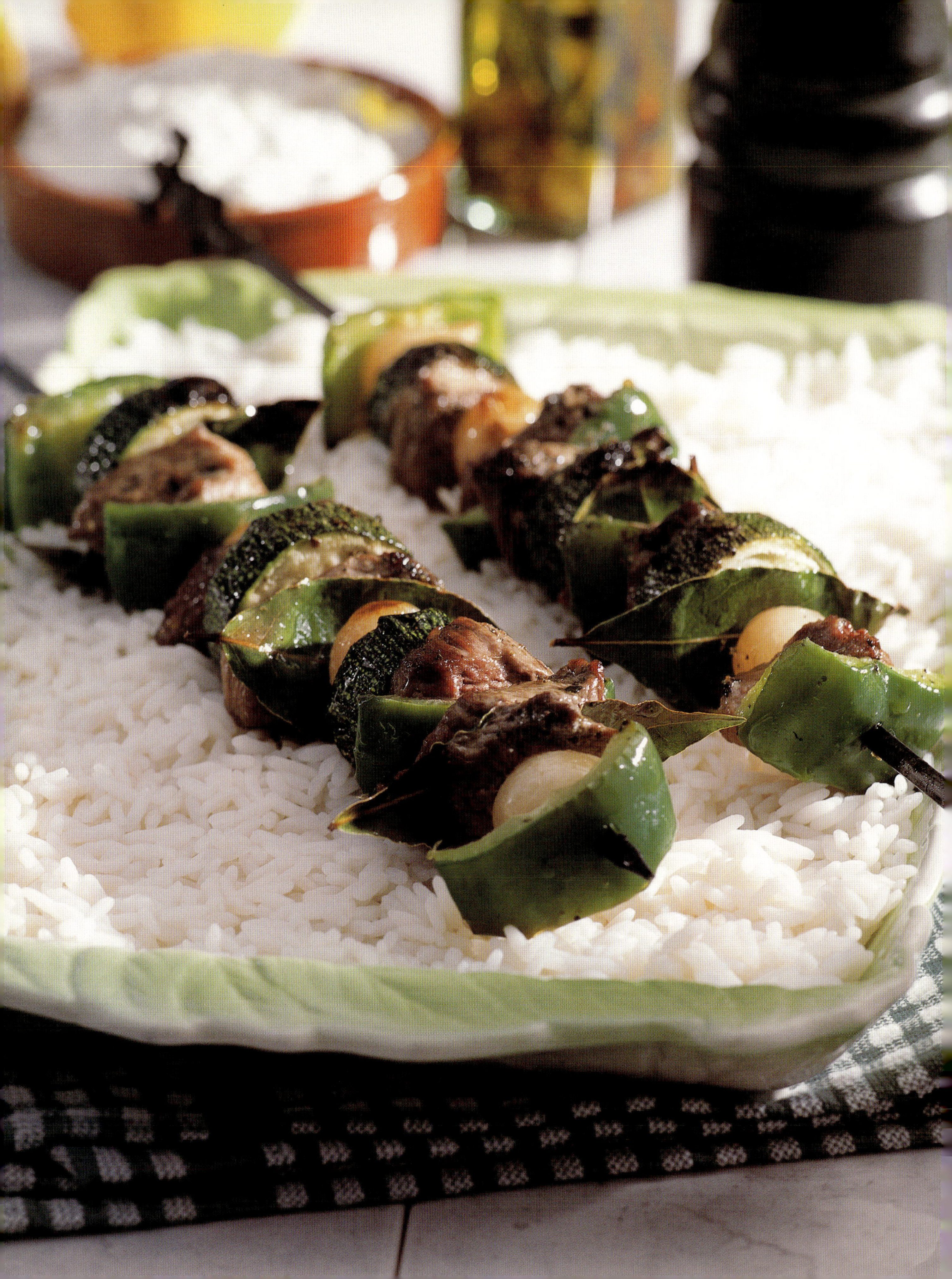

meat & poultry dishes

marinated lamb and vegetable kabobs
souvlákia

Souvlákia comes from the Greek word, souvlá, meaning spit or skewer. These kabobs are very popular in Greece and are ideal for cooking on a barbecue. Serve with their traditional accompaniment of Tzatzíki, rice or a pilaf, and a salad.

1. Put the lemon juice, oil, garlic, oregano or mint, salt, and pepper in a bowl and whisk together. Trim and cut the lamb into 1½-inch/4-cm cubes and add to the marinade.

2. Toss the lamb in the marinade, cover and refrigerate overnight or for at least 8 hours. Stir occasionally to coat the lamb.

3. When ready to serve, core, seed the bell peppers, and cut into 1¼-inch/3-cm cubes. Cut the zucchini into 1-inch/2.5-cm pieces. Thread the lamb, bell peppers, zucchini, onions, and bay leaves onto 8 flat, greased metal kabob skewers, alternating and dividing the ingredients as evenly as possible. Place on a greased broiler pan.

4. Preheat the broiler then put the kabobs under the broiler for 10–15 minutes, turning frequently and basting with any remaining marinade, until cooked. Serve hot, garnished with lemon wedges, with a bowl of Tzatzíki.

SERVES 4

juice of 2 large lemons

⅓ cup olive oil

1 garlic clove, crushed

1 tbsp chopped fresh oregano or mint

salt and pepper

1 lb 9 oz/700 g boned leg or fillet of lamb

2 green bell peppers

2 zucchini

12 pearl onions

8 large bay leaves

lemon wedges, to garnish

Tzatzíki (see page 47), to serve

cinnamon lamb casserole
arní me kanéla

The combination of spicy cinnamon, raisins, wine, tomatoes, and vinegar produces a rich, pungent stew, which is topped with a spoonful of garlicky yogurt. Serve with potatoes, rice, or a pilaf to mop up the delicious aromatic juices.

SERVES 6

2 tbsp all-purpose flour

pepper

2 lb 4 oz/1 kg lean boned lamb, cubed

2 tbsp olive oil

2 large onions, sliced

1 garlic clove, chopped finely

1¼ cups full-bodied red wine

2 tbsp red wine vinegar

14 oz/400 g canned chopped tomatoes in juice

⅓ cup seedless raisins

1 tbsp ground cinnamon

pinch of sugar

1 bay leaf

salt

paprika, to garnish

topping

⅔ cup authentic Greek yogurt

2 garlic cloves, crushed

salt and pepper

1. Put the flour and pepper in a plastic bag, add the lamb, and shake well to coat each piece. Heat the oil in a large, flameproof casserole or Dutch oven. Add the onions and garlic and fry for 5 minutes, until softened. Add the lamb to the casserole and fry for about 5 minutes, stirring frequently, until browned on all sides.

2. Pour in the wine, vinegar, and tomatoes, stirring in any glazed bits from the bottom of the casserole, and bring to the boil. Reduce the heat and add the raisins, cinnamon, sugar, and bay leaf. Season with salt and pepper.

3. Cover the casserole with a lid and simmer gently for 2 hours, until the lamb is tender.

4. Meanwhile, make the topping. Put the yogurt into a small serving bowl, stir in the garlic, and season with salt and pepper. Chill in the fridge until ready to serve.

5. Serve the casserole hot, topped with a spoonful of the garlic yogurt, and dust with paprika.

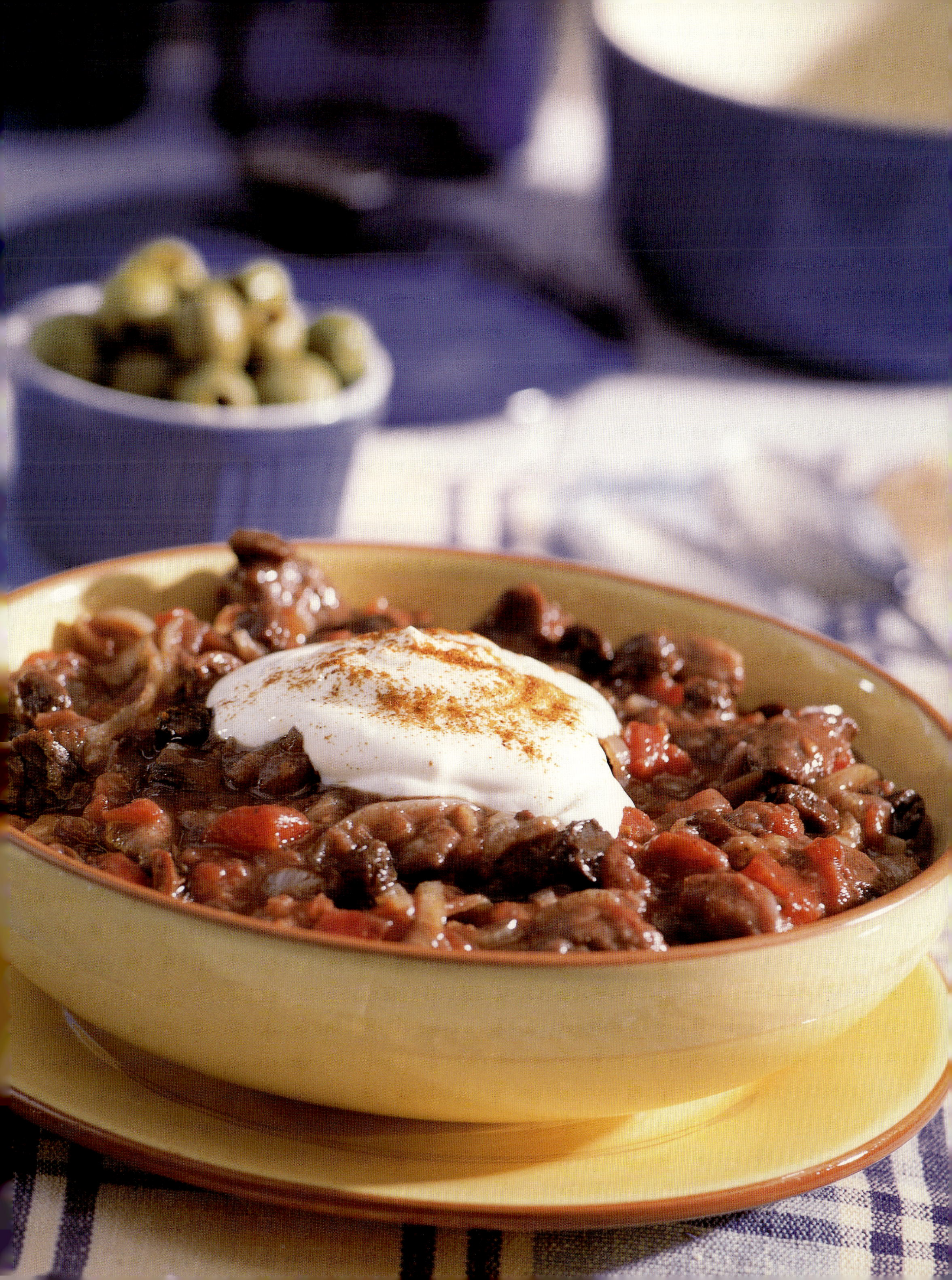

roast lamb with orzo
arní me giouvétsi

Orzo is a very small form of pasta which looks like flat wheat grains. It is used in soup and meat dishes and served as an accompaniment. In this recipe it is baked with lamb and absorbs the meat juices, giving it the most wonderful flavor. It is an immensely popular dish in Greece, where it is also made with kid and beef.

SERVES 4

- 1 lb 10 oz/750 g boned leg or shoulder of lamb
- ½ lemon, sliced thinly
- 1 tbsp chopped fresh oregano
- 4 large garlic cloves, 2 chopped finely and 2 sliced thinly
- salt and pepper
- 1 lb 12 oz/800 g canned chopped tomatoes in juice
- pinch of sugar
- 1 bay leaf
- 2 tbsp olive oil
- 1⅓ cups orzo or short grain rice

1. If necessary, untie the leg of lamb and open out. Place the lemon slices down the middle, sprinkle over half the oregano, the chopped garlic, salt and pepper. Roll up the meat and tie with string. Using the tip of a sharp knife, make slits in the lamb, and insert the garlic slices.

2. Calculate the cooking time, allowing 25 minutes per 1 lb/450 g plus 25 minutes.

3. Put the tomatoes and their juice, ⅔ cup cold water, the remaining oregano, sugar, and the bay leaf in a large roasting tin. Place the lamb on top, drizzle over the olive oil, and season with salt and pepper.

4. Roast the lamb in a preheated oven, 350°F/180°C, for the calculated cooking time. Fifteen minutes before the lamb is cooked, stir ⅔ cup boiling water and the orzo into the tomatoes. Add a little extra water if the sauce seems too thick. Return to the oven for a further 15 minutes, until the lamb and orzo are tender and the tomatoes reduced to a thick sauce.

5. To serve, carve the lamb into slices and serve hot with the orzo and tomato sauce.

Steps down to the alluring Aegean Sea

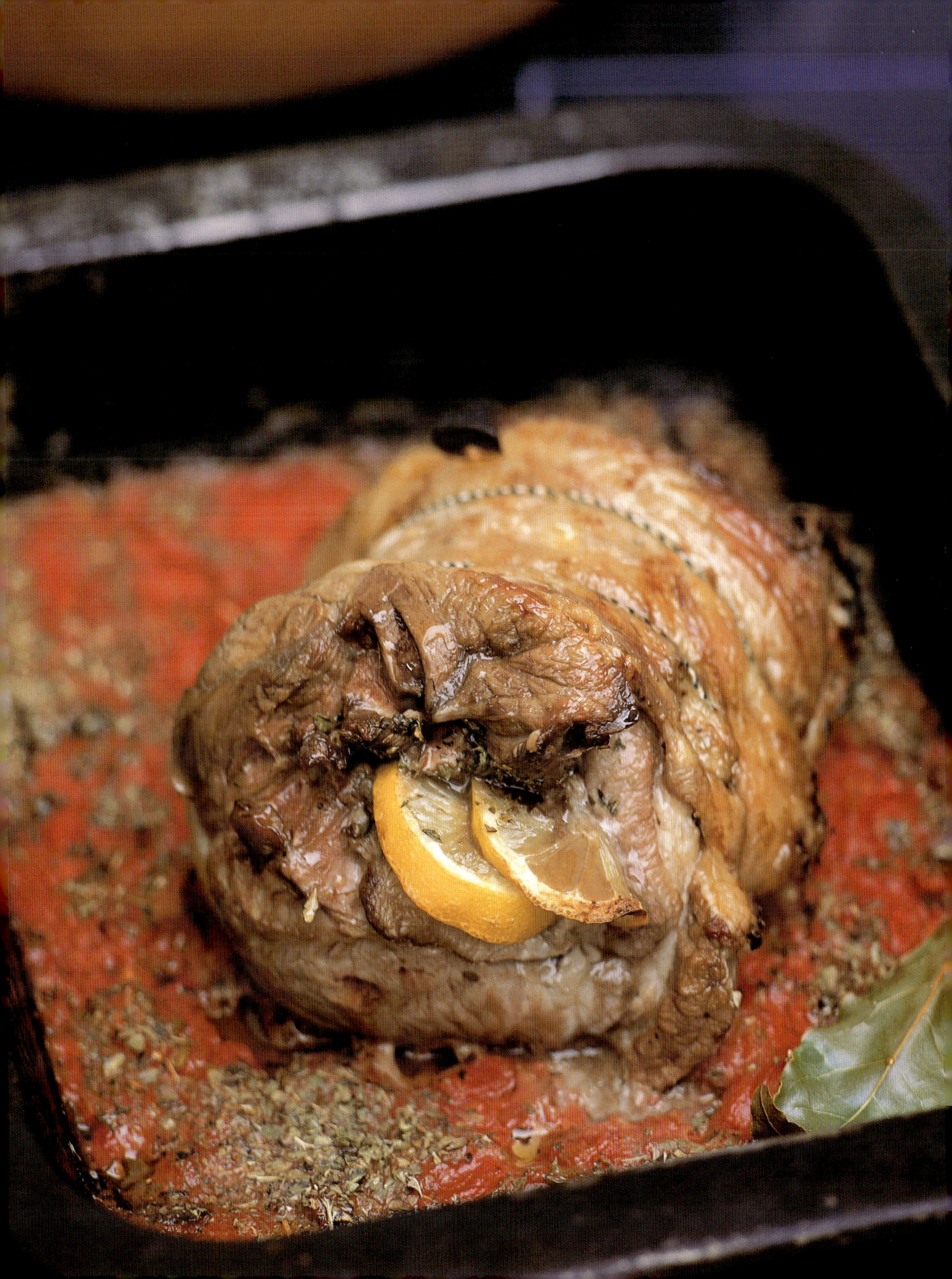

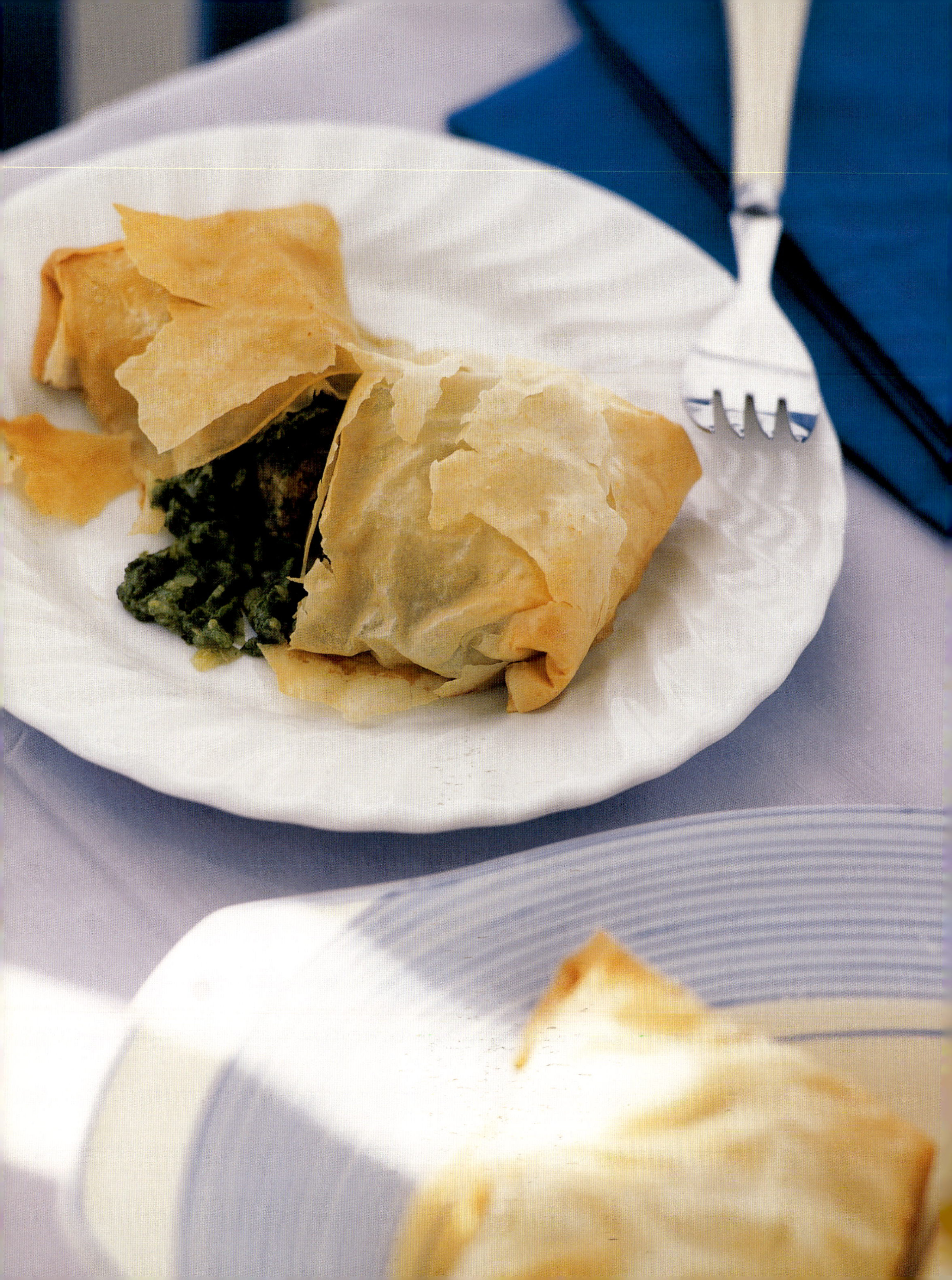

meat & poultry dishes

rosemary lamb in phyllo pastry
arní me dendrolívano se fílo

Lamb fillet, encased in phyllo pastry with a spinach purée, can only be described as truly delicious!

SERVES 4

3 tbsp olive oil

1 small onion, chopped finely

1 garlic clove, chopped finely

6 oz/175 g fresh spinach leaves

pinch of freshly grated nutmeg

2 tbsp authentic Greek yogurt

salt and pepper

4 lamb fillets, each weighing about 4 oz/115 g

1 tsp finely chopped fresh rosemary leaves

2½ oz/70 g butter

8 sheets authentic Greek phyllo pastry

1. Heat 2 tablespoons of the olive oil in a heavy-bottomed saucepan, add the onion and garlic, and fry for about 5 minutes, until softened. Add the spinach leaves and nutmeg and cook for 3 minutes, stirring.

2. Turn the spinach mixture into a food processor or blender, add the yogurt, salt, and pepper and blend until smooth. Let cool.

3. Meanwhile, heat the remaining tablespoon of oil in a skillet. Add the lamb fillets and rosemary and fry for 3 minutes on each side. Remove from the skillet, drain on kitchen towels and let cool.

4. When the lamb fillets are cool, slash each fillet 4 times, almost all the way through. Fill each slash with the spinach mixture, spreading any remaining mixture on top. Season the fillets with salt and pepper.

5. Melt the butter. Take 1 sheet of pastry and cover the remaining sheets with a damp dish towel. Brush the sheet with a little of the melted butter. Place a second sheet on top, brush with butter and fold in half. Put a lamb fillet in the center and wrap to form a parcel. Place on a baking tray and brush with butter. Repeat with the remaining pastry and lamb to form 4 parcels.

6. Bake the lamb parcels in a preheated oven, 375°F/190°C, for 25 minutes, until golden. Serve hot.

variations

Pork tenderloin can be used in exactly the same way as the lamb and, instead of the spinach paste, you could use a leek paste with either meat. Prepare this in the same way as the spinach paste in the recipe but substitute the spinach leaves with the same quantity of sliced leeks and cook for 10 minutes until tender.

lamb with eggplant and black olive sauce
arní me melitzána kai eliés

Choose firm, juicy Kalamáta olives to add to the sauce of this dish. Pasta would make an ideal accompaniment.

SERVES 4

1 eggplant
salt and pepper
4–8 lamb chops
3 tbsp olive oil
1 onion, chopped coarsely
1 garlic clove, chopped finely
14 oz/400 g canned chopped tomatoes in juice
pinch of sugar
16 black olives preferably Kalamáta, pitted and chopped coarsely
1 tsp chopped fresh herbs such as basil, flat-leaf parsley, or oregano

1. Cut the eggplant into ¾-inch/2-cm cubes, put in a colander standing over a large plate, and sprinkle each layer with salt. Cover with a plate and place a heavy weight on top. Leave for 30 minutes.

2. Preheat the broiler. Rinse the eggplant slices under cold running water, then pat dry with paper towels. Season the lamb chops with pepper.

3. Place the lamb chops on the broiler pan and cook under medium heat for 10–15 minutes until tender, turning once during the cooking time.

4. Meanwhile, heat the olive oil in a saucepan, add the eggplant, onion, and garlic, and fry for 10 minutes, until softened and starting to brown. Add the tomatoes and their juice, the sugar, olives, chopped herbs, salt, and pepper and simmer for 5–10 minutes.

5. To serve, spoon the sauce onto 4 warmed serving plates and top with the lamb chops.

lamb's liver in red wine and orange sauce
sikotakiá me sáltsa

Choose lamb's liver for a midweek meal and calf's liver for a special occasion. They are two quite different dishes! Serve with pasta or rice.

SERVES 4

2 oranges
8 thin slices lamb's or calf's liver
2 tbsp all-purpose flour
1 tsp paprika
3 tbsp olive oil
¾ cup dry red wine
2 tbsp chopped fresh flat-leaf parsley, plus extra to garnish
2 tbsp chopped fresh oregano
salt and pepper

1. Using a zester, remove the zest from the oranges. Put the zest in a small saucepan of boiling water, boil for 1 minute, then drain and set aside. Squeeze the juice from the oranges and set aside.

2. Remove and discard any ducts and membrane from the liver slices. Put the flour and paprika in a plastic bag, add the liver, and shake well to coat each piece.

3. Heat the oil in a large skillet. Add the liver and fry over a medium heat for 4–5 minutes, stirring constantly, until lightly browned all over but still moist in the center. Remove from the skillet with a slotted spoon and place on 4 warmed serving plates.

4. Add the wine to the skillet, stirring in any glazed bits from the bottom. Boil briskly for 1 minute. Reduce the heat and stir in the orange juice, parsley, oregano, salt, and pepper. Heat gently until reduced slightly, then spoon over the liver and garnish with the reserved orange zest and parsley. Serve hot.

baked pasta with spicy meat sauce
pastítsio

SERVES 4-6

2 tbsp olive oil

1 onion, chopped finely

2 garlic cloves, chopped finely

1 lb 7 oz/650 g lean minced lamb or beef

14 oz/400 g canned chopped tomatoes in juice

pinch of sugar

2 tbsp chopped fresh flat-leaf parsley

1 tbsp chopped fresh marjoram

1 tsp ground cinnamon

$1/2$ tsp grated nutmeg

$1/4$ tsp ground cloves

salt and pepper

8 oz/225 g long, hollow Greek macaroni or other short pasta

2 eggs, beaten

$1 1/4$ cups authentic Greek yogurt

2 oz/55 g authentic Greek feta cheese, grated

1 oz/25 g kefalotiri or pecorino cheese, grated

*This traditional dish of cooked pasta (*makarónia*) and a spicy lamb or beef sauce, topped with a cheese sauce, is not dissimilar to moussaká. It only needs a simple green salad to accompany it.*

1 Heat the oil in a saucepan, add the onion and garlic, and fry for 5 minutes, until softened. Add the lamb or beef and fry for about 5 minutes, until browned all over, stirring frequently and breaking up the meat.

2 Add the tomatoes to the saucepan, the sugar, parsley, marjoram, cinnamon, nutmeg, cloves, salt, and pepper. Bring to the boil then simmer, uncovered, for 30 minutes, stirring occasionally.

3 Meanwhile, cook the macaroni in a large saucepan of boiling salted water for 10-12 minutes or as directed on the package, until tender, then drain well. Beat together the eggs, yogurt, and feta cheese. Season with salt and pepper.

4 When the meat is cooked, transfer it to a large ovenproof dish. Add the macaroni in a layer to cover the meat then pour over the sauce. Sprinkle over the kefalotiri or pecorino cheese.

5 Bake in a preheated oven, 375°F/190°C, for 30-45 minutes, until golden brown. Serve hot or warm, cut into portions.

Few visitors will fail to be awed by the classical landscape of Greece

Overleaf A beautiful town clings spectacularly to volcanic cliffs that spill down to the sea

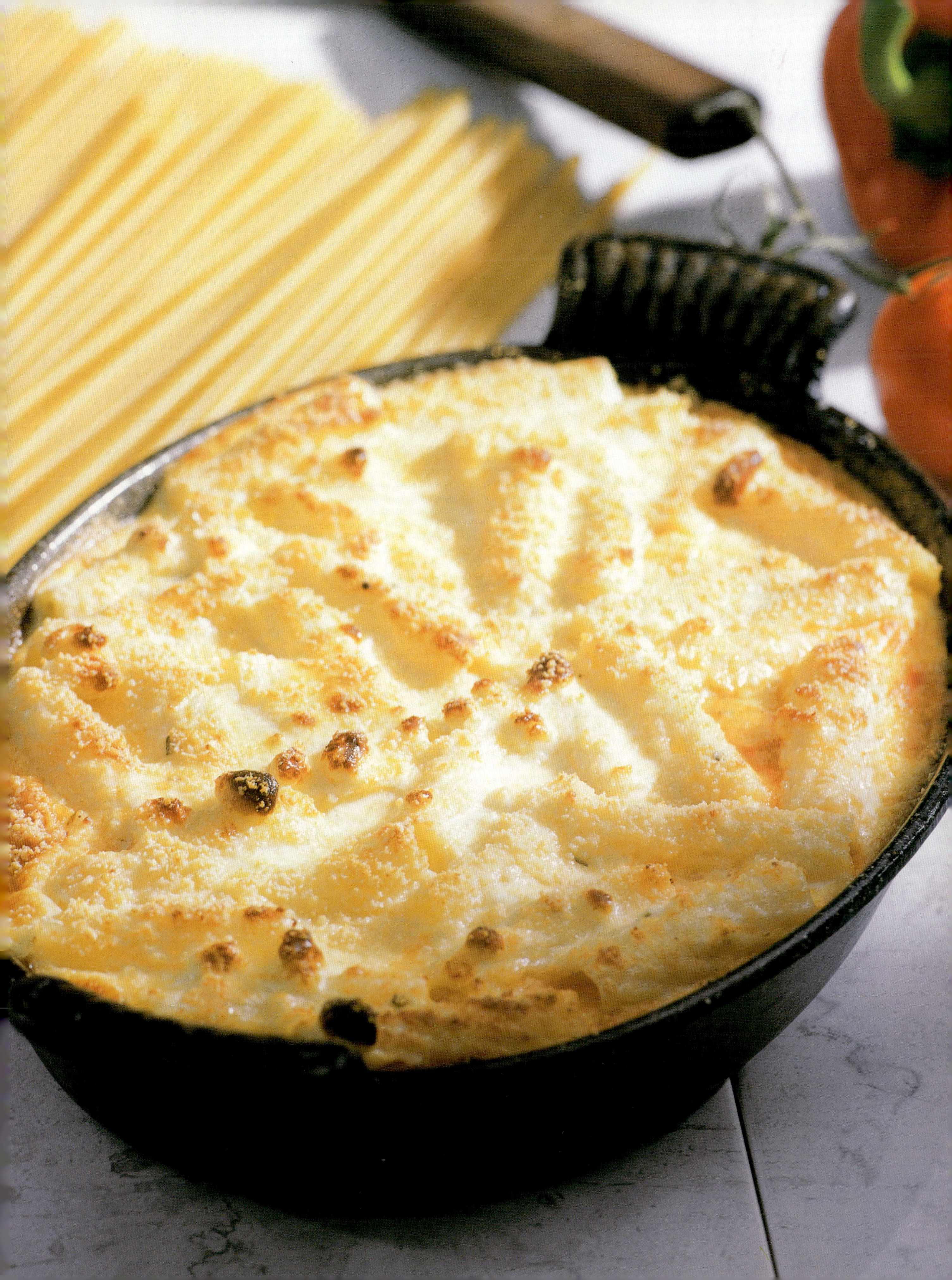

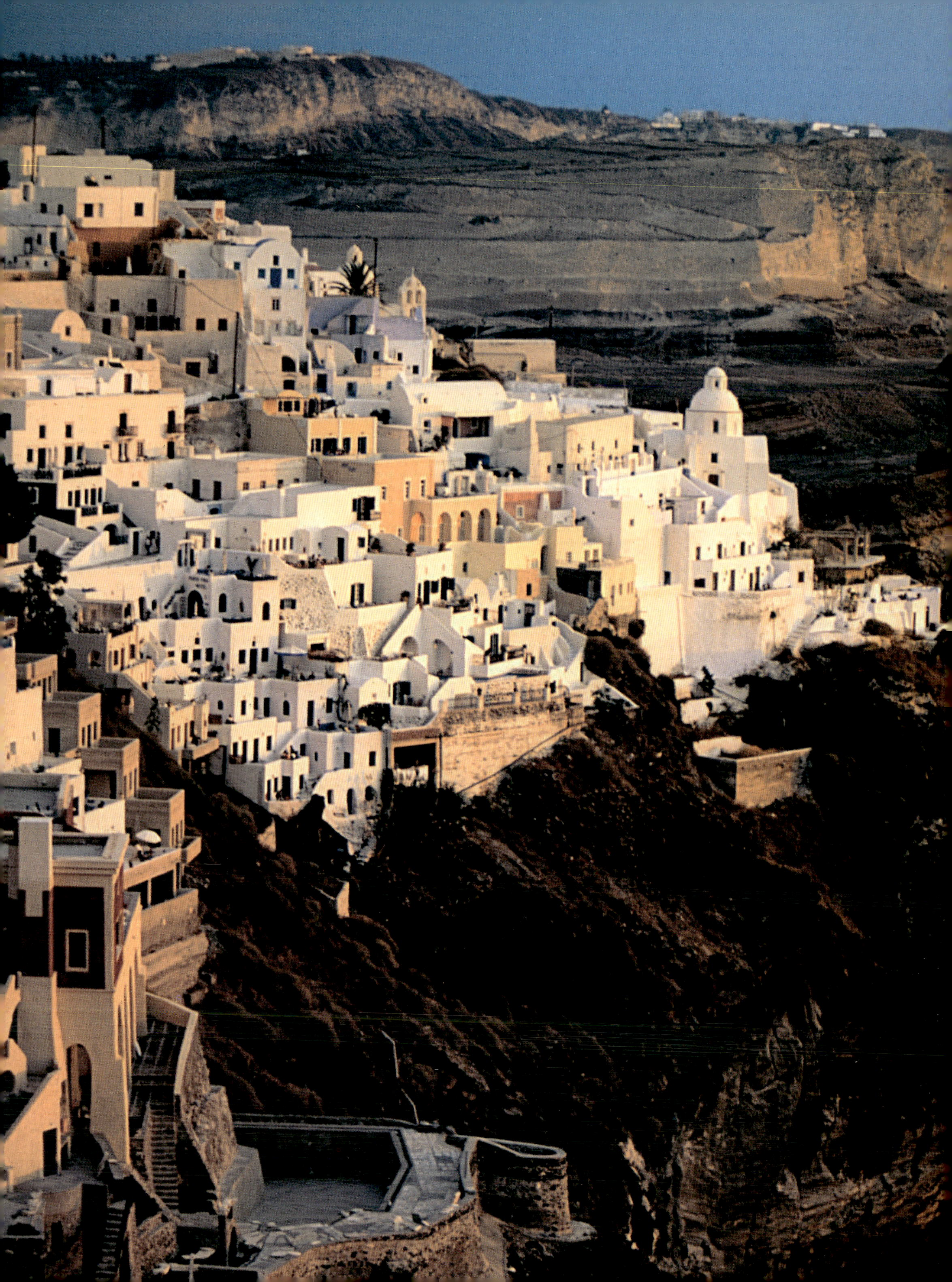

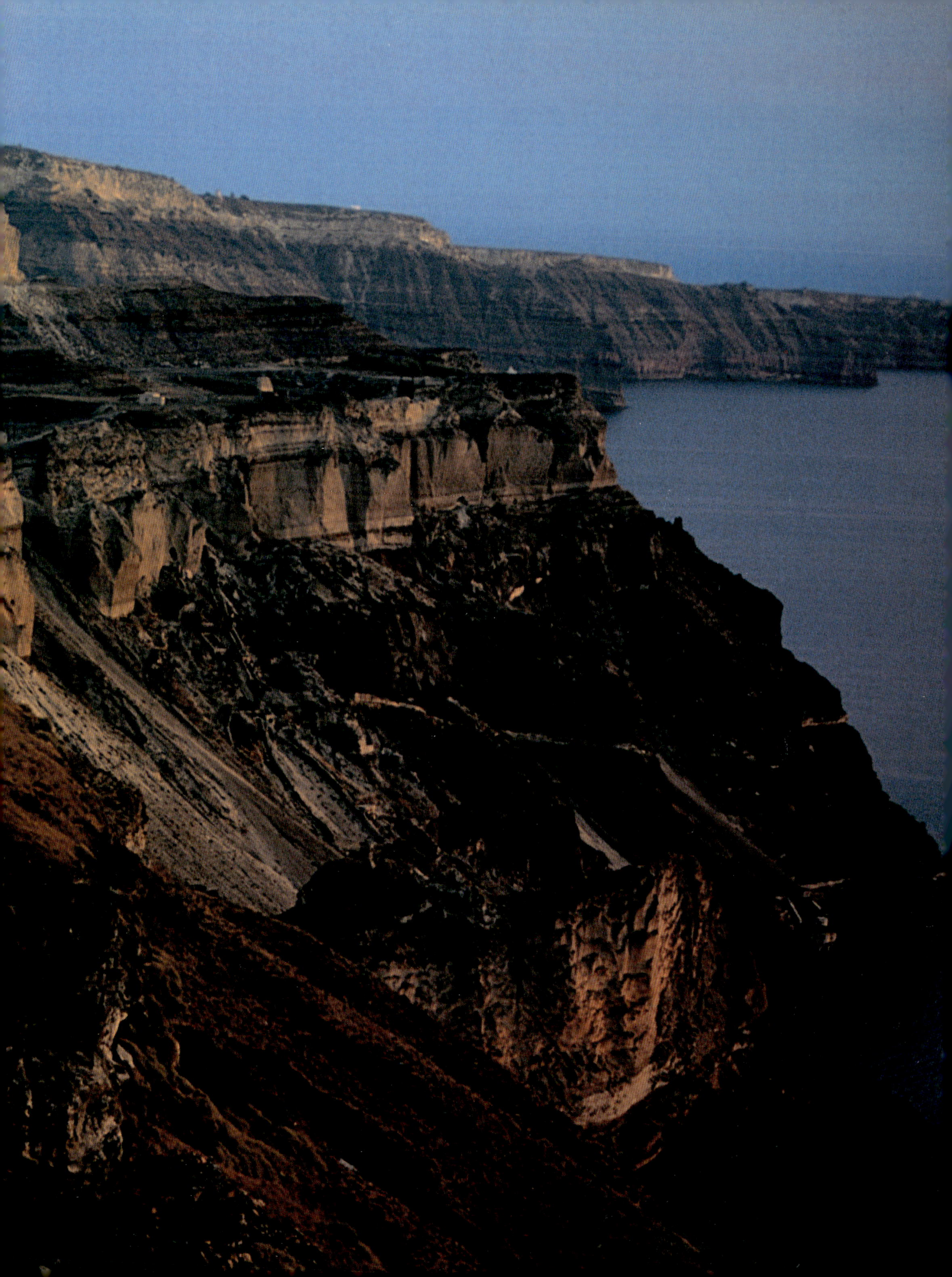

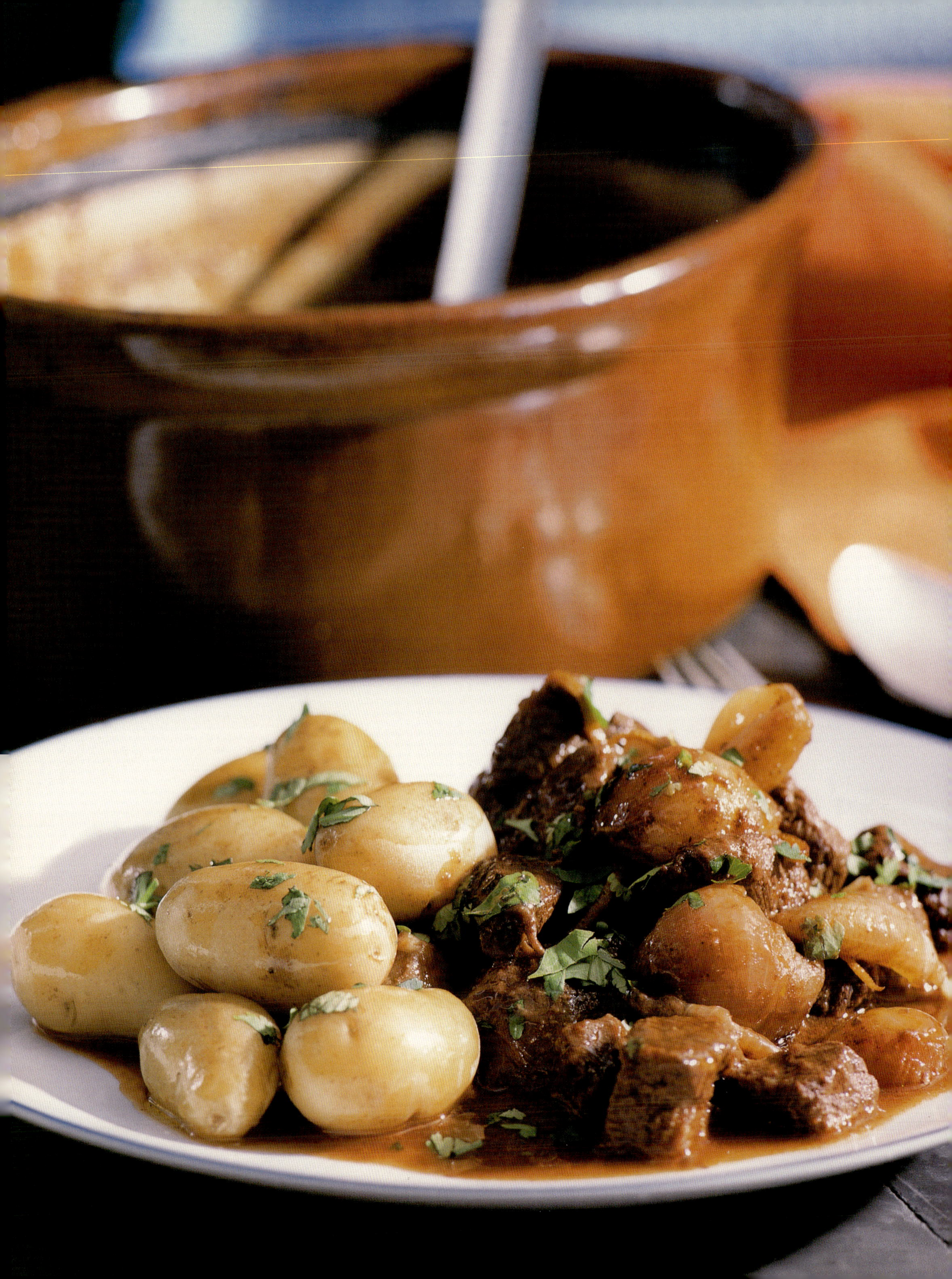

meat & poultry dishes

thick beef and pearl onion casserole
stifádo

A stifádo, *made with onions and red wine and spiced with cinnamon, cloves, and cumin, is a warming casserole ideal for serving in winter. The lid is removed toward the end of the cooking time to allow some of the liquid to reduce and thicken. It can also be prepared with rabbit, chicken, pork, or beef. Serve it with boiled or mashed potatoes.*

1 Heat the oil in a large flameproof casserole or Dutch oven. Add the whole onions and the garlic and fry for 5 minutes until softened and beginning to brown. Add the beef to the casserole and fry for about 5 minutes, stirring frequently, until browned on all sides.

2 Stir the cinnamon, cloves, cumin, tomato purée, salt, and pepper into the casserole. Pour in the wine, stirring in any glazed bits from the bottom, then add the grated orange rind and juice and the bay leaf. Bring to the boil then cover the casserole.

3 Cook in a preheated oven, 300°F/150°C, for about 1¼ hours. Remove the lid and cook the casserole for a further hour, stirring once or twice during this time, until the meat is tender. Garnish with chopped fresh parsley and serve hot, with boiled or mashed potatoes.

*cook's tip
If you find it difficult to skin the pearl onions, bring a large saucepan of water to a boil, remove from the heat then plunge the onions quickly into the hot water, then into cold, before skinning.

SERVES 6

2 tbsp olive oil

1 lb/450 g pearl onions

2 garlic cloves, halved

2 lb/900 g stewing beef, cubed

½ tsp ground cinnamon

1 tsp ground cloves

1 tsp ground cumin

2 tbsp tomato purée

salt and pepper

1 bottle full-bodied red wine

grated rind and juice of 1 orange

1 bay leaf

chopped fresh flat-leaf parsley, to garnish

braised veal in red wine
moshári me kókkino krási

SERVES 6

- 4 tbsp all-purpose flour
- 2 lb/900 g stewing veal or beef, cubed
- 4 tbsp olive oil
- 12 oz/350 g pearl onions
- 2 garlic cloves, chopped finely
- 2 cups sliced carrots
- 1¼ cups dry red wine
- ⅔ cup beef or chicken stock
- 14 oz/400 g canned chopped tomatoes with herbs in juice
- pared rind of 1 lemon
- 1 bay leaf
- 1 tbsp chopped fresh flat-leaf parsley
- 1 tbsp chopped fresh basil
- 1 tsp chopped fresh thyme
- salt and pepper

This is a classic casserole of meat braised in wine with garlic, tomatoes, and a liberal amount of herbs. You can use stewing veal or beef and it goes particularly well with rice.

1 Put the flour and pepper in a plastic bag, add the meat and shake well to coat each piece. Heat the oil in a large flameproof casserole or Dutch oven. Add the meat and fry, in batches, for 5–10 minutes, stirring constantly, until browned on all sides. Remove with a slotted spoon and set aside.

2 Add the whole onions, the garlic, and carrots to the casserole and fry for 5 minutes until beginning to soften. Return the meat to the casserole.

3 Pour in the wine, stirring in any glazed bits from the bottom, then add the stock, the tomatoes with their juice, lemon rind, bay leaf, parsley, basil, thyme, salt, and pepper. Bring to the boil then cover the casserole.

4 Cook in a preheated oven, 350°F/180°C, for about 2 hours, until the meat is tender. Serve hot with rice.

cook's tip

This is a perfect casserole for cooking in advance and then reheating. Once cooked, let cool and store in the refrigerator. Reheat by bringing to a boil then simmering for 15 minutes.

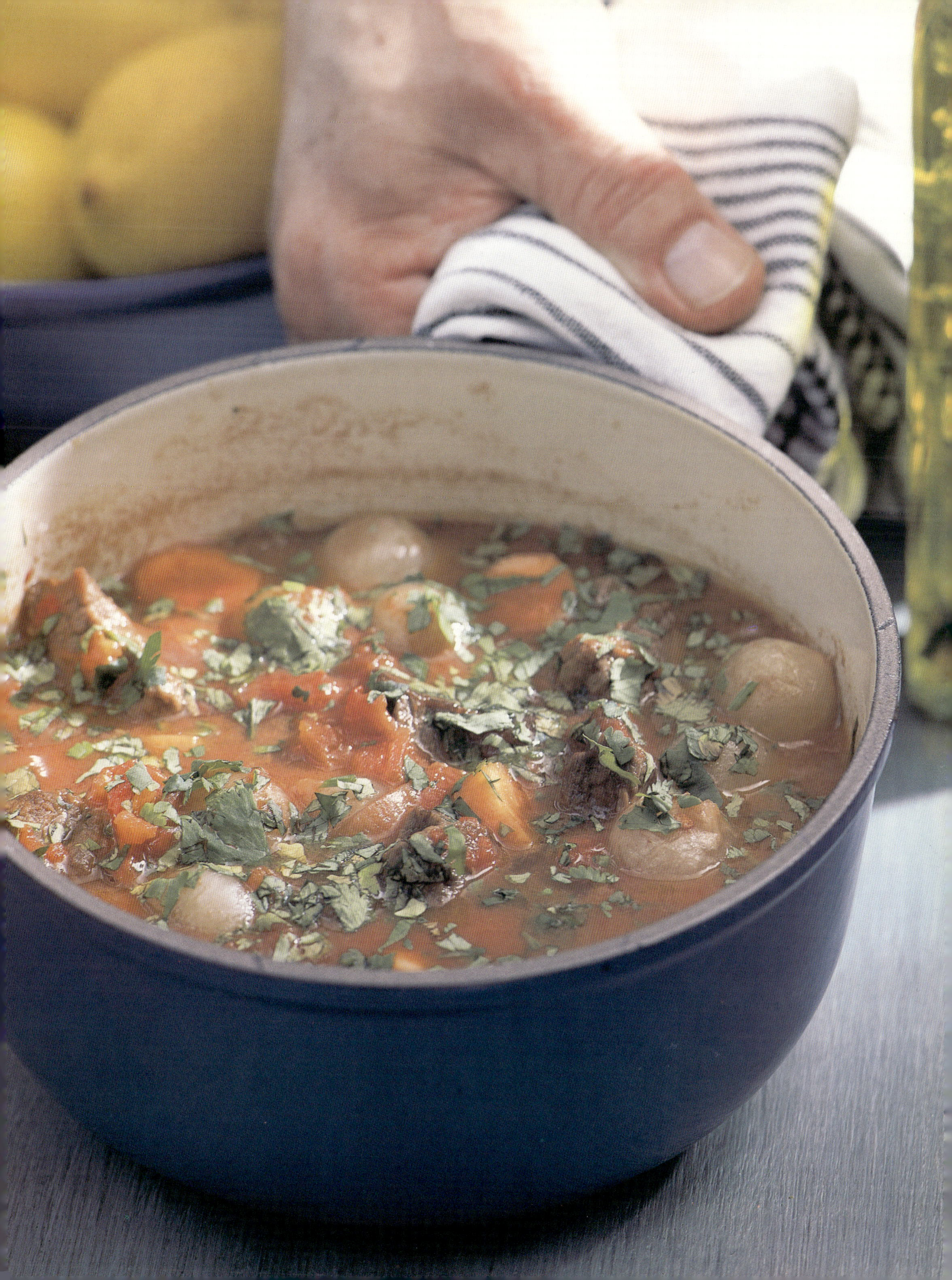

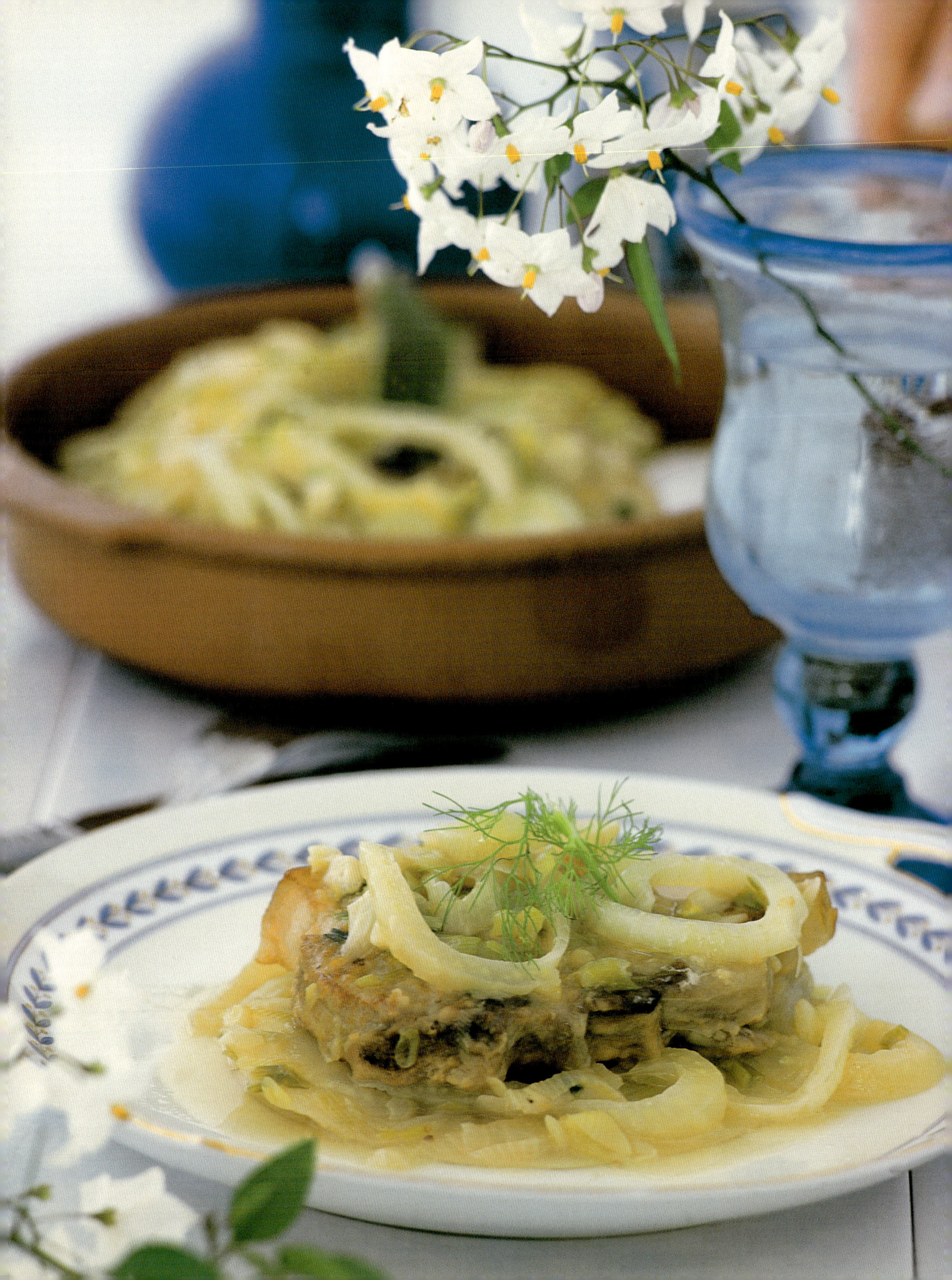

braised pork with fennel
hirinó me aníthos

In Greek cooking, the fronds, bulb, and seeds of fennel are all used. They combine particularly well with pork, as this recipe illustrates.

SERVES 4
1 tsp fennel seeds
grated rind of 1 lemon
salt and pepper
4 pork chops
1 tbsp all-purpose flour
2 tbsp olive oil
2 bunches scallions, sliced thinly
1 garlic clove, chopped finely
2 fennel bulbs, sliced thinly with fronds reserved
1 cup dry white wine
1 bay leaf

1 Crush the fennel seeds and mix with the lemon rind, salt, and pepper. Spread the mixture over both sides of the pork chops and let marinate for about 1 hour.

2 Dust the pork chops with the flour. Heat the oil in a flameproof casserole or Dutch oven, add the pork, and fry until browned on both sides. Remove from the casserole. Add the onions, garlic, and fennel to the casserole and fry for 5–10 minutes until softened and beginning to brown. Return the chops to the casserole.

3 Pour in the wine, stirring in any glazed bits from the bottom of the casserole, and bring to the boil. Reduce the heat and add the bay leaf. Cover the casserole with a lid and simmer for 45 minutes, until the pork chops are tender. Serve sprinkled with the reserved snipped fennel fronds.

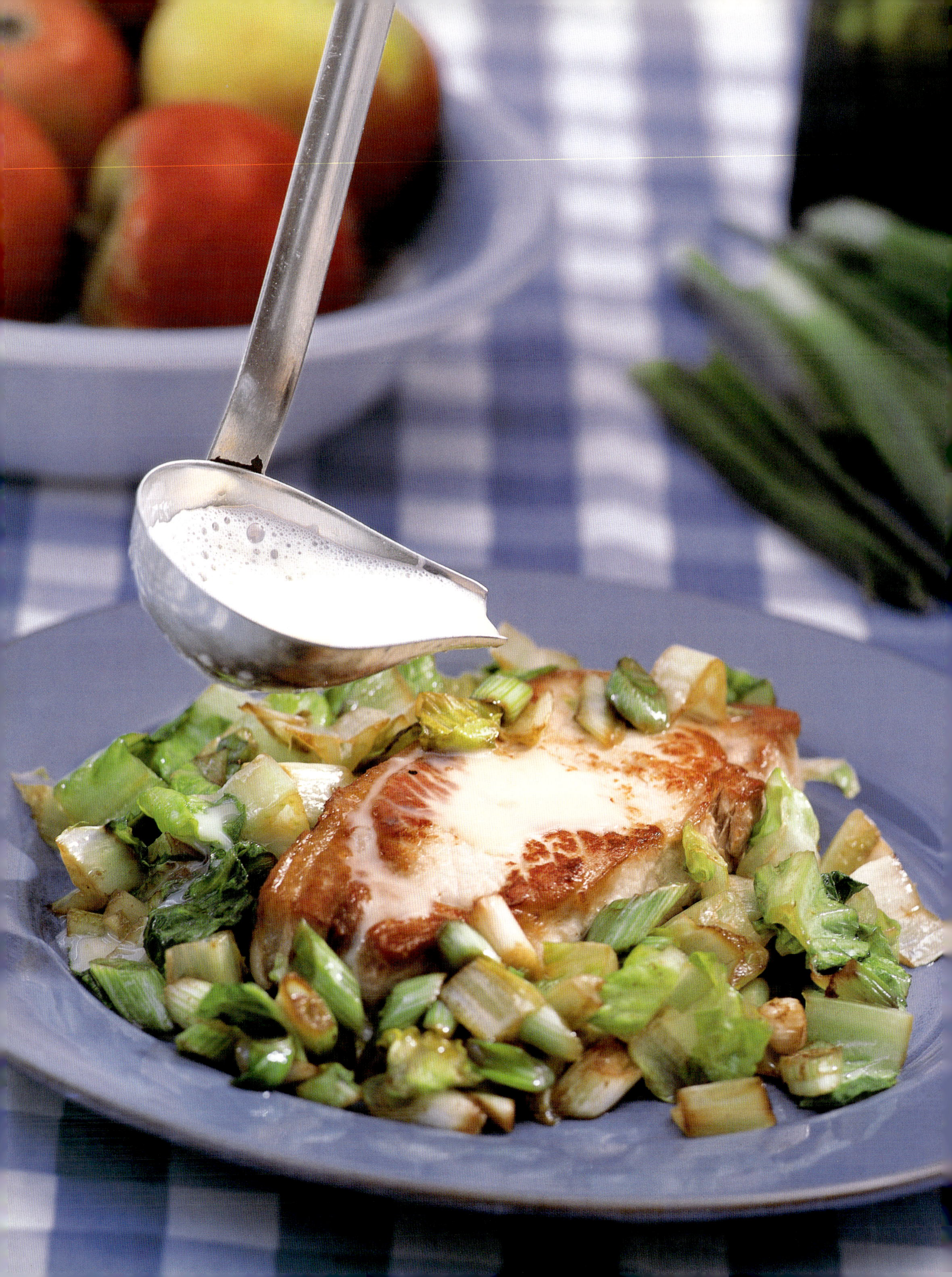

pork and cos lettuce in egg and lemon sauce
hirinó avgolémono

Avgolémono is Greece's traditional egg and lemon sauce that is served with meat, poultry, fish, and vegetable dishes, or added to soups and casseroles. It is perhaps best-known served with lamb or chicken but it also marries well with pork as this recipe illustrates. Serve with boiled new potatoes.

1. Season the pork steaks with pepper. Heat the oil in a large, heavy-bottomed skillet, add the scallions and fry for 2 minutes until softened. Add the pork steaks and fry for 10 minutes, turning the steaks several times, until browned on both sides and tender.

2. When the pork steaks are cooked, add the lettuce, dill, and stock to the skillet. Bring to the boil, cover, and then simmer for 4–5 minutes, until the lettuce has wilted.

3. Meanwhile, put the eggs and lemon juice in a large bowl and whisk together.

4. When the lettuce has wilted remove the pork steaks and lettuce from the skillet with a slotted spoon, put in a warmed serving dish and keep warm in a low oven. Strain the cooking liquid into a measuring jug.

5. Gradually add 4 tablespoons of the hot cooking liquid to the lemon mixture, whisking all the time. Pour the egg mixture into the skillet and simmer for 2–3 minutes, whisking all the time, until the sauce thickens. (Do not boil or the sauce will curdle.) Season with salt and pepper. Pour the sauce over the pork steaks and lettuce and serve hot.

SERVES 4

4 pork loin steaks
pepper
2 tbsp olive oil
bunch scallions, white parts only, sliced thinly
1 romaine lettuce, sliced thinly widthwise
1 tbsp chopped fresh dill
1 cup chicken stock
2 eggs
juice of 1 large lemon
salt

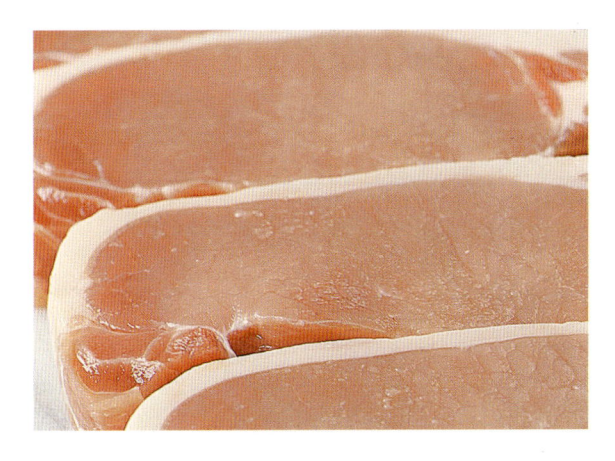

grilled chicken with lemon
kotópoulo scharás me lemóni

Since chicken is popular and lemons grow in abundance in Greece, chicken and lemon are a natural combination. This tangy, sharp lemon marinade complements the broiled chicken perfectly. If preferred, the chicken pieces can also be cooked on a barbecue. Serve with rice or a pilaf.

SERVES 4

4 chicken quarters
grated rind and juice of 2 lemons
4 tbsp olive oil
2 garlic cloves, crushed
2 sprigs fresh thyme
salt and pepper

1 Prick the skin of the chicken quarters all over with a fork. Put the chicken pieces in a dish, add the lemon juice, oil, garlic, thyme, salt, and pepper and mix well. Cover and let marinate in the fridge for at least 2 hours.

2 To cook the chicken, preheat the broiler or barbecue. Put the chicken in a broiler pan or on the barbecue grid and baste with the marinade. Cook for 30–40 minutes, basting and turning occasionally, until the chicken is tender. (To test if the chicken is cooked, pierce the thickest part of the chicken pieces with a skewer. If the juices run clear, they are ready.) Serve hot, with any remaining marinade spooned over, and garnished with the grated lemon rind.

meat & poultry dishes

spicy aromatic chicken
kotópoulo pikántiko

The spices give this chicken dish a true Balkan flavor. It is thought to have been invented by nomadic tribes who once wandered all over the Balkans and Greece. Serve with rice, pasta, or new potatoes.

SERVES 4

4–8 chicken pieces, skinned

½ lemon, cut into wedges

4 tbsp olive oil

1 onion, chopped coarsely

2 large garlic cloves, chopped finely

½ cup dry white wine

14 oz/400 g canned chopped tomatoes in juice

pinch of sugar

½ tsp ground cinnamon

½ tsp ground cloves

½ tsp ground allspice

salt and pepper

14 oz/400 g canned artichoke hearts or okra, drained

8 black olives, pitted

1 Rub the chicken pieces with the lemon. Heat the oil in a large flameproof casserole or lidded skillet. Add the onion and garlic and fry for 5 minutes, until softened. Add the chicken pieces and fry for 5–10 minutes, until browned on all sides.

2 Pour in the wine and add the tomatoes with their juice, the sugar, cinnamon, cloves, allspice, salt, and pepper and bring to the boil. Cover the casserole and simmer for 45 minutes–1 hour, until the chicken is tender.

3 Meanwhile, if using artichoke hearts, cut them in half. Add the artichokes or okra and the olives to the casserole 10 minutes before the end of cooking, and continue to simmer until heated through. Serve hot.

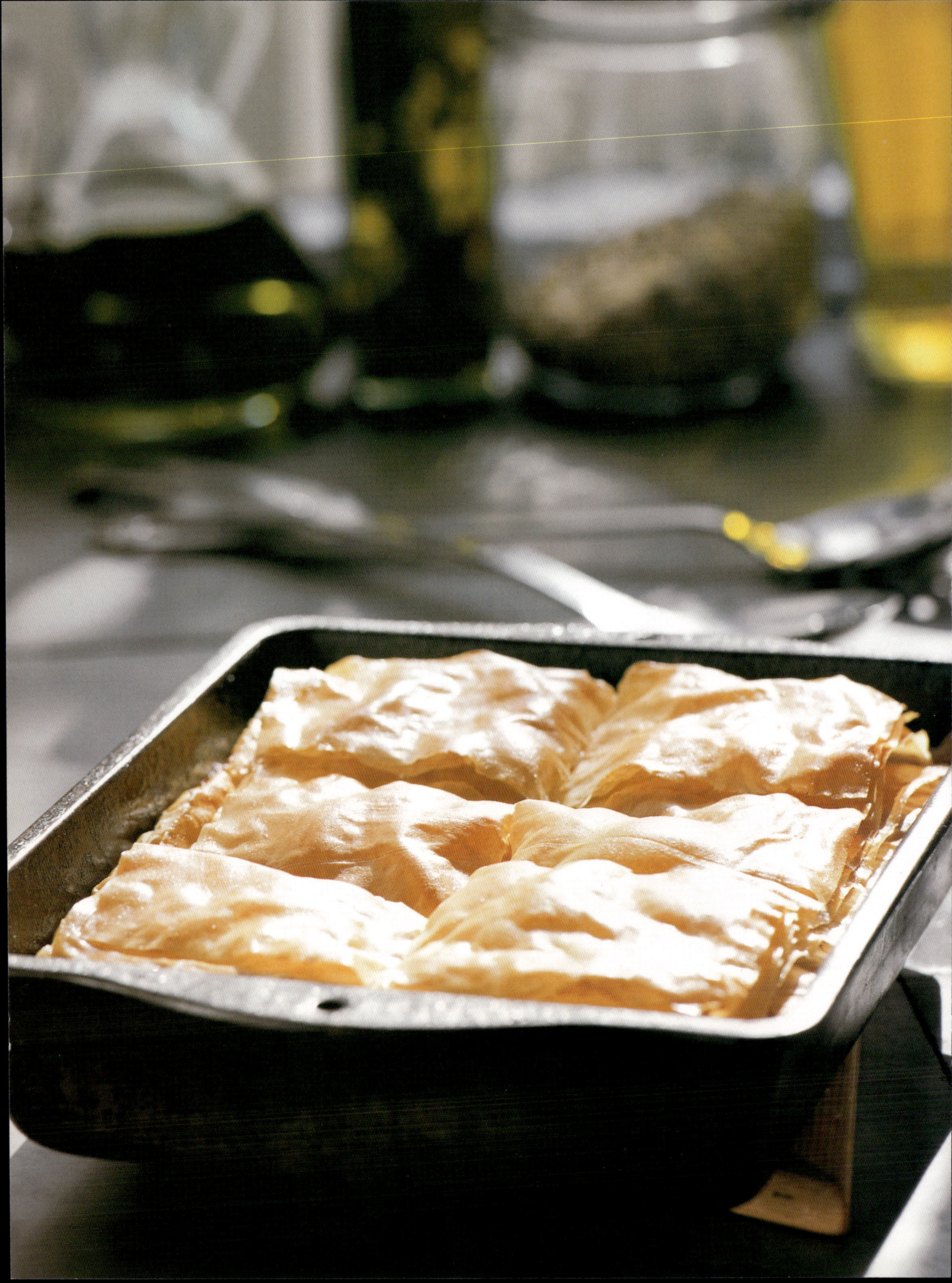

phyllo chicken pie
kotópita

This is the equivalent to the recipe for Spanakópita, *the Spinach and Feta Pie (see page 190), but here phyllo pastry is filled with chicken in an onion and cheese sauce for an equally delicious, mouth-watering dish.*

SERVES 6-8

3 lb 5 oz/1.5 kg whole chicken

1 small onion, halved, and 3 large onions, chopped finely

1 carrot, sliced thickly

1 celery stalk, sliced thickly

1 bay leaf

pared rind of 1 lemon

10 peppercorns

5½ oz/155 g butter

scant ½ cup all-purpose flour

⅔ cup milk

salt and pepper

⅓ cup kefalotiri or pecorino cheese, grated

3 eggs, beaten

8 oz/225 g authentic Greek phyllo pastry

1 Put the chicken in a large saucepan and add the halved onion, carrot, celery, bay leaf, lemon rind, and peppercorns. Pour in enough cold water to just cover the chicken legs and bring to the boil. Cover with a lid and simmer for about 1 hour. (To test if the chicken is cooked, pierce a thigh with a skewer. If the juices run clear it is ready.) Remove the chicken from the saucepan and set aside to cool.

2 Bring the stock to the boil and boil until reduced to about 2½ cups. Strain and reserve the stock.

3 When the chicken is cool enough to handle, remove the flesh, discarding the skin and bones. Cut the flesh into small bite-size pieces.

4 To make the filling, heat 2 oz/55 g of the butter in a saucepan, add the chopped onions, and fry for 5-10 minutes, until softened. Stir in the flour and cook gently, stirring, for 1-2 minutes. Remove from the heat and gradually stir in the reserved stock and the milk. Return to the heat, bring to the boil, stirring constantly, then simmer for 1-2 minutes until thick and smooth.

5 Remove the saucepan from the heat, stir in the chicken, and season with salt and pepper. Let cool. When the mixture has cooled, stir the cheese and eggs into the sauce and mix well together.

6 Melt the remaining 3½ oz/100 g butter and use a little to lightly grease a deep 12 x 8-inch-30 x 20-cm metal baking pan.

7 Cut the pastry sheets in half widthwise. Take one sheet of pastry and cover the remaining sheets with a damp dish towel. Use the sheet to line the pan and brush with a little of the melted butter. Repeat with half of the pastry sheets, brushing each with butter.

8 Spread the chicken filling over the pastry, then top with the remaining pastry sheets, brushing each with butter and tucking down the edges. Using a sharp knife, score the top layers of the pastry into 6 squares.

9 Bake the pie in a preheated oven, 375°F/190°C, for about 50 minutes, until golden brown. Remove from the oven and leave in a warm place for 5-10 minutes then serve hot, cut into squares.

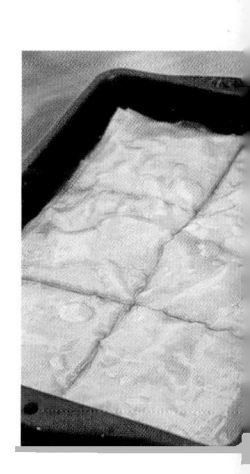

chicken kabobs with yogurt sauce
kotópoulo souvláki me sáltsa yaóurti

Kabobs, small cubes of meat broiled on a spit or skewer, have been popular in Greece since ancient times. Lamb is the usual choice but this recipe uses chicken, which is marinated in, cooked, and then served with a traditional yogurt sauce. The yogurt tenderizes the meat and makes it more succulent. The chicken can be threaded onto metal or wooden skewers or stalks of rosemary, which grow wild in the Greek hills. This dish couldn't be easier to prepare yet the result is delicious. Serve with rice or a pilaf.

SERVES 4

1¼ cups authentic Greek yogurt

2 garlic cloves, crushed

juice of ½ lemon juice

1 tbsp chopped fresh herbs such as oregano, dill, tarragon, or parsley

salt and pepper

4 large skinned, boned chicken breasts

8 firm stems of fresh rosemary, optional

shredded romaine lettuce, to serve

lemon wedges, to garnish

1. To make the sauce, put the yogurt, garlic, lemon juice, oregano, salt, and pepper in a large bowl and mix well together.

2. Cut the chicken breasts into chunks measuring about 1½ inches/4 cm square. Add to the yogurt mixture and toss well together until the chicken pieces are coated. Cover and leave to marinate in the fridge for about 1 hour. If you are using wooden skewers, soak them in cold water for 30 minutes.

3. Preheat the broiler. Thread the pieces of chicken onto 8 flat, greased, metal kabob skewers, wooden skewers, or rosemary stems and place on a greased broiler pan.

4. Cook the kabobs under the broiler for about 15 minutes, turning and basting with the remaining marinade occasionally, until lightly browned and tender.

5. Pour the remaining marinade into a saucepan and heat gently but do not boil. Serve the kabobs on a bed of shredded lettuce and garnish with lemon wedges. Accompany with the yogurt sauce.

variation

If liked, a selection of vegetables could be added to the kebobs. For an attractive and delicious combination try adding 8 cherry tomatoes, 1 thickly sliced zucchini, and 1 yellow bell pepper, cut into chunky pieces.

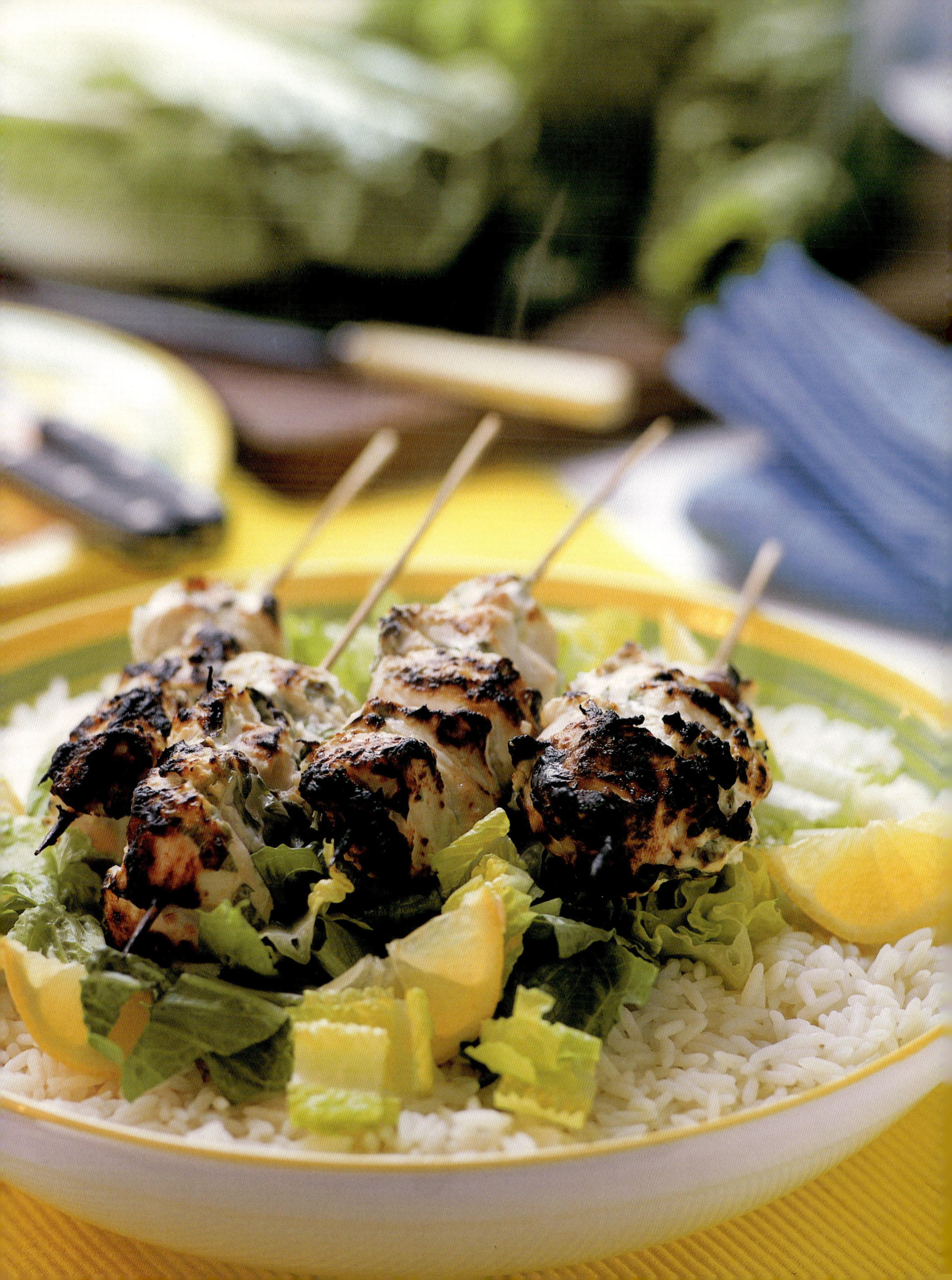

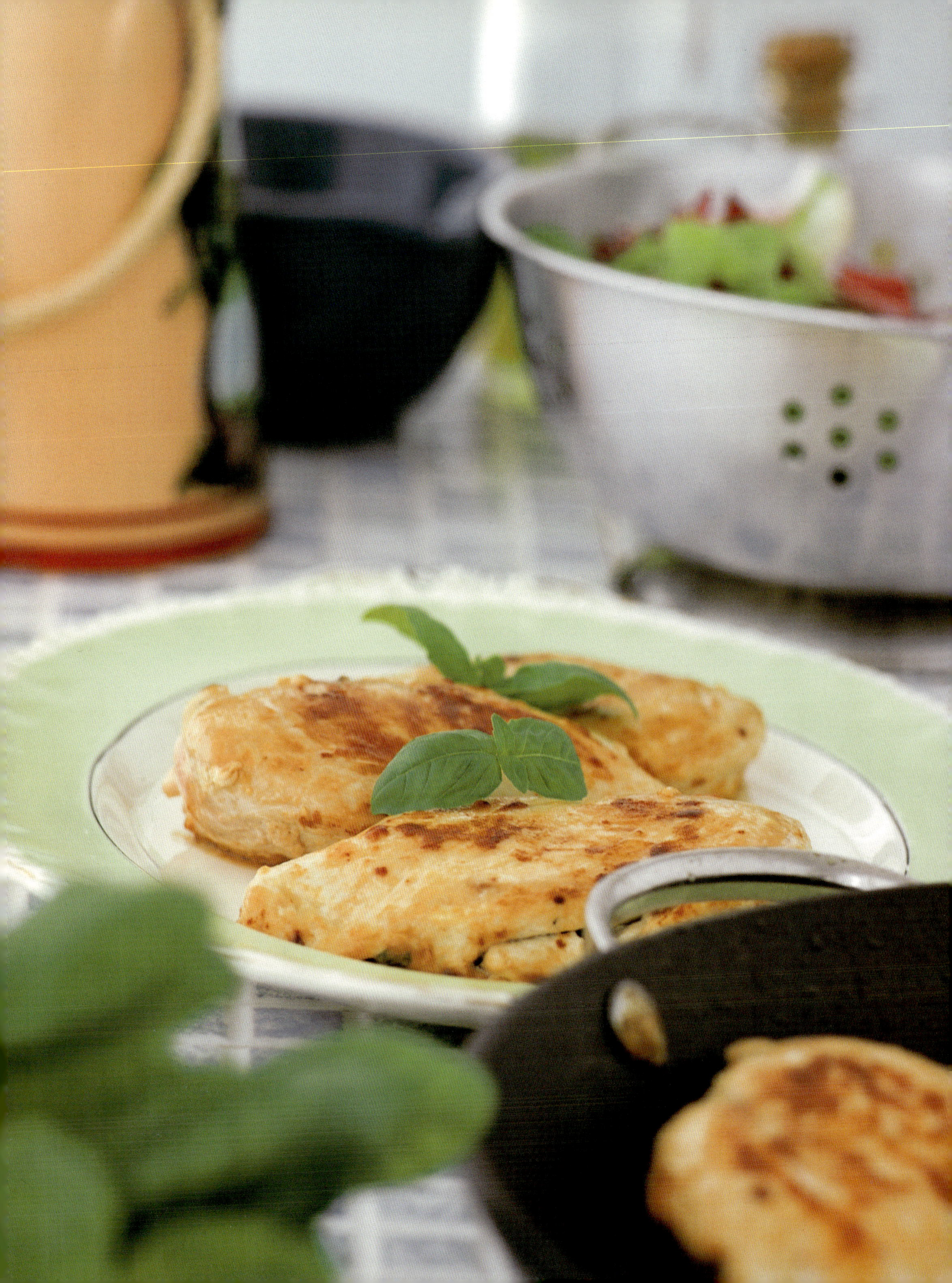

chicken with goat cheese and basil
kotópoulo me tirí próvio kai vasilikó

Basil is seldom used in cooked dishes but here, combined with soft goat cheese which makes the chicken succulent, it imparts the most wonderful fresh flavor.

SERVES 4

4 skinned chicken breast fillets
3½ oz/100 g soft goat cheese
small bunch fresh basil
salt and pepper
2 tbsp olive oil

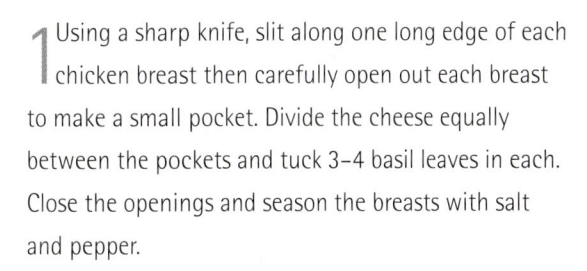

1 Using a sharp knife, slit along one long edge of each chicken breast then carefully open out each breast to make a small pocket. Divide the cheese equally between the pockets and tuck 3–4 basil leaves in each. Close the openings and season the breasts with salt and pepper.

2 Heat the oil in a skillet, add the chicken breasts and fry gently for 15–20 minutes, turning several times, until golden and tender. Serve warm, garnished with a sprig of basil.

Many Greek towns wind up mountain sides

chicken with walnut sauce
kotópoulo me karídia

In Greece, this dish would be served in the fall, when fresh walnuts are harvested. Shelled walnuts, available in packages all year round, make a perfectly acceptable substitute. Serve with rice or pilaf.

SERVES 4

4–8 skinned chicken pieces

½ lemon, cut into wedges

3 tbsp olive oil

⅔ cup dry white wine

1¼ cups chicken stock

1 bay leaf

salt and pepper

¾ cup walnut pieces

2 garlic cloves

⅔ cup authentic Greek yogurt

chopped fresh flat-leaf parsley, to garnish

1 Rub the chicken pieces with the lemon. Heat the oil in a large skillet, add the chicken pieces, and fry quickly until lightly browned on all sides.

2 Pour the wine into the skillet and bring to the boil. Add the stock, bay leaf, salt, and pepper and simmer for about 20 minutes, turning several times, until the chicken is tender.

3 Meanwhile, put the walnuts and garlic in a food processor and blend to form a fairly smooth purée.

4 When the chicken is cooked, transfer to a warmed serving dish and keep warm. Stir the walnut mixture and yogurt into the pan juices and heat gently for about 5 minutes until the sauce is fairly thick. (Do not boil or the sauce will curdle.) Season with salt and pepper.

5 Pour the walnut sauce over the chicken pieces and serve hot, garnished with chopped parsley.

roast chicken with oregano
kotópoulo me rígani

A simple roast chicken, flavored with the Greek cook's favorite herb and, of course, lemon and garlic, is always one of the most popular dishes for a family meal.

SERVES 4

3½–4 lb/1.6–1.8 kg whole chicken

1 lemon

4 tbsp chopped fresh oregano

1 garlic clove, crushed

2 tbsp butter

3 tbsp olive oil

salt and pepper

1. To calculate the cooking time, allow 20 minutes per 1 lb/450 g, plus 20 minutes.

2. Grate the rind from the lemon and cut the lemon in half. Put the chicken in a large roasting pan and squeeze the lemon juice from 1 lemon half into the cavity. Add the lemon rind, 3 tablespoons of the oregano, and the garlic. Rub the butter, the juice from the remaining lemon half, and the oil over the chicken. Sprinkle with the remaining oregano, salt, and pepper. Put the squeezed lemon halves inside the chicken cavity.

3. Roast the chicken in a preheated oven, 375°F/190°C, for the calculated cooking time, basting occasionally, until golden brown and tender. (To test if the chicken is cooked, pierce the thickest part of a thigh with a skewer. If the juices run clear it is ready.)

4. Allow the chicken to rest in a warm place for 5–10 minutes then carve into slices or serving pieces. Stir the remaining juices in the pan and serve spooned over the chicken.

rabbit, roast tomato, and sage pie
kounéli me domáta kai mirodiká

A recipe inspired by ingredients that are typically found in Greece. As a variation, chicken could be used instead of the rabbit.

SERVES 4

1 lb/450 g cherry tomatoes
3 tbsp olive oil
½ tsp sugar
1½ lb/700 g boned rabbit, cubed
1 tbsp all-purpose flour
1 onion, chopped
1 garlic clove, chopped finely
3 tbsp pine nuts
⅔ cup chicken or vegetable stock
1 tbsp lemon juice
12 fresh sage leaves, snipped finely
salt and pepper
3 tbsp butter
3½ oz/100 g authentic Greek phyllo pastry

1. Put the tomatoes in a roasting pan and sprinkle with 1 tablespoon of the olive oil and the sugar. Roast in a preheated oven, 400°F/200°C, for 30 minutes.

2. Meanwhile, put the flour in a plastic bag and toss the rabbit in the flour until coated. Heat 1 tablespoon of the oil in a large, heavy-bottomed skillet, add the onion and garlic, and fry for 5 minutes, until softened. Add the pine nuts and fry for a further 1 minute. Using a slotted spoon, transfer the mixture to a 2½-pint/1.4-litre pie dish.

3. Add the remaining oil to the skillet and fry the rabbit for 5–10 minutes, until browned on all sides. Add the stock and lemon juice, bring to the boil, then simmer for 2–3 minutes. Transfer the mixture to the pie dish.

4. When the tomatoes have roasted, gently stir them into the pie dish. Add the sage and season with salt and pepper.

5. Reduce the oven temperature to 375°F/190°C. Melt the butter. Take one sheet of pastry and cover the remaining sheets with a damp dish towel. Brush the sheet with butter, and then cut into 1-inch/2.5-cm strips. Arrange on top of the pie. Repeat with the remaining pastry sheets, brushing each with butter and arranging on top of the pie in the opposite direction each time. Make sure that the filling is covered and tuck in the edges.

6. Bake the pie in the oven for about 30 minutes, until golden brown. Serve hot.

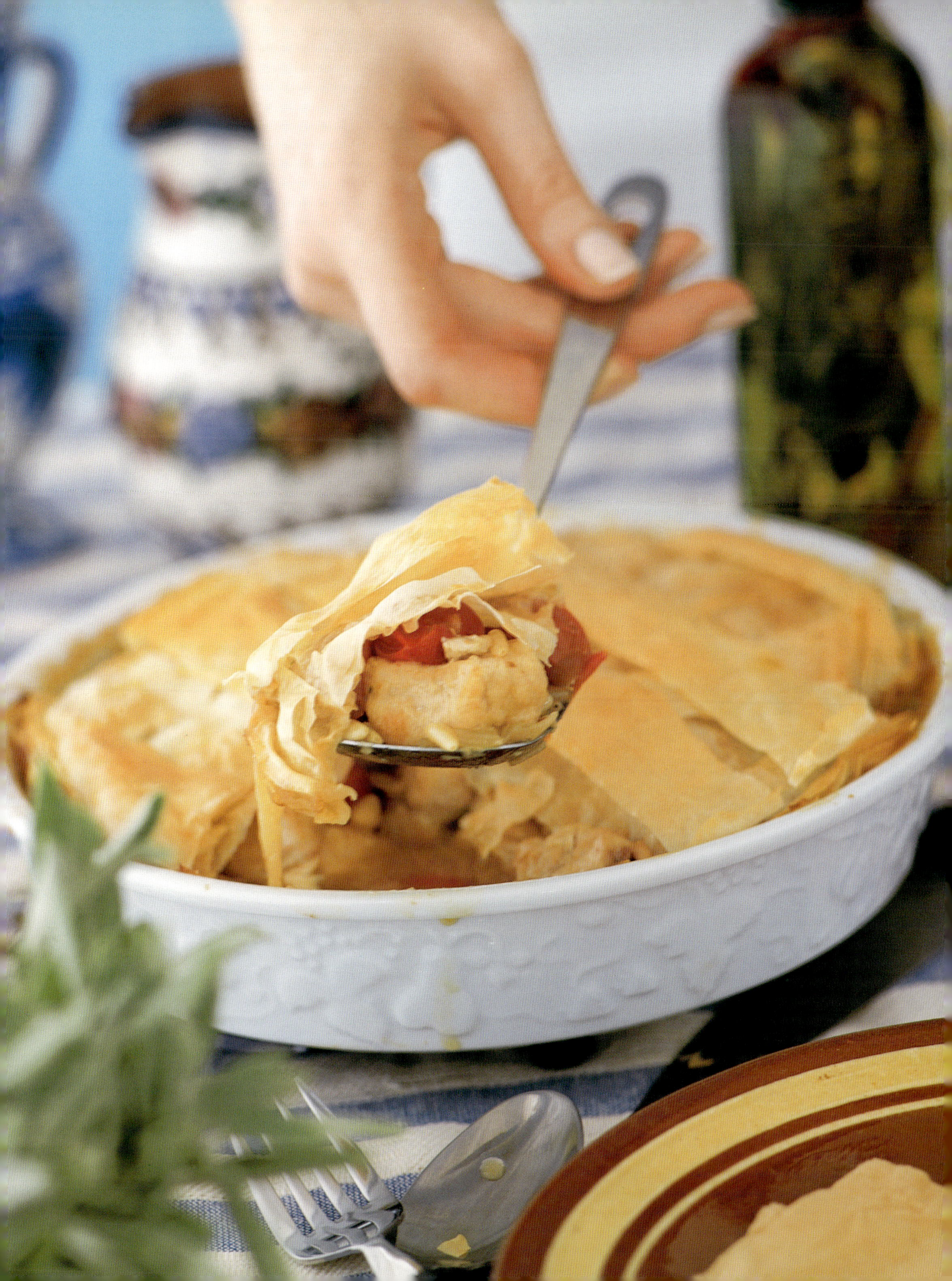

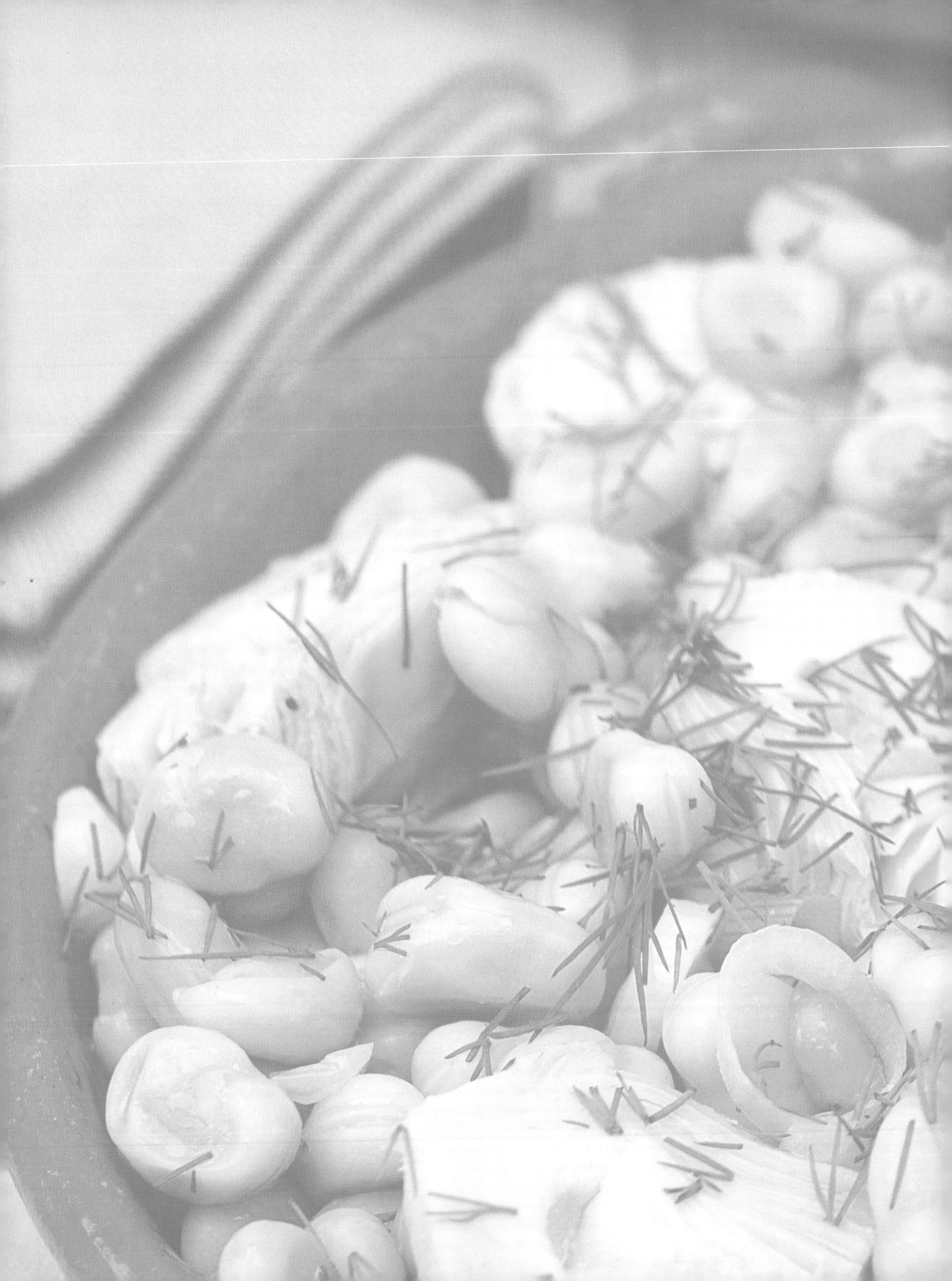

VEGETABLES & SALADS

Vegetables play a central role in the Greek diet. They are at their best seen on the market stall, shiny dark eggplants, plump polished bell peppers, piles of rosy red tomatoes, large fat radishes, garlic, and more garlic, and bunches of herbs perfuming the air. Vegetables often take center stage on a table.

Vegetables are often served as a dish in their own right rather than alongside a main dish. There are many reasons for this, one being their wider availability in comparison to meat and another being the abstinence from eating meat during the fasting traditions, which was imposed on its followers by the Greek Orthodox Church. Fasting days, particularly Lent, are still observed in Greece, especially on the islands, and this means that Greek cuisine includes many vegetables. In fact, it is said that the Greeks eat more vegetables than any other Western country.

When people lived off the land and grew their own produce, vegetables were part of the daily diet and in times of hardship they lived on a diet of vegetables and grain. Even today, people living in apartments in Athens and other large cities have herbs growing in pots on their windowsills and tomatoes on their balconies. Perhaps the most popular vegetables are eggplants, scallions, artichokes, tomatoes, zucchini, bell peppers, onions, garlic, cabbage, okra, fava beans, and Great Northern beans. They can be eaten on their own, or sometimes as an accompaniment to a main dish, although more usually they are served separately from the main course. They are often used in combination with other vegetables, and with garlic and herbs.

The Greeks show great ingenuity in the cooking of vegetables. They prepare them in an enormous variety of ways, from broiling and baking to frying and serving with a sauce. Seldom are they simply boiled or steamed. At the top of the list must be stuffed vegetables, for just about any vegetable can be stuffed in some way, even zucchini flowers. Take, for example, Stuffed Cabbage Leaves (see page 182), Roasted Red Bell peppers with Halloumi (see page 197), Baked Stuffed Eggplant (see page 184) and Stuffed Zucchini with Walnuts and Feta (see page 195). They can be braised, as in Braised Okra with Tomatoes (see page 176) and baked, as in *Spanakópita* (see page 190), the well-known Spinach and Feta Pie. There is even a meatless Roasted Vegetable Moussaka (see page 189).

Then we come to the various popular fresh and dried beans and grains that are frequently eaten in Greece. In particular, these include fava beans, cannellini beans, chickpeas, black-eyed peas, lima beans, gigandes beans, butter beans, and brown lentils that are used in vegetable stews and salads. Rice is the most commonly eaten grain, often served with chickpeas or with tomatoes and olives and as a pilaf. (A pilaf is a savory rice dish made with

The Greeks show great ingenuity in the cooking of vegetables. They prepare them in an enormous variety of ways...Seldom are they simply boiled or steamed

Eggplants, tomatoes, bell peppers, and garlic are some of the staple vegetables used in many Greek savory dishes

long-grain rice that is always cooked in olive oil and stock or water by the same basic method, to which vegetables, meat, or fish are added.) Vegetables such as zucchini, spinach, eggplant, and tomatoes (see page 200) are all popular additions and are served as accompaniments as well as dishes on their own.

Vegetarians can be in their element with Greek vegetable dishes. Many of the recipes are suitable for serving as a vegetarian main course, several of which include cheese. Greek cheeses are usually made with goat's or sheep's milk and most are soft cheeses, made locally for local consumption. Feta and halloumi cheese are two exceptions since they are made commercially and exported. Other Greek cheeses include Kasséri, Kefalotíri, Graviéra, and Manoúri cheese.

Fresh vegetables or salad leaves tossed in olive oil and lemon juice are also popular Greek vegetable and salad dishes. Even today, wild greens, called *hórta*, and herbs are collected from the fields and hillsides and used in salads. According to the season, this might include dandelion leaves, mustard greens, wild asparagus, arugula, mint, wild marjoram, dill, and sage, and even wild flowers such as the blue grape

Above and right *Market stallholders mass together dried mushrooms* (above) *and fresh vegetables in colorful display*

Overleaf *Greek homes extend into the streets by their use of plants to adorn their steps and balconies*

hyacinth. The most famous Greek salad is, of course, the classic *Saláta Horiátiki* (see page 203) which has a mixture of ingredients, such as tomatoes, cucumber, onion, bell peppers, and sometimes green salad leaves, but always feta cheese and black olives. In the Traditional Greek Salad the green salad leaves, if included, are always shredded, not separated. It is dressed with an olive oil and lemon juice dressing. This is simple to make but when you are short of time or do not have the ingredients, bottles of Greek lemon dressing can be bought from Greek delicatessens and from larger supermarkets.

In fact many of the dishes that the Greeks call salads are actually a purée of ingredients, such as *Taramasaláta* (see page 48), a dip made with cod roe, and *Melitzanosaláta* (see page 53), an eggplant dip. They are served as a mezze and you will find the recipes for these in the mezze chapter.

vegetables & salads

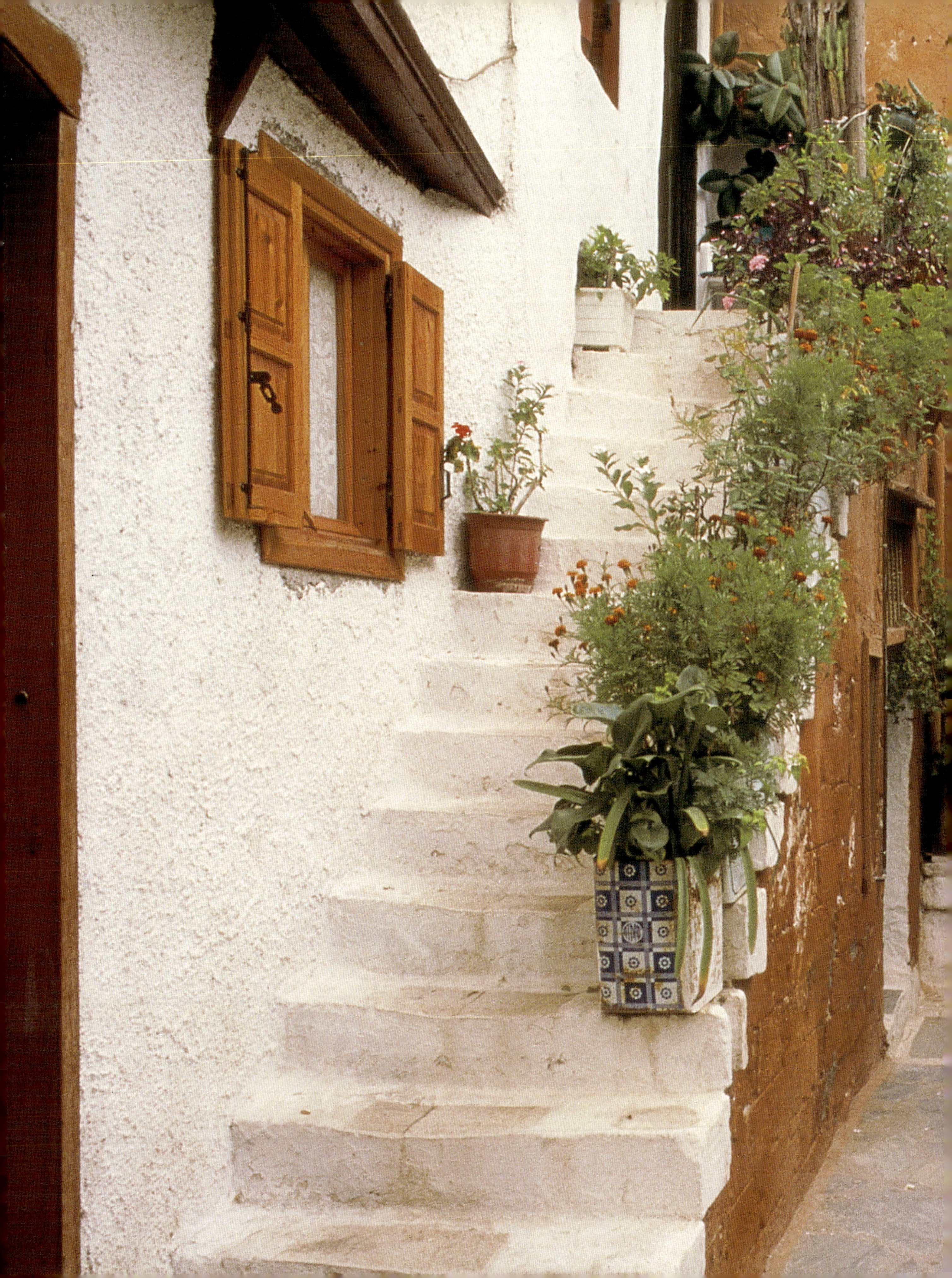

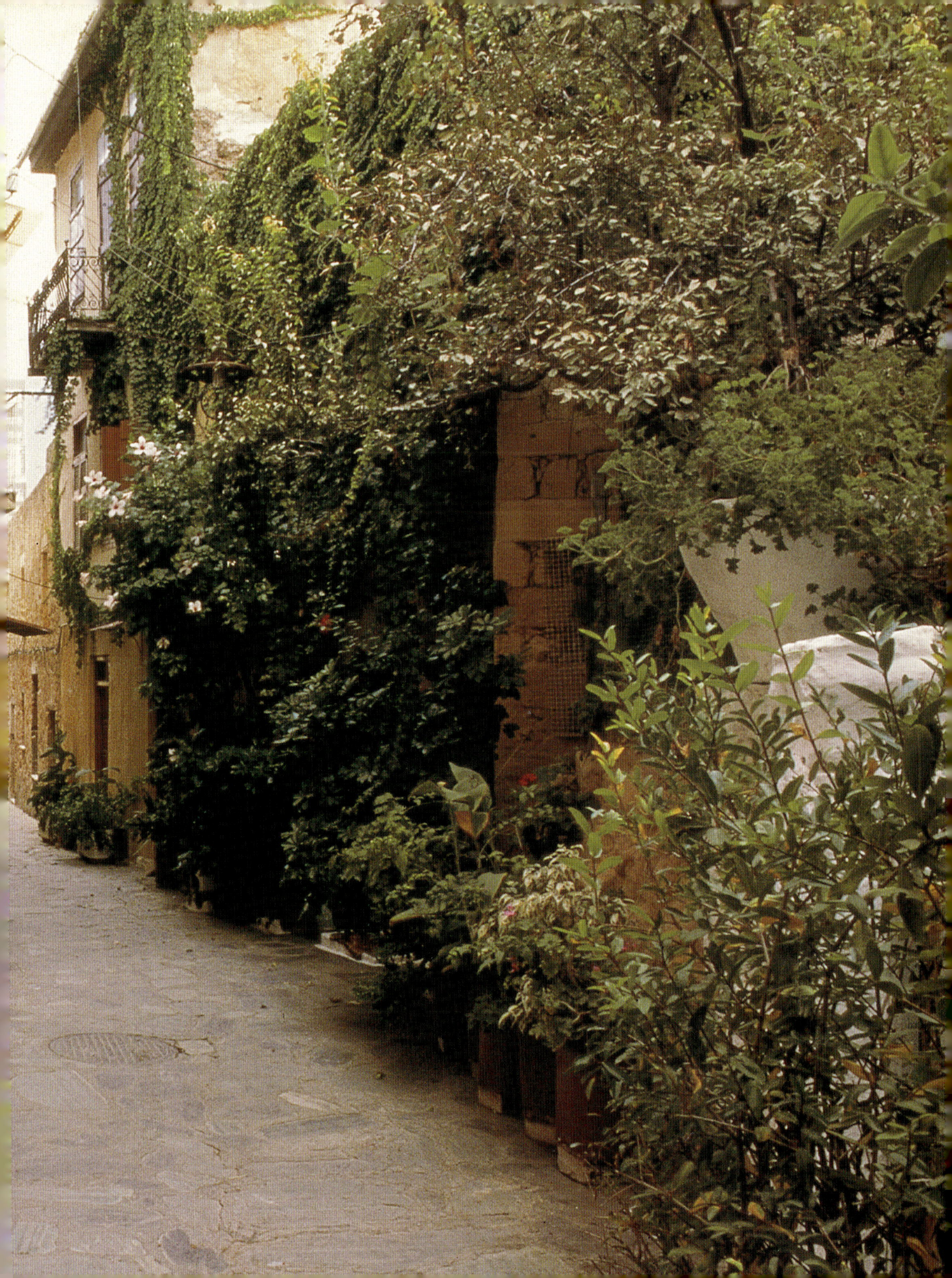

braised okra with tomatoes
bámies kokkinístes

Okra, although originally from the West Indies, is a popular vegetable in Greece. It is particularly good served with lamb. Green beans, another popular vegetable in Greece, can be prepared in the same way. Follow the recipe but omit soaking in vinegar.

SERVES 4–6

1 lb/450 g okra

²/₃ cup white wine vinegar

3 tbsp olive oil

1 large onion, chopped coarsely

1 large garlic clove, chopped finely

14 oz/400 g canned chopped tomatoes in juice

pinch of sugar

salt and pepper

chopped fresh flat-leaf parsley, to garnish

1 Trim off the tops and tails of the okra but do not cut into the flesh. Put in a bowl, pour over the vinegar, and leave in a warm place for 30 minutes. Rinse the okra well under cold running water and drain.

2 Heat the oil in a large skillet, add the onion and garlic, and fry for 5–10 minutes until softened. Add the okra and fry for about 5 minutes, stirring occasionally, until beginning to brown.

3 Add the tomatoes with their juice, the sugar, salt, and pepper then simmer for 15–20 minutes, until the okra is tender and the sauce reduced slightly. Do not boil or the okra will burst. Serve hot or cold, garnished with chopped parsley.

zucchini slices with greek garlic sauce
kolokíthia me skordaliá

Zucchini grow in abundance in Greece and are therefore used a great deal, either deep-fried, stuffed, sautéed, or grated. They are eaten hot and also served cold in salads.

SERVES 4

1 lb/450 g baby zucchini
3 tbsp all-purpose flour
olive oil, for shallow-frying
grated rind and juice of ½ lemon
salt and pepper
½ recipe Greek Garlic Sauce (see page 64)

1. Cut the zucchini lengthwise into ¼-inch/5-mm thick strips. Dust with the flour to coat.

2. Pour enough oil into a large skillet to cover the bottom, heat, then add the zucchini and fry for 5–10 minutes until golden brown, stirring occasionally.

3. When cooked, add the lemon rind and juice and season with salt and pepper. Serve the zucchini hot, with the Greek Garlic Sauce spooned on top.

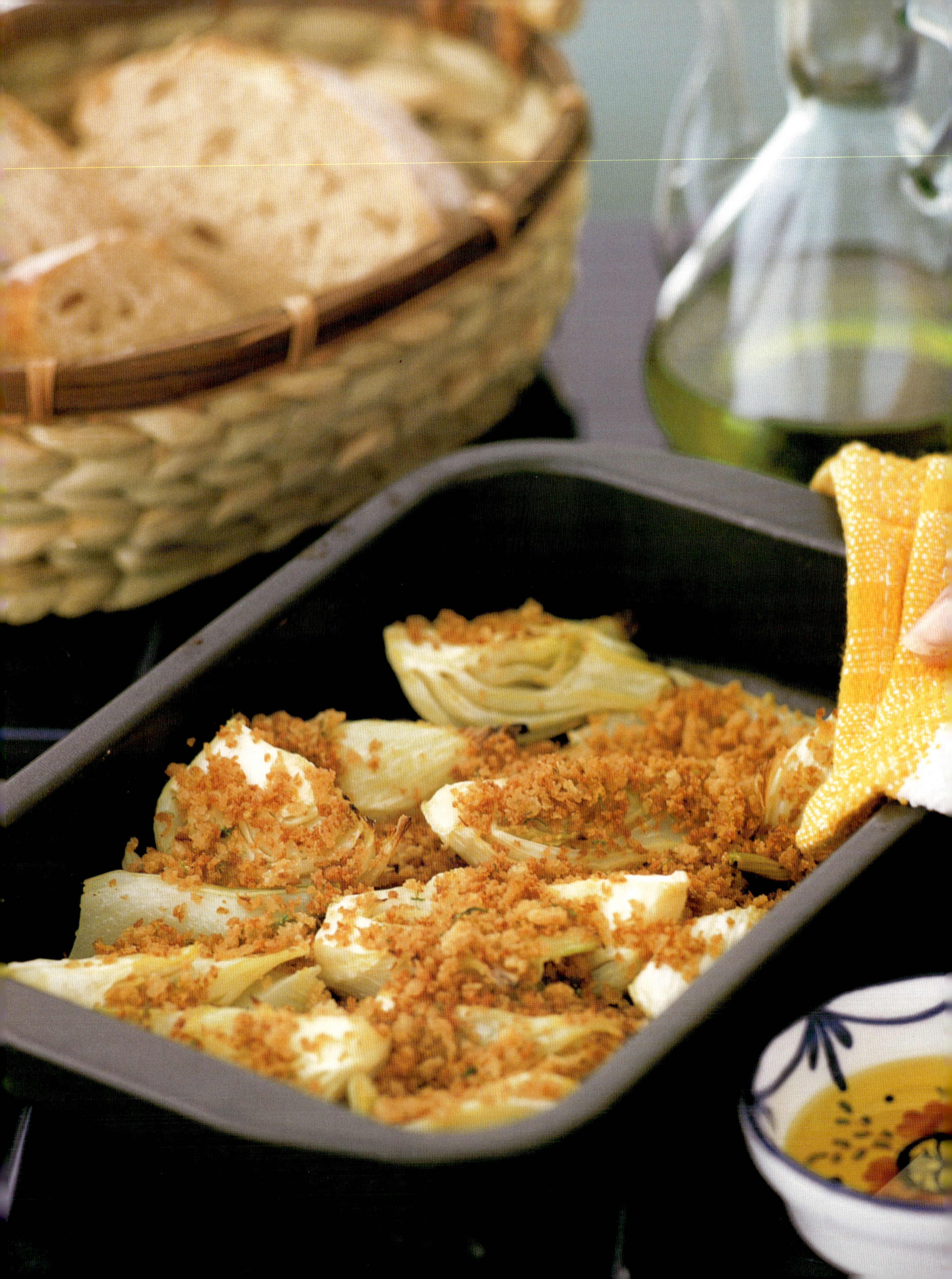

vegetables & salads

Fennel was known in ancient Greece. With its mild anise flavor, it makes a delicious vegetable accompaniment to many meat and fish dishes or a dish in its own right.

crispy roasted fennel
psitó traganistó aníthos

SERVES 4-6

3 large fennel bulbs

4 tbsp olive oil

finely grated rind and juice of 1 small lemon

1 garlic clove, chopped finely

1 cup fresh white breadcrumbs

salt and pepper

1 Trim the fennel bulbs, reserving the green feathery fronds, and cut into quarters. Cook the bulbs in a large saucepan of boiling salted water for 5 minutes until just tender then drain well.

2 Heat 2 tablespoons of the olive oil in a small roasting pan or skillet with flameproof handle, add the fennel and turn to coat in the oil. Drizzle over the lemon juice. Roast the fennel in a preheated oven, 400°F/200°C, for about 35 minutes, until beginning to brown.

3 Meanwhile, heat the remaining oil in a skillet. Add the garlic and fry for 1 minute, until lightly browned. Add the breadcrumbs and fry for about 5 minutes, stirring frequently, until crispy. Remove from the heat and stir in the lemon rind, reserved snipped fennel fronds, salt and pepper.

4 When the fennel is cooked, sprinkle the breadcrumb mixture over the top and return to the oven for a further 5 minutes. Serve hot.

*cook's tip

It is said that the male fennel has more flavor than the female fennel and to recognize one from the other, the male is long and thin whilst the female is bulbous, as though it has hips.

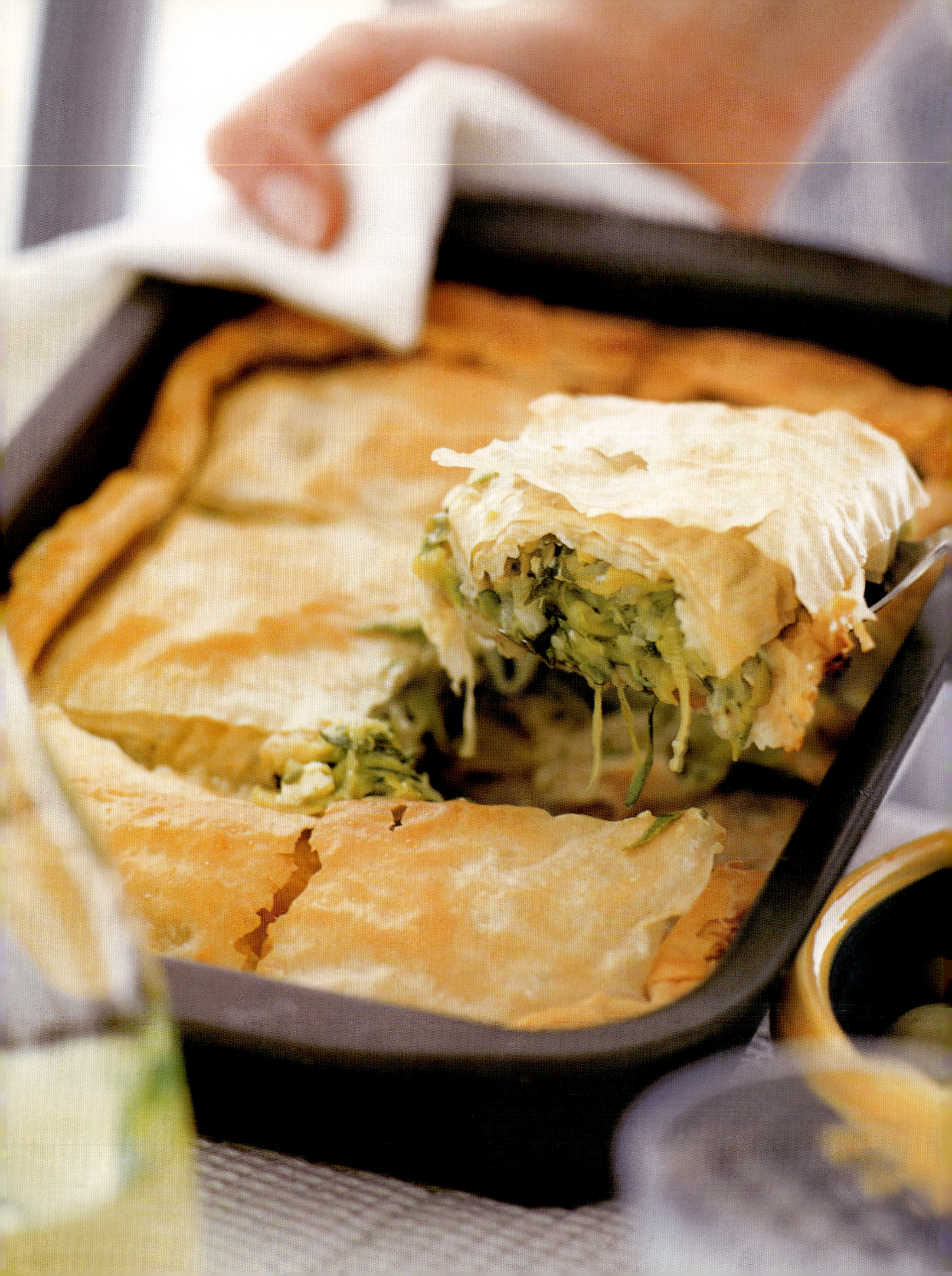

vegetables & salads

zucchini pie
kolokithópita

The Greeks' great fondness for zucchini is illustrated in this pie, which needs only a salad to accompany it.

SERVES 6–8

2 tbsp olive oil

2 bunches scallions, sliced thinly

1/3 cup arborio or other short-grain rice

3/4 cup hot vegetable or chicken stock

1 lb 10 oz/750 g zucchini, grated coarsely and left to drain in a colander for 5–10 mins

4 tbsp chopped fresh flat-leaf parsley

2 tbsp chopped fresh mint

3 eggs, beaten

3 1/2 oz/300 g authentic Greek feta cheese

salt and pepper

3 1/2 oz/100 g butter

7 oz/200 g authentic Greek phyllo pastry

1. Heat the oil in a saucepan, add the scallions and fry for 5 minutes, until softened. Add the rice and cook for 1 minute, stirring to coat in the oil.

2. Add the stock to the saucepan and simmer for about 15 minutes until the stock has been absorbed and the rice is tender but still firm to the bite. Remove the saucepan from the heat and stir in the zucchini. Let cool.

3. When the mixture has cooled, add the parsley, mint, and eggs. Crumble in the cheese, season with salt and pepper, and mix well together.

4. Melt the butter and use a little to lightly grease a deep 12 x 8-inch/30 x 20-cm metal baking pan.

5. Cut the pastry sheets in half widthwise. Take 1 sheet of pastry and cover the remaining sheets with a damp dish towel. Use to line the base and sides of the pan and brush the sheet with a little of the melted butter. Repeat with half of the pastry sheets, brushing each with butter.

6. Spread the zucchini mixture over the pastry, then top with the remaining pastry sheets, brushing each with butter and tucking down the edges. Using a sharp knife, score the top layers of the pastry into 6–8 squares.

7. Bake the pie in a preheated oven, 375°F/190°C, for about 35 minutes, until golden brown. Serve hot.

The warm glow of lights as darkness descends creates a romantic scene

stuffed cabbage leaves
láhano dolmádes

The láhana cabbage grows in Greece and the Middle East and is perfect for stuffing, as in this recipe, because its large leaves soften when boiled but do not collapse.

SERVES 4

8 large cabbage leaves such as láhana, Chinese cabbage or romaine lettuce

1 lb 12 oz/800 g canned tomatoes in juice

2 tbsp olive oil

2 onions, chopped finely

1 large garlic clove, chopped finely

¼ cup arborio or other short-grain rice

⅓ cup golden raisins

1 tbsp chopped fresh mint

1¼ cups vegetable or chicken stock

1 tsp dried oregano

salt and pepper

⅓ cup pine nuts

1 Plunge the cabbage into a large saucepan of boiling water, return to the boil, then boil for 3–4 minutes until softened. Drain well, plunge into ice water, then drain well again. If necessary, cut out any hard cores.

2 Take 3–4 of the canned tomatoes and chop into fairly small pieces. Heat 1 tablespoon of the oil in a saucepan. Add half the onions and the garlic and fry for 5–10 minutes until softened and browned. Stir in the chopped tomatoes, the rice, golden raisins, and mint.

3 Add the stock to the saucepan, bring to the boil, then simmer for 15–20 minutes until the rice is tender and the stock has been absorbed.

4 Meanwhile, make the tomato sauce. Heat the remaining oil in a saucepan, add the remaining onion, and fry for 5–10 minutes until softened and browned. Stir in the remaining canned tomatoes and their juice, the oregano, salt, and pepper and bring to the boil, then simmer for about 10 minutes. Allow to cool slightly then purée in a food processor, blender, or with a hand-held blender.

5 When the rice is cooked, remove from the heat, stir in the pine nuts, and season with salt and pepper. Divide the stuffing mixture between the cabbage leaves and roll up and fold the leaves to form 8 neat packets. Place seam-side down, side by side, in a shallow ovenproof dish.

6 Pour the tomato sauce over the stuffed cabbage leaves. Cover the dish and bake in a preheated oven, 350°F/180°C, for 1 hour. Serve hot or warm.

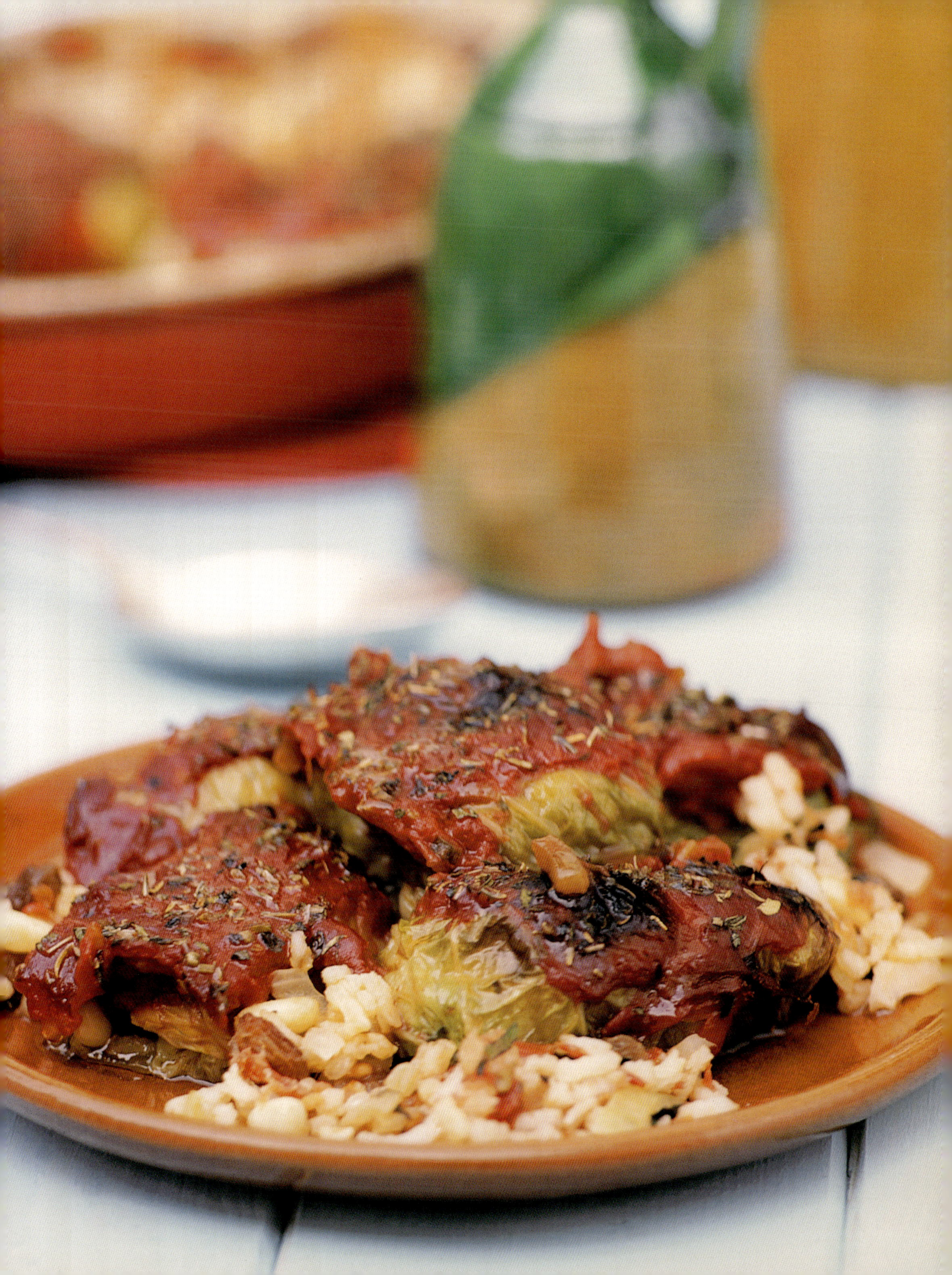

baked stuffed eggplant
melitzánes gémistes

Stuffed eggplants, called Imam Baildí, are often served in Greek restaurants and acclaimed as a Greek specialty. However, they are Turkish in origin, Imam being the Turkish word for Priest and the literal translation meaning the fainting priest. (It is alleged that the priest fainted at the sight of the quantity of oil used, or through over-indulgence.) Whichever nationality claims the dish, it is truly delicious.

SERVES 4

4 large, long, thin eggplants

salt

4 tbsp olive oil plus ⅔ cup olive oil or sunflower oil

3 large onions, sliced thinly

2 large garlic cloves, chopped finely

1 green bell pepper, cored, seeded, and sliced thinly

14 oz/400 g canned tomatoes in juice, drained

1 tsp dried oregano

¼ tsp dried thyme

4 tbsp chopped fresh flat-leaf parsley, plus extra to garnish

pepper

2 tbsp lemon juice

1 Cut the eggplants in half lengthwise. Scoop out the flesh, leaving a shell to hold the stuffing, and reserve. Sprinkle the insides with salt and place upside down on a plate. Coarsely chop the scooped out flesh and place in a colander standing over a large plate, and sprinkle each layer with salt. Cover with a plate and place a heavy weight on top. Leave both the shells and flesh for 30 minutes.

2 Rinse the eggplant shells and chopped flesh under cold running water, and then pat dry with paper towels. Heat the 4 tablespoons of olive oil in a saucepan. Add the onions, garlic, and green bell pepper and cook for 10–15 minutes until softened, stirring occasionally.

3 Add the eggplant flesh, the tomatoes, breaking them up with a fork, the oregano, thyme, parsley, salt, and pepper. Simmer for 20–30 minutes until the mixture has reduced and thickened slightly.

4 Spoon the stuffing into the eggplant shells and place them, side by side, in a shallow ovenproof dish.

5 Pour the remaining oil around the eggplants. Add the lemon juice and enough boiling water to come halfway up the sides of the eggplants. Cover the dish and cook in a preheated oven, 300°F/150°C, for 1 hour, until tender. Let cool in the liquid, but do not chill.

6 To serve, lift out the eggplants with a slotted spoon, discarding the liquid, and garnish with chopped parsley.

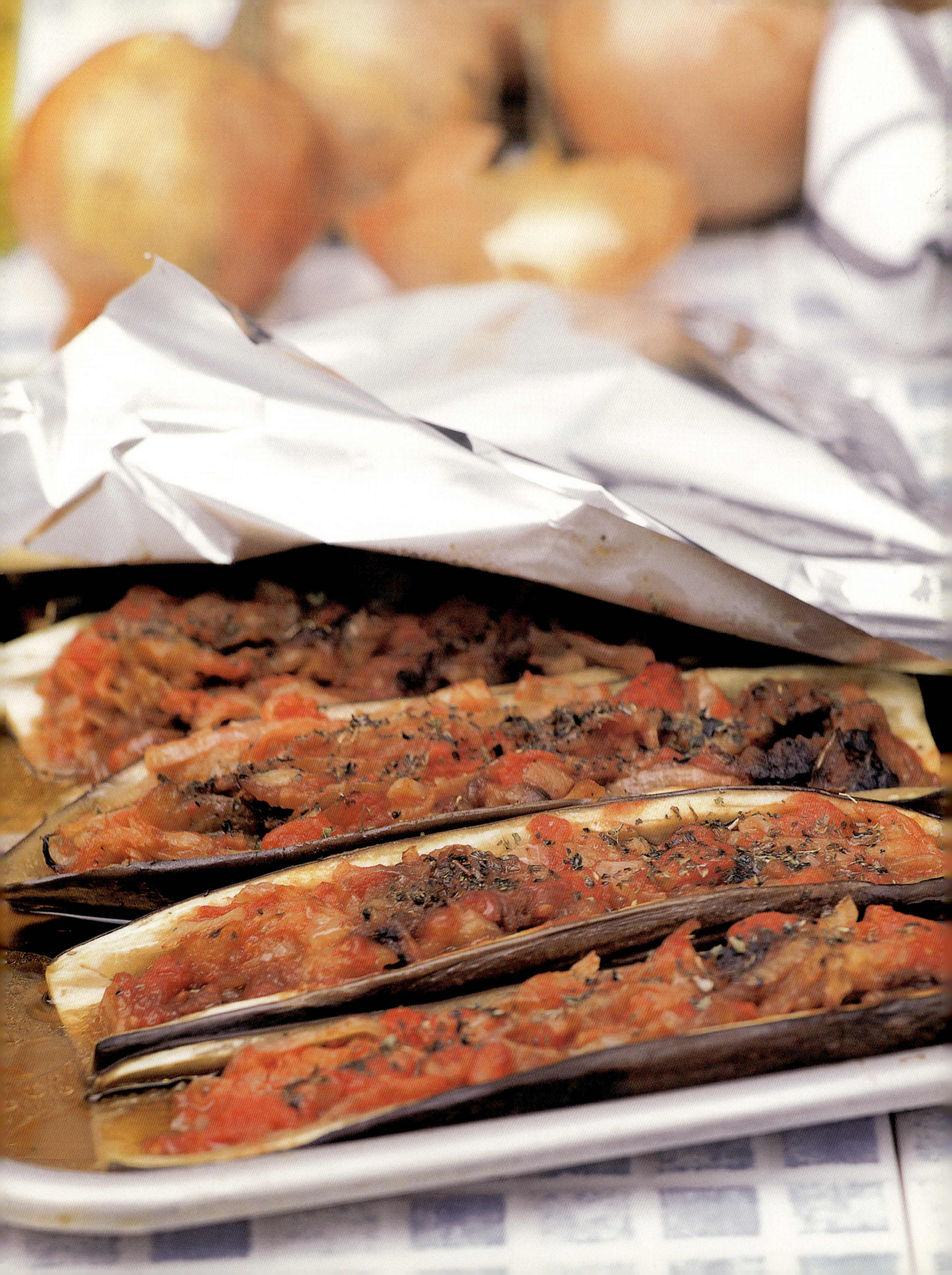

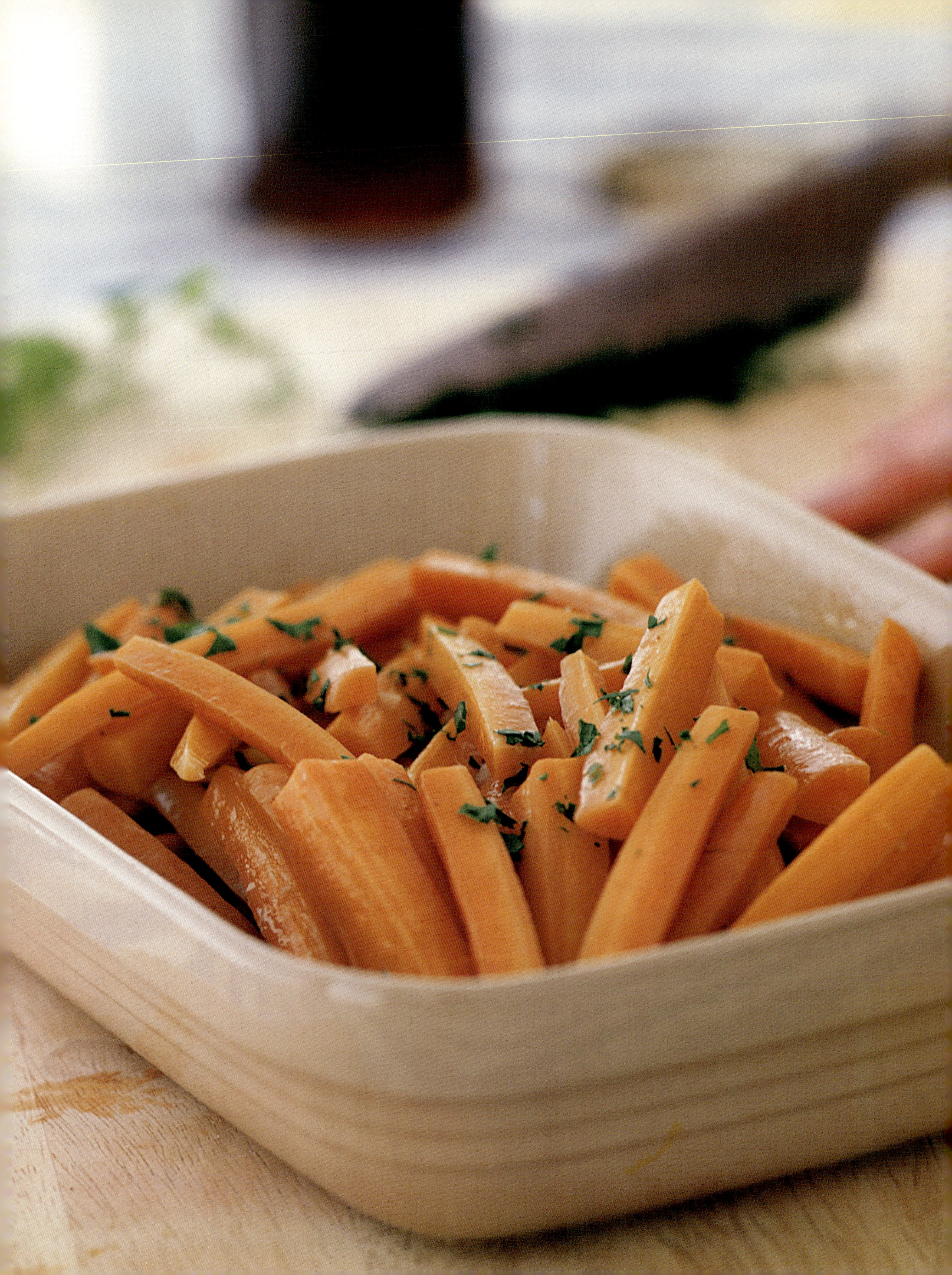

carrots à la grecque
karóta á la grecque

This style of cooking vegetables, where the vegetables are cooked in an aromatic liquid, allowed to marinate and then chilled, is well known. Other vegetables can be cooked in just the same way and examples include cauliflower, zucchini, green beans, leeks, eggplant, pearl onions, and mushrooms. The cooking time varies, depending on the tenderness of the vegetables.

SERVES 4

1 lb 9 oz/700 g young carrots
¼ cup olive oil
1¾ cups dry white wine
1 tbsp Greek honey
2 sprigs fresh thyme
6 sprigs fresh parsley
1 bay leaf
2 garlic cloves, chopped finely
1 tbsp coriander seeds, crushed lightly
salt and pepper
chopped fresh herbs, to garnish

1 Cut the carrots in half and then into quarters to form fingers of equal thickness. Put the carrots and all the remaining ingredients in a large saucepan and bring to the boil, then simmer, uncovered, for about 20 minutes until the carrots are tender.

2 Using a slotted spoon, transfer the carrots to a serving dish. Return the cooking liquid to the boil and boil until reduced by about half.

3 Strain the cooking liquid over the carrots and let cool. When cool, chill in the fridge for 3–4 hours or overnight. Serve at room temperature, garnished with chopped fresh herbs.

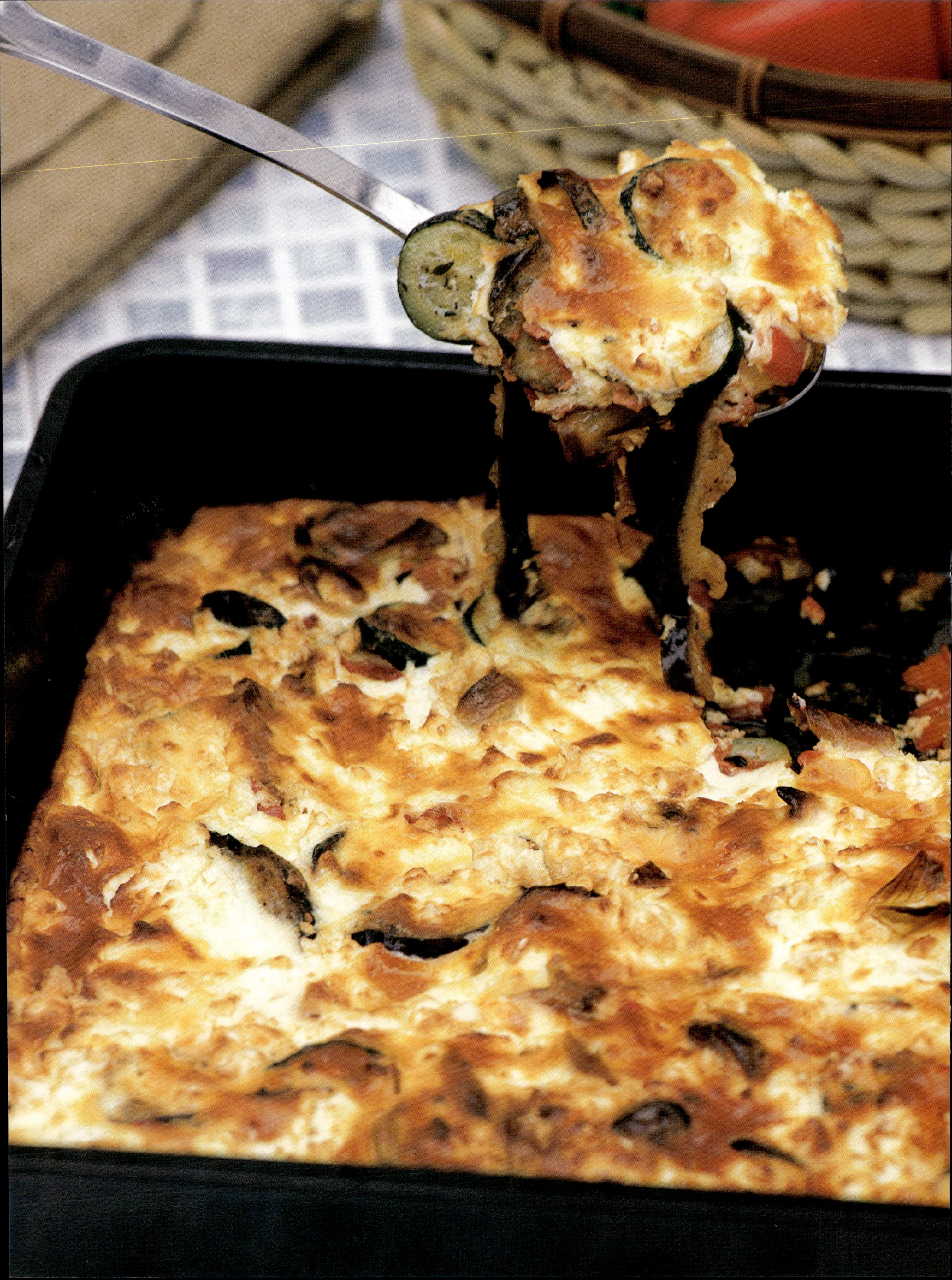

roasted vegetable moussaka
moussakás lahanikón

This is a vegetarian version of the famous dish which is just as delicious and satisfying as the meat version.

SERVES 4–6

1 large eggplant

salt

2 medium zucchini, sliced thickly

2 onions, cut into small wedges

2 red bell peppers, cored, seeded and chopped coarsely

2 garlic cloves, chopped coarsely

5 tbsp olive oil

1 tbsp chopped fresh thyme

pepper

2 eggs, beaten

1 1/4 cups authentic Greek yogurt

14 oz/400 g canned chopped tomatoes in juice

2 oz/55 g authentic Greek feta cheese

1 Cut the eggplant into slices, about 1/4 inch/5 mm thick. Put in a colander standing over a large plate, and sprinkle each layer with salt. Cover with a plate and place a heavy weight on top. Leave for 30 minutes.

2 Rinse the eggplant slices under cold running water, then pat dry with paper towels.

3 Put the eggplant, zucchini, onions, bell peppers, and garlic in a roasting pan. Drizzle over the oil, toss together, and then sprinkle over the thyme and season with salt and pepper. Roast in a preheated oven, 425°F/ 220°C, for 30–35 minutes, turning half-way through the cooking, until golden brown and tender.

4 Meanwhile, beat together the eggs, yogurt, salt, and pepper. When the vegetables are cooked, reduce the oven temperature to 350°F/180°C.

5 Put half the vegetables in a layer in a large ovenproof dish. Spoon over the canned chopped tomatoes and their juice then add the remaining vegetables. Pour over the yogurt mixture and crumble over the feta cheese. Bake in the oven for 45 minutes– 1 hour, until golden brown. Serve hot, warm, or cold.

*cook's tip
When it comes to seasoning the egg and yogurt mixture, add salt sparingly as the feta cheese is already salty and may provide enough.

spinach and feta pie
spanakópita

This recipe makes one large pie but you can make individual pastries to serve as a mezze. Follow the recipe for Hot Cheese Pastries (Tirópites) on page 60, using the filling in this recipe to stuff them.

SERVES 6

2 tbsp olive oil

1 large onion, chopped finely

2 lb 4 oz/1 kg fresh young spinach leaves, washed or 1 lb 2 oz/500 g frozen spinach, thawed

4 tbsp chopped fresh flat-leaf parsley

2 tbsp chopped fresh dill

3 eggs, beaten

7 oz/200 g authentic Greek feta cheese

salt and pepper

3½ oz/100 g butter

8 oz/225 g authentic Greek phyllo pastry

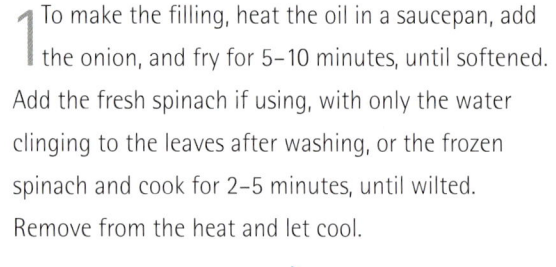

1 To make the filling, heat the oil in a saucepan, add the onion, and fry for 5–10 minutes, until softened. Add the fresh spinach if using, with only the water clinging to the leaves after washing, or the frozen spinach and cook for 2–5 minutes, until wilted. Remove from the heat and let cool.

2 When the mixture has cooled, add the parsley, dill, and eggs. Crumble in the cheese, season with salt and pepper, and mix well together.

3 Melt the butter and use a little to lightly grease a deep 12 x 8-inch/30 x 20-cm metal baking pan.

4 Cut the pastry sheets in half widthwise. Take 1 sheet of pastry and cover the remaining sheets with a damp dish towel. Line the pan with the pastry sheet and brush it with a little of the melted butter. Repeat with half of the pastry sheets, brushing each with butter.

5 Spread the spinach and cheese filling over the pastry, then top with the remaining pastry sheets, brushing each with butter and tucking down the edges. Using a sharp knife, score the top layers of the pastry into 6 squares.

6 Bake in a preheated oven, 375°F/190°C, for about 40 minutes, until golden brown. Serve hot or cold.

Overleaf Picturesque Preveli beach on the southern coast of Crete

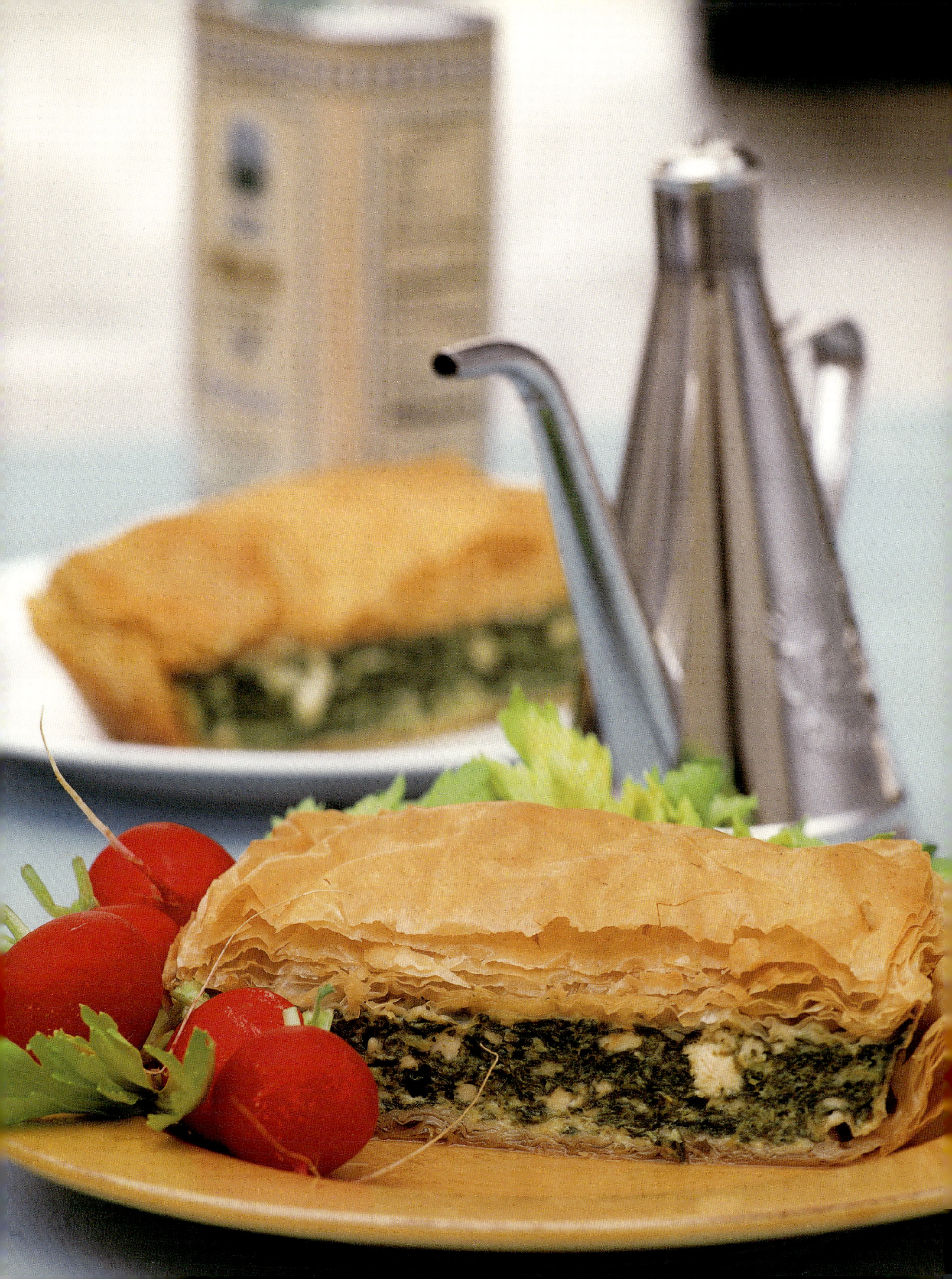

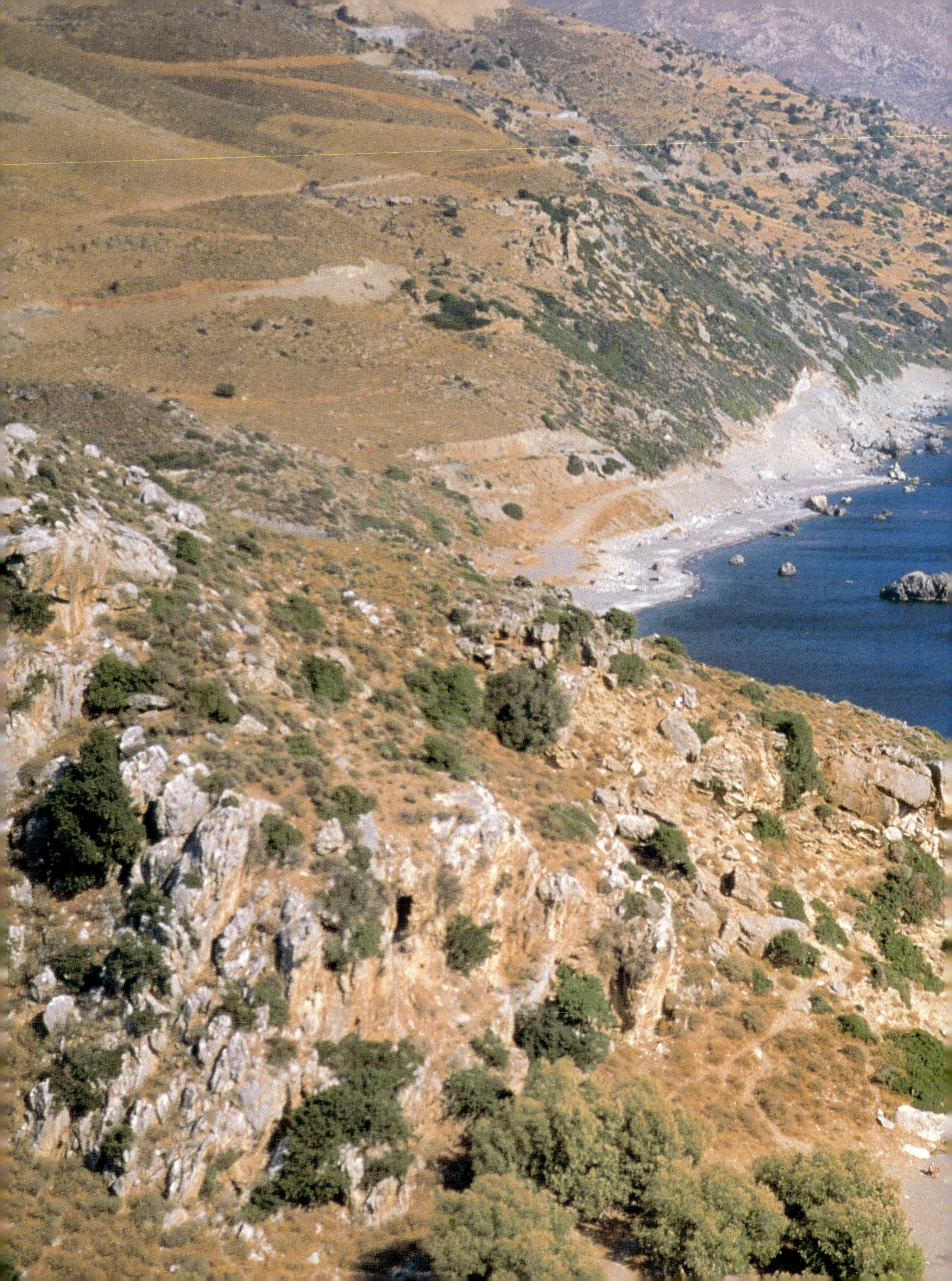

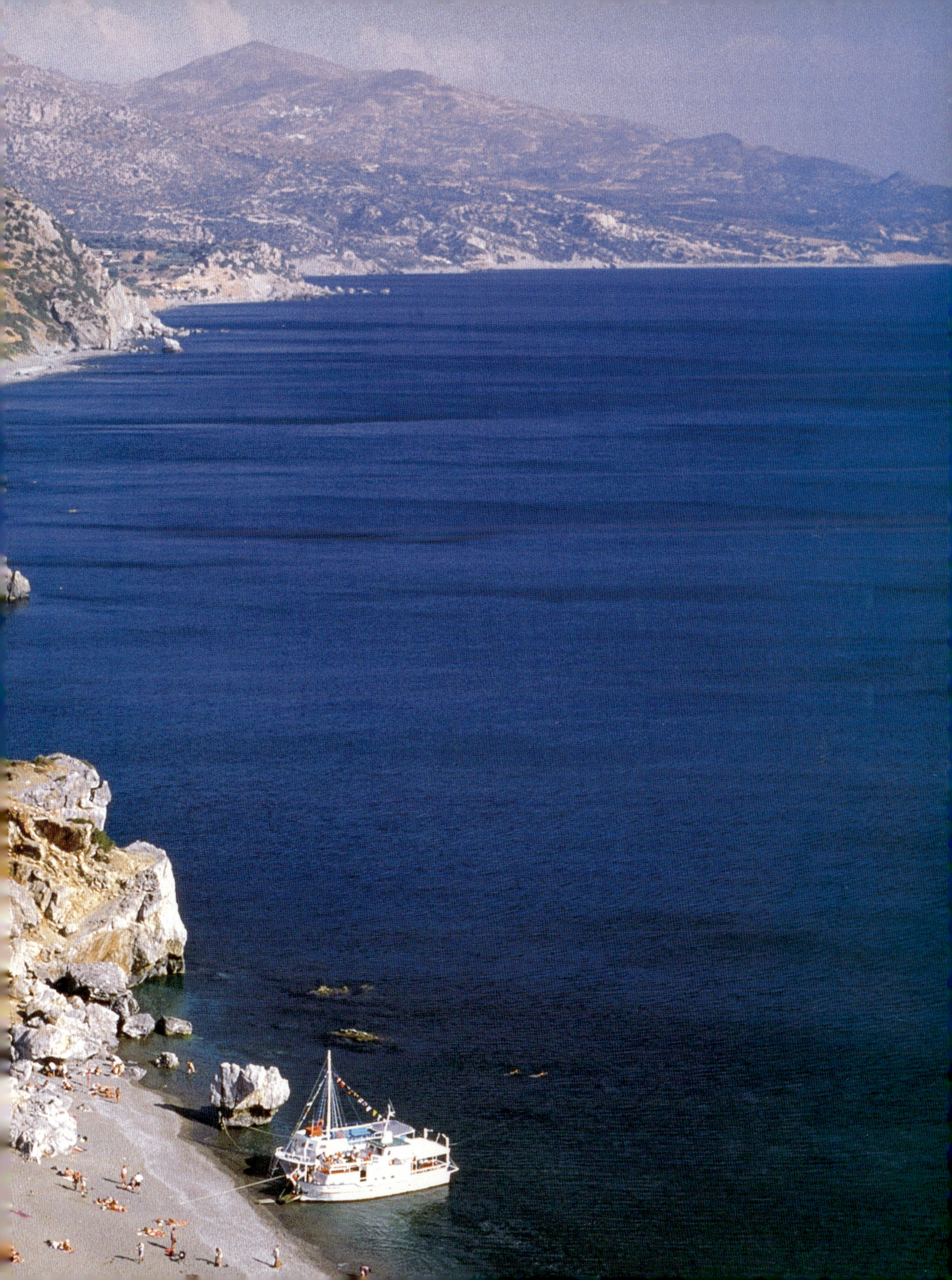

artichoke hearts with fava beans
agináres me koukiá

This recipe uses canned artichoke hearts and frozen fava beans for convenience. It is an ideal vegetable accompaniment for serving with a fish or meat dish.

SERVES 4

4 tbsp olive oil
1 bunch scallions, white parts only, sliced thinly
1 lb/450 g frozen fava beans
$\frac{1}{2}$ cup water
juice of 1 lemon
14 oz/400 g canned artichoke hearts, drained and halved
2 tbsp chopped fresh dill
salt and pepper

1. Heat the oil in a large saucepan. Add the scallions and fry for 5 minutes, until softened. Add the beans and stir to coat in the oil. Pour in the water and lemon juice; bring to the boil and boil, uncovered, for 5 minutes.

2. Add the artichoke hearts to the saucepan and gently boil for 5 minutes, until the beans are tender and most of the liquid has evaporated. Add the dill and season to taste with salt and pepper. Serve hot.

vegetables & salads

stuffed zucchini with walnuts and feta
kolokíthia gemistá

You can serve these as a vegetable accompaniment with, for example, cold meats, broiled meat or fish, or as a light lunch or supper dish.

SERVES 4

4 fat, medium zucchini

3 tbsp olive oil

1 onion, chopped finely

1 garlic clove, chopped finely

2 oz/55 g authentic Greek feta cheese, crumbled

¼ cup walnut pieces, chopped

1 cup white breadcrumbs

1 egg, beaten

1 tsp chopped fresh dill

salt and pepper

1 Put the zucchini in a saucepan of boiling water, return to the boil, and then boil for 3 minutes. Drain, rinse under cold water, and drain again. Let cool.

2 When the zucchini are cool enough to handle, cut a thin strip off the top side of each one with a sharp knife and gently score around the inside edges to help scoop out the flesh. Using a teaspoon, scoop out the flesh, leaving a shell to hold the stuffing. Chop the zucchini flesh.

3 Heat 2 tablespoons of the oil in a saucepan. Add the onion and garlic and fry for 5 minutes, until softened. Add the zucchini flesh and fry for 5 minutes, until the onion is golden brown. Remove from the heat and let cool slightly. Stir in the cheese then the walnuts, breadcrumbs, egg, dill, salt, and pepper. Use the stuffing to fill the zucchini shells and place side by side in an ovenproof dish. Drizzle over the remaining oil.

4 Cover the dish with foil and bake in a preheated oven, 375°F/190°C, for 30 minutes. Remove the foil and bake for a further 10–15 minutes or until golden brown. Serve hot.

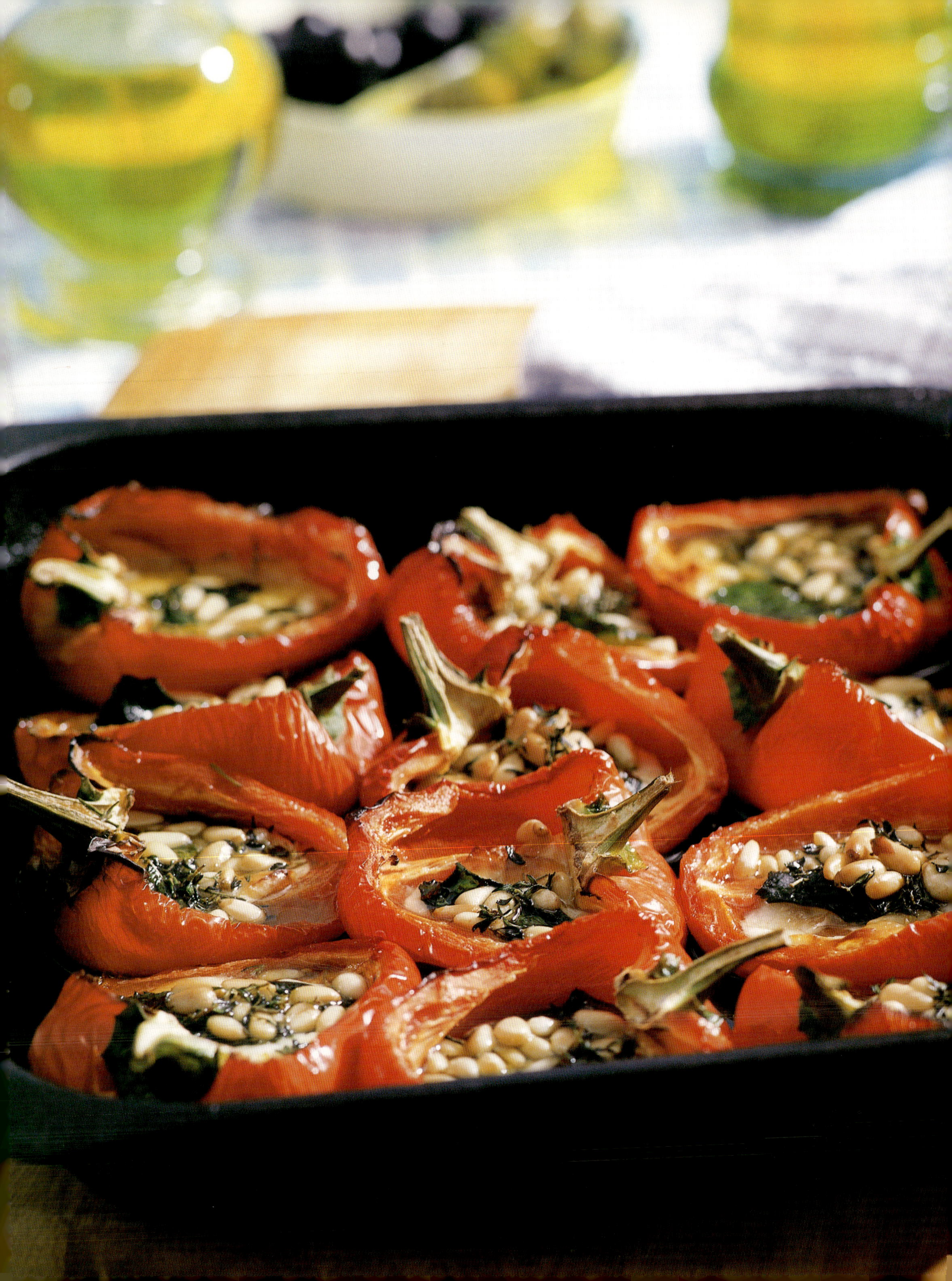

roasted red bell peppers with halloumi
pipéries gemistés me hallóumi

Red bell peppers are filled with halloumi cheese, lemon, and pine nuts and are ideal served as a light lunch dish with some bread to mop up the juices. Halloumi cheese is a soft cheese that is similar to feta but less salty. Feta cheese can be used as an alternative if preferred.

SERVES 6

6 small red bell peppers

2 tbsp olive oil

3 garlic cloves, sliced thinly

9 oz/250 g halloumi, provolone, or feta cheese, sliced thinly

12 fresh mint leaves

grated rind and juice of 1 lemon

1 tbsp chopped fresh thyme

3 tbsp pine nuts

pepper

1 Cut the bell peppers in half lengthwise and remove the core and seeds. Rub the skins of the bell peppers with a little of the oil then arrange the bell peppers, skin-side down, on a large greased baking sheet.

2 Scatter half the garlic into the bell peppers; add the cheese then the mint leaves, lemon rind, remaining garlic, the thyme, pine nuts, and pepper. Drizzle over the remaining oil and the lemon juice.

3 Roast the bell peppers in a preheated oven, 400°F/200°C, for 30 minutes, until tender and beginning to char around the edges. Serve warm.

greek country beans
fasólia yahní

Dried beans are very popular in Greece, especially white beans. Choose whichever beans are your favorite. Serve as an accompaniment to a meat or fish dish.

SERVES 4

6 oz/175 g white beans, such as Great Northern, cannellini, black-eyed peas, or butter beans, covered with water and soaked overnight

$1/3$ cup olive oil

1 large onion, chopped coarsely

1 large garlic clove, chopped finely

2 carrots, chopped finely

2 celery stalks, finely sliced

14 oz/400g canned chopped tomatoes in juice

pinch of sugar

1 tsp dried oregano

1 tbsp chopped fresh flat-leaf parsley

salt and pepper

to serve
Greek olives
lemon wedges

1 Drain the beans, put in a saucepan, and cover with cold water. Bring to the boil then boil for 10 minutes. Drain and return to the saucepan.

2 Heat the oil in a saucepan, add the onion and garlic, and fry for 5 minutes, until softened. Add the carrots and celery and fry for a further 10 minutes, until browned.

3 Add the beans, tomatoes, sugar, oregano, and parsley, and enough boiling water to just cover the beans. (Do not add salt at this stage as it toughens the beans.) Bring to the boil then simmer for 1–1$1/2$ hours, until the beans are really tender and the sauce is thick. The beans should be coated in sauce but add a little extra water during cooking if the sauce becomes too thick. (The time will vary, depending on the type of bean and its age.) Season with salt and pepper. Allow to cool slightly before serving with olives and lemon wedges.

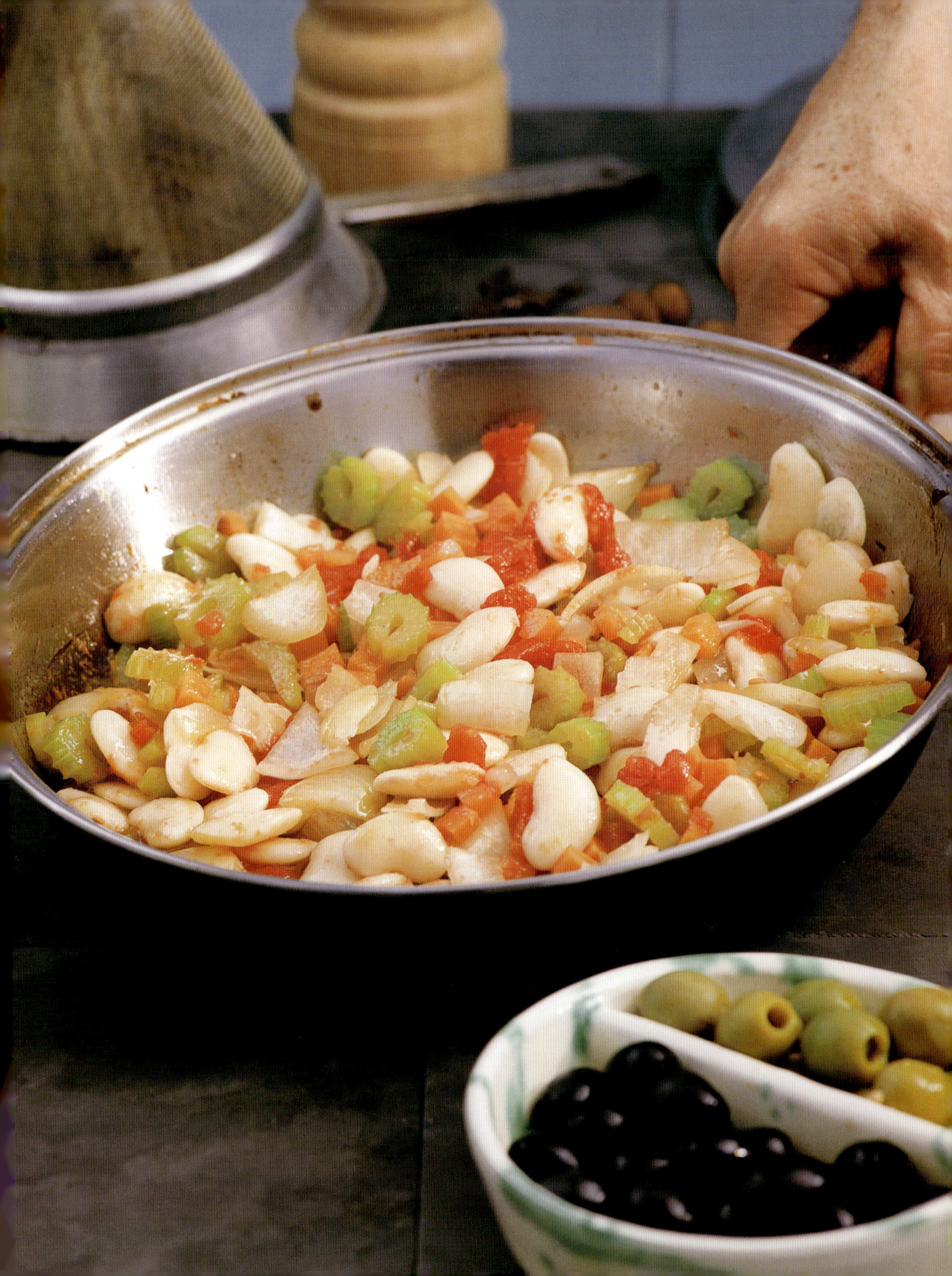

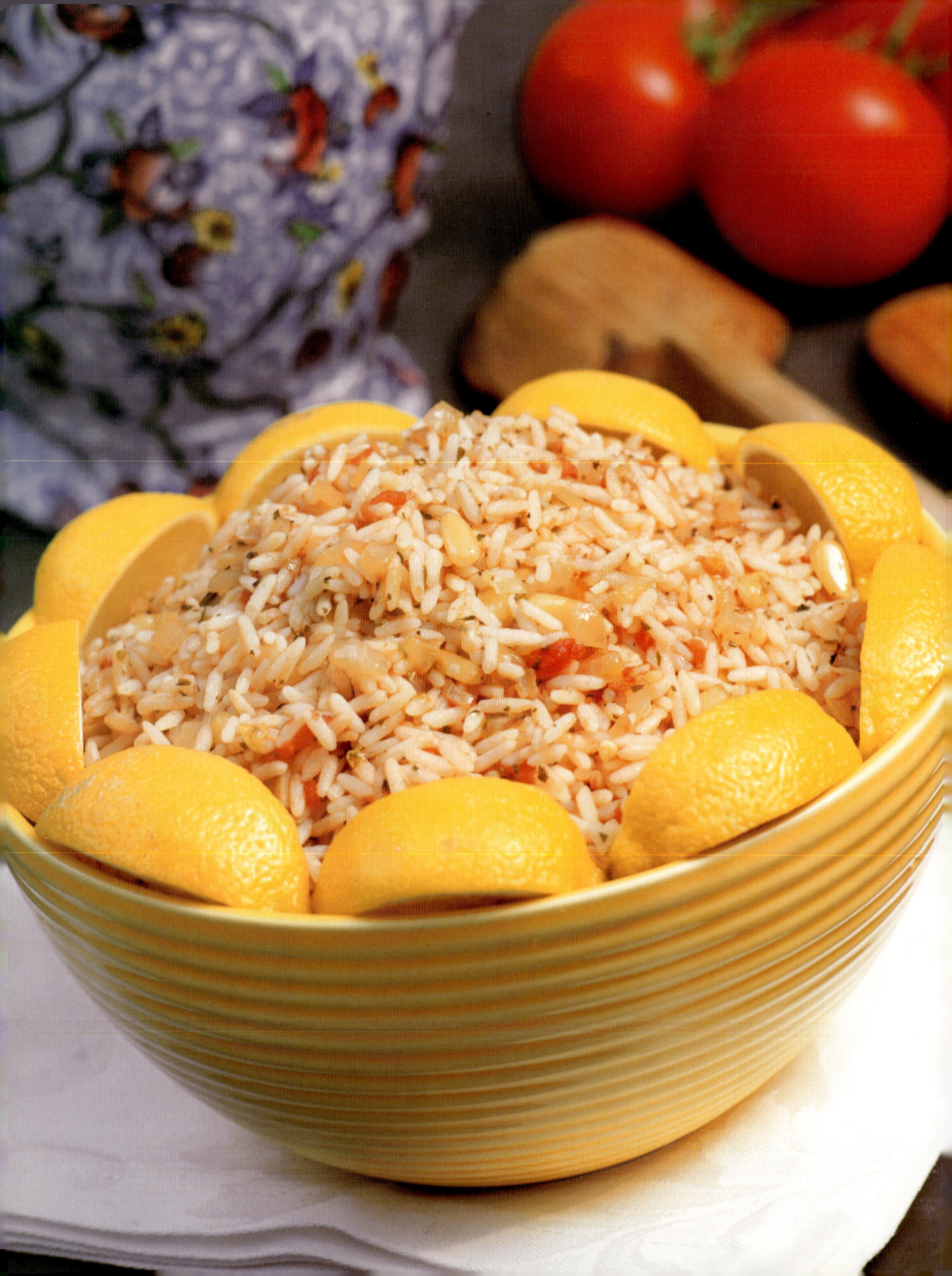

tomato pilaf
piláfi me domáta

Piláfi *is the Greek name given to savory rice dishes, and tomatoes, spinach, eggplant, and zucchini are all popular additions. This recipe uses canned tomatoes for convenience. Serve as an accompaniment or with slices of feta cheese as a main dish.*

SERVES 4

3 tbsp olive oil

1 onion, chopped finely

1 garlic clove, chopped finely

generous 1 cup long-grain white rice

14 oz/400 g canned chopped tomatoes in juice

pinch of sugar

2½ cups chicken or vegetable stock

1 tsp dried mint

salt and pepper

2 tbsp pine nuts

lemon wedges, to serve

1 Heat the oil in a large, heavy-bottomed saucepan, add the onion and garlic, and fry for 5 minutes, until softened. Add the rice and cook for 2–3 minutes, stirring all the time, until the rice looks transparent.

2 Add the tomatoes with their juice, the sugar, stock, mint, salt, and pepper. Bring to the boil then cover the saucepan with a tightly fitting lid and simmer for about 15 minutes, until the rice is tender and the liquid has been absorbed. Do not stir during cooking. When cooked, gently stir in the pine nuts.

3 Remove the lid, cover the saucepan with a clean dish towel, replace the lid, and leave in a warm place for 10 minutes to dry out. Stir with a fork to separate the grains and serve with lemon wedges to squeeze over.

variation
An additional scattering of toasted pine nuts would enhance this pilaf. To prepare these, heat 1 tablespoon olive oil in a skillet, add 1 cup pine nuts, and fry until golden brown, shaking the skillet constantly.

tomato salad with fried feta
domatasaláta me féta

The addition of fried feta turns this popular Greek salad into a light lunch or supper dish. Make it when tomatoes are at their best.

SERVES 4

3 tbsp extra virgin olive oil

juice of ½ lemon

2 tsp chopped fresh oregano

pinch of sugar

pepper

12 plum tomatoes, sliced

1 very small red onion, sliced very thinly

½ oz/15 g arugula leaves

20 Greek black olives

7 oz/200 g authentic Greek feta cheese

1 egg

3 tbsp all-purpose flour

2 tbsp olive oil

1. Make the dressing by whisking together the extra virgin olive oil, the lemon juice, oregano, sugar, and pepper in a small bowl. Set aside.

2. Prepare the salad by arranging the tomatoes, onion, arugula, and olives on 4 individual plates.

3. Cut the feta cheese into cubes about 1-inch/2.5-cm square. Beat the egg in a dish and put the flour on a separate plate. Toss the cheese first in the egg, shake off the excess, and then toss in the flour.

4. Heat the olive oil in a large skillet, add the cheese and fry over a medium heat, turning over the cubes of cheese until they are golden on all sides.

5. Scatter the fried feta over the salad. Whisk together the prepared dressing, spoon over the salad, and serve warm.

vegetables & salads

traditional greek salad
saláta horiátiki

203

This is Greece's most ubiquitous salad. Recipes vary enormously and in fact the Greeks use whatever they have on hand. Any kind of salad leaves will do but whichever lettuce you choose, it should be sliced rather than separated into leaves.

SERVES 4

6 tbsp extra virgin olive oil

2 tbsp fresh lemon juice

1 garlic clove, crushed

pinch of sugar

salt and pepper

7 oz/200g authentic Greek feta cheese

½ head of iceberg lettuce or 1 lettuce such as romaine or escarole, shredded or sliced

4 tomatoes, quartered

½ cucumber, sliced

12 Greek black olives

2 tbsp chopped fresh herbs such as oregano, flat-leaf parsley, mint, or basil

1. Make the dressing by whisking together the oil, lemon juice, garlic, sugar, salt, and pepper in a small bowl. Set aside.

2. Cut the feta cheese into cubes about 1-inch/2.5-cm square. Put the lettuce, tomatoes, and cucumber in a salad bowl. Scatter over the cheese and toss together.

3. Just before serving, whisk the dressing, pour over the salad leaves, and toss together. Scatter over the olives and chopped herbs and serve.

fava bean salad
saláta me koukiá

SERVES 4

6 tbsp extra virgin olive oil

grated rind of 1 lemon and 2 tbsp lemon juice

1 small garlic clove, crushed

pinch of sugar

pepper

3 lb/1.3 kg fresh young fava beans or 1½ lb/675 g frozen baby fava beans

5½ oz/150 g authentic Greek feta cheese

1 bunch scallions, sliced thinly

2 tbsp chopped fresh dill or mint

2 hard-boiled eggs, quartered

to serve

lemon wedges

authentic Greek yogurt

Prepare this salad with fresh fava beans when they are in season or use frozen fava beans when they are not. Serve the salad as a light lunch or supper dish.

1. Make the dressing by whisking together the oil, lemon rind and juice, garlic, sugar, and pepper in a small bowl. Set aside.

2. Shell the fresh fava beans, if using, and cook in boiling salted water for 5–10 minutes, until tender. If using frozen fava beans, cook in boiling salted water for 4–5 minutes. Drain the cooked beans and put in a salad bowl.

3. Whisk the dressing and pour over the beans while they are still warm. Crumble over the feta cheese, add the scallions and toss together. Sprinkle over the chopped dill and arrange the egg quarters around the edge.

4. Serve warm with lemon wedges and a bowl of yogurt to spoon on top, if desired.

*cook's tip

If using mint in this salad, sprinkle a very little sugar over it as you chop to bring out its full aroma.

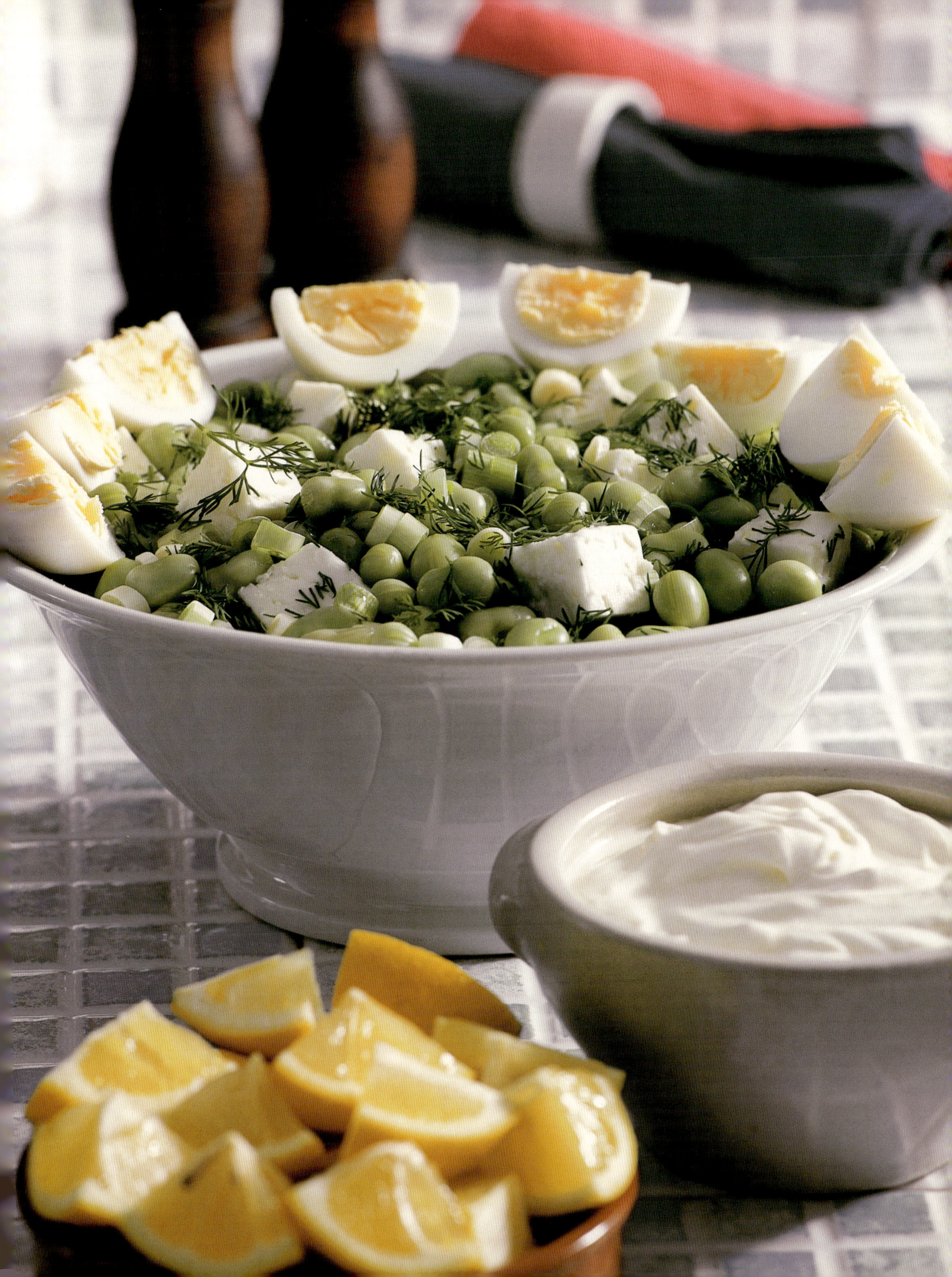

salad of greens with lemon dressing
hórta me ladolémono

In Greece, wild greens and herbs are collected from the hillsides and used in salads. You can use any variety of small salad leaves for this recipe. Freshly made lemon dressing is, of course, preferable but, for convenience, you can buy bottles of lemon dressing in supermarkets selling Greek products. If desired, a handful of broken walnuts or croûtons can be added.

SERVES 4

7 oz/200 g mixed baby salad leaves such as maché, spinach, watercress, and wild arugula

4 tbsp mixed chopped fresh herbs such as flat-leaf parsley, mint, cilantro, and basil

about 4 tbsp extra virgin olive oil

juice of about ½ lemon

1 garlic clove, crushed

salt and pepper

1. Wash the salad leaves and discard any thick stems. Dry and put in a salad bowl. Add the chopped herbs.

2. Make the dressing by whisking together the oil, lemon juice, garlic, salt, and pepper in a small bowl. Taste and add more oil or lemon juice if necessary.

3. Just before serving, whisk the dressing; pour over the salad leaves, toss, and serve.

vegetables & salads

orange and olive salad
saláta me portokali kai eliés

As both oranges and olives grow in abundance in Greece, this unusual salad is often prepared.

SERVES 4

4 thick-skinned oranges
1 small red onion, sliced very thinly
16 large black Greek olives, pitted
2 tbsp extra virgin olive oil
1 tbsp lemon juice
pinch of sugar
salt and pepper
lettuce leaves, to serve
chopped fresh herbs such as flat-leaved parsley, mint, or dill, to garnish

1 Using a sharp knife, remove the peel and pith from the oranges then cut the flesh into ¼-inch/ 5-mm thick slices, discarding the seeds and white membrane. Put the oranges and any juice, the onion slices, and the olives in a large bowl.

2 To make the dressing, whisk together the oil, lemon juice, sugar, salt, and pepper and drizzle over the salad ingredients. Gently toss together then chill in the fridge for 2–3 hours before serving in a shallow dish lined with lettuce leaves. Garnish with chopped fresh herbs.

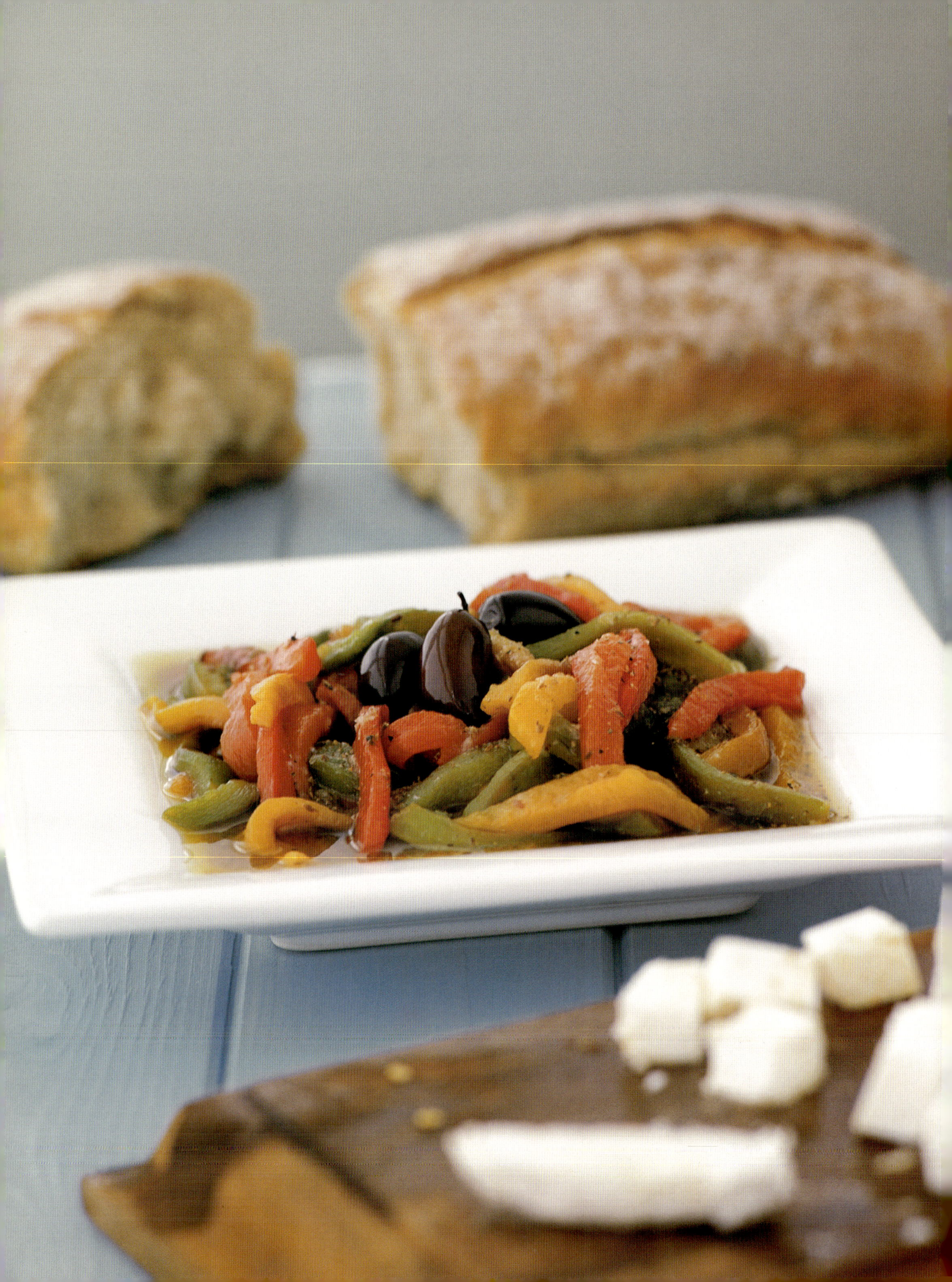

charred bell pepper salad
saláta me psités piperiés

Bell peppers are much used in Greek cooking, perhaps stuffed bell peppers being the recipe that most people are familiar with. Here they take center stage in a delicious salad. The dressing can be flavored with cumin or marjoram—the choice is yours.

SERVES 4–6

2 green bell peppers

2 red bell peppers

2 yellow bell peppers

½ tsp cumin seeds or 2 tbsp chopped fresh marjoram

5 tbsp extra virgin olive oil

2 tbsp lemon juice

2 garlic cloves, crushed

pinch of sugar

salt and pepper

Greek olives, to garnish

1 Preheat the broiler. Broil the bell peppers, turning frequently, until the skins are charred all over. Put the bell peppers in a bowl, cover with a damp dish towel and leave until cold.

2 When the bell peppers are cold, hold them over a clean bowl to collect the juices and peel off the skin. Remove the stem, core, and seeds and cut the peppers into thin strips. Arrange the bell pepper strips on a flat serving plate.

3 If using cumin seeds, dry-toast them in a dry skillet until they turn brown and begin to pop. Shake the skillet continuously to prevent them from burning and do not allow them to smoke. Lightly crush the toasted seeds with a pestle and mortar.

4 Add the toasted cumin seeds or marjoram, the olive oil, lemon juice, garlic, sugar, salt, and pepper to the bell pepper juices and whisk together.

5 Pour the dressing over the bell peppers and chill in the fridge for 3–4 hours or overnight. Serve at room temperature, garnished with olives.

cook's tip

A selection of different colored bell peppers have been used in this recipe but this isn't essential—they just look attractive.

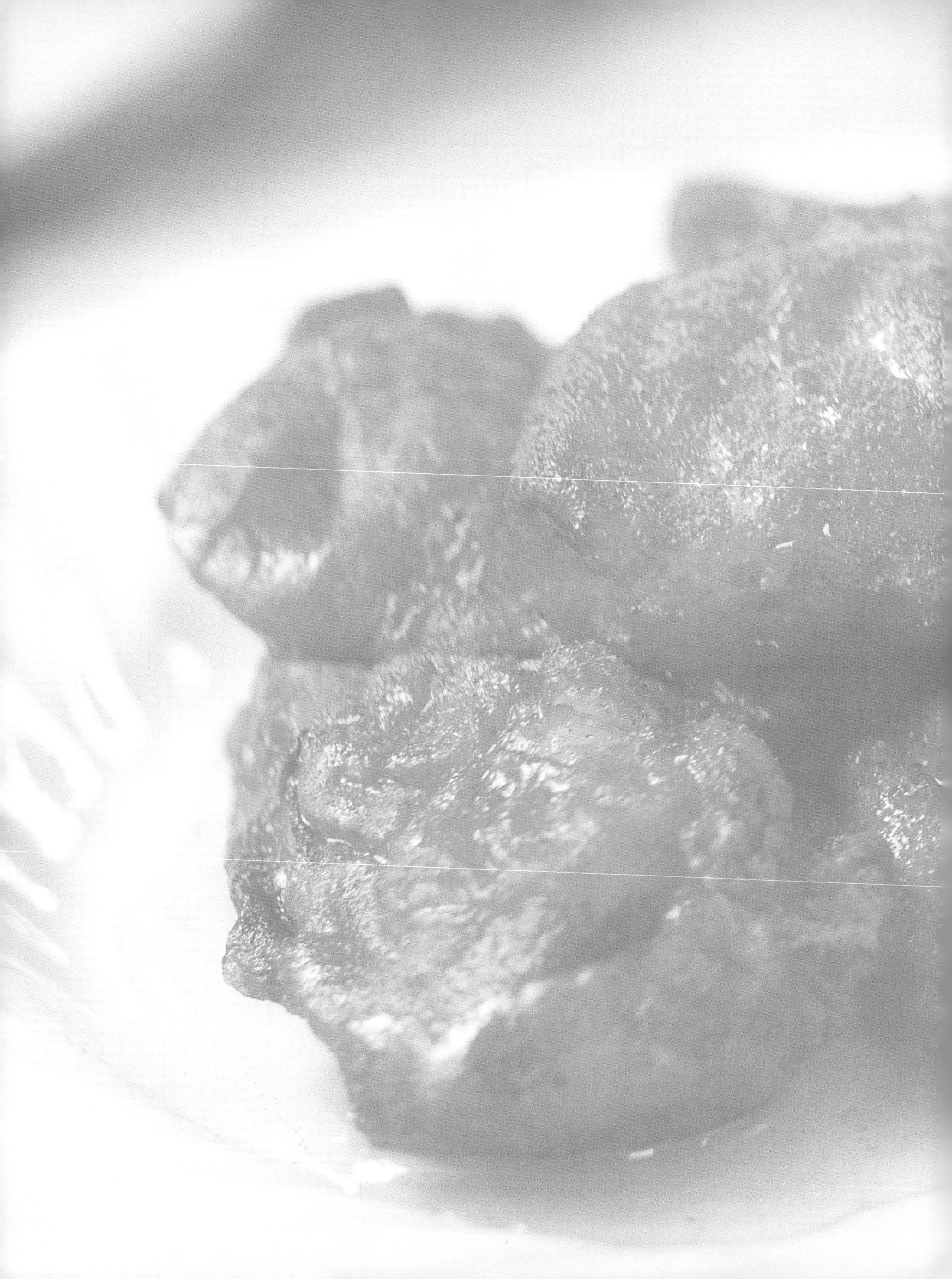

SWEET THINGS

The fruits of Greece, like the vegetables, are best seen on the market stalls—piles of yellow lemons, fat fresh figs and dried ones too, perfectly round melons, and large bunches of juicy grapes. They are so fresh and magnificent, and grow in such abundance that they make desserts almost superfluous.

In Greece, the meal usually concludes with a bowl of fresh, seasonal fruit rather than a dessert, and sometimes this is extended to include some dried fruit and nuts. The choice may be both black and white grapes, cherries, fresh figs, apricots, peaches, oranges, tangerines, dates, loquats, apples, pears, melons, pomegranates, and strawberries. Crete, in particular, is renowned for its sweet fruit.

the Greeks have a particular fondness for sweet things. Most of them are based on honey, nuts, and sesame seeds

This does not, however, mean that desserts are not eaten but those that are will often be based on fresh fruit, and, of course, there is always *yaoúrti kai mél*, which is simply yogurt with Greek honey drizzled over the top and sprinkled with a few crushed pistachio nuts or almonds, or there is ice cream.

Fruits are also served as *glyká tou koutalióu*, meaning "spoon sweets," which are fruits preserved in a heavy syrup. They are a Greek speciality and were the traditional way of offering hospitality to guests. They were served in small bowls with spoons and accompanied by a glass of water, generally followed by a glass of liqueur and then coffee. Nowadays, particularly in Athens and other large cities, the visitor is more likely to be offered another type of sweet and coffee but some islanders still serve spoon sweets in the traditional way. Fruits that are popular for making into spoon sweets are those that cannot be eaten fresh, such as bitter oranges, lemons, and quinces, but also figs, cherries, strawberries, apricots, pears, and oranges.

Nevertheless, many excellent desserts, cakes, and pastries are prepared in Greece, for the Greeks have a particular fondness for sweet things. Most of them are based on honey, nuts, and sesame seeds and they are eaten in large quantities. They are sold at the popular pastry shops, known as *zaharoplastion*, and are served with coffee during the day or in the evening. They may be eaten on the premises or bought and taken home, where they are eaten as a snack, after the afternoon siesta, served to visitors or guests, or eaten one or two hours after a meal, with coffee.

Cakes and pastries are particularly enjoyed at festive occasions such as Christmas, New Year, and Easter. *Kourambiédes* (see page 219) are Greek Shortbread Cookies which are liberally dusted with confectioners' sugar and eaten during these celebrations. Mind you, they are enjoyed all year round and a batch stored in a cookie tin will soon disappear!

Freshly caught local fish and seafood is the order of the day at the restaurants that line the waterfront in a seaside town

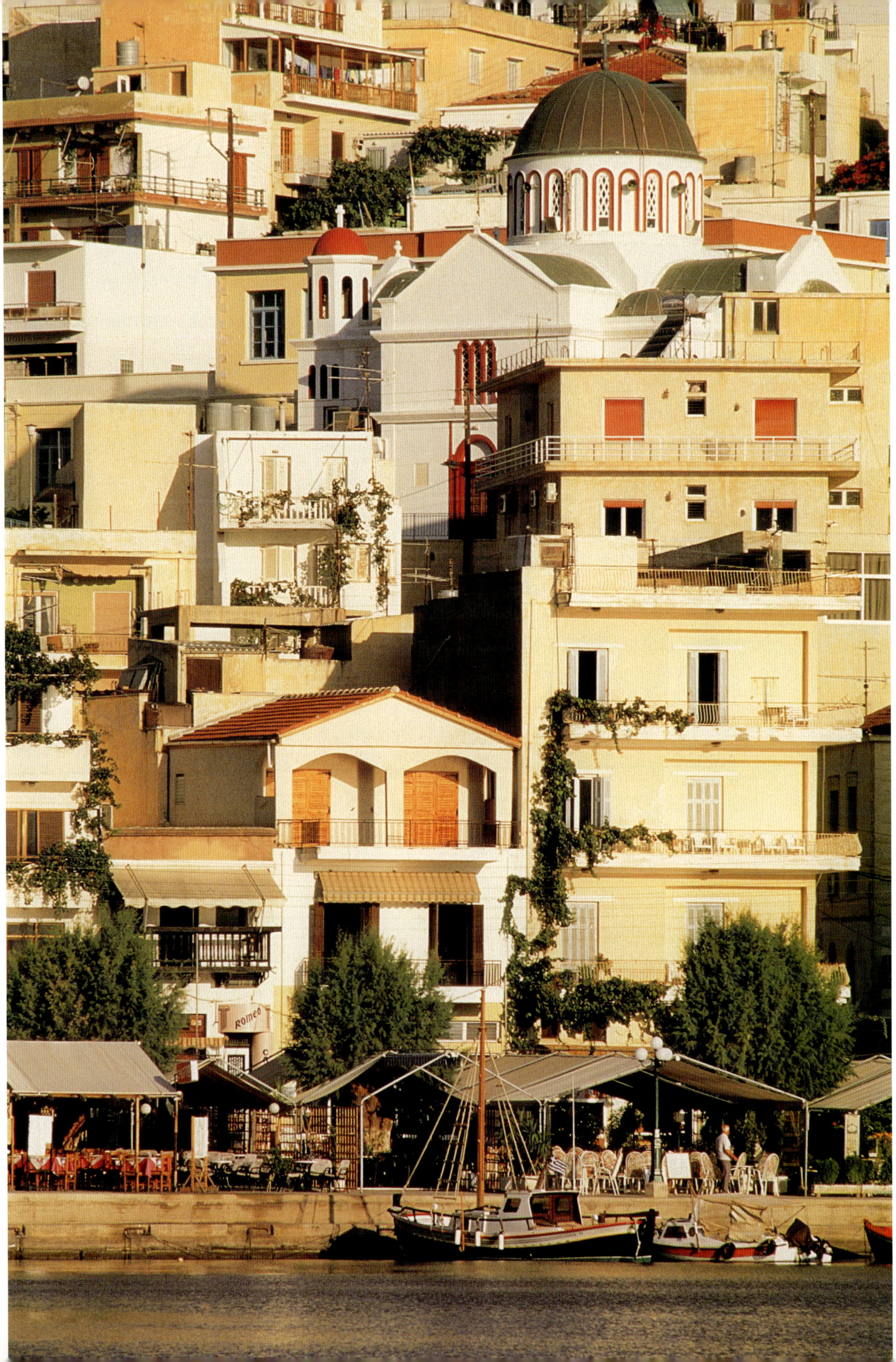
Romeo

Many Greek cakes and pastries are based on nuts such as walnuts, pistachios, and almonds and many of them have been steeped in a honey syrup, for Greek honey is another ingredient used in large quantities. There is no doubt that the Greeks have a sweet tooth, as the majority of the traditional cakes and pastries are sweet and sticky. These sweet concoctions include the well-known *Baklavás* (see page 240), made with layers of phyllo pastry and walnuts in a honey syrup, *Halvás* (see page 243), the Semolina and Almond Cake with a lemon syrup, and *Loukoumádes* (see page 225), deep-fried doughnuts in a warm honey syrup. All these cakes and pastries make wonderful desserts.

Finally, tucked into the end of this chapter, there are a couple of drink recipes. These are Lemonade (see page 252), which was an obvious choice because there is such as abundance of lemons grown in Greece and, of course, coffee. Greek coffee (see page 253), also known as Turkish coffee, is the most popular drink in Greece and is drunk at all hours of the day at home and in cafés. It is traditionally made in a *briki*, which is a small, long-handled brass or copper pot with a narrow top and broad lip. However, this is not essential and any small saucepan with a lip can be used. The coffee used is very finely ground and sugar is added, according to taste, to the coffee grounds at the same time as the water. It may be *métrio* if you want a medium-sweet coffee, *skéto* if you don't want sugar in it and *varies glyko* if you want it very sweet. Greek coffee is always served in small cups and left for a few moments to allow the coffee grounds to settle. It is never stirred, as the last thing you want to do is swallow the grounds, so spoons are not necessary and it is accompanied with glasses of ice water and often with Turkish delight or a sweet cake or pastry.

Religion plays a major role in Greek life and churches abound

Overleaf Handmade lace on sale in the town of Kritsá, Crete

sweet things

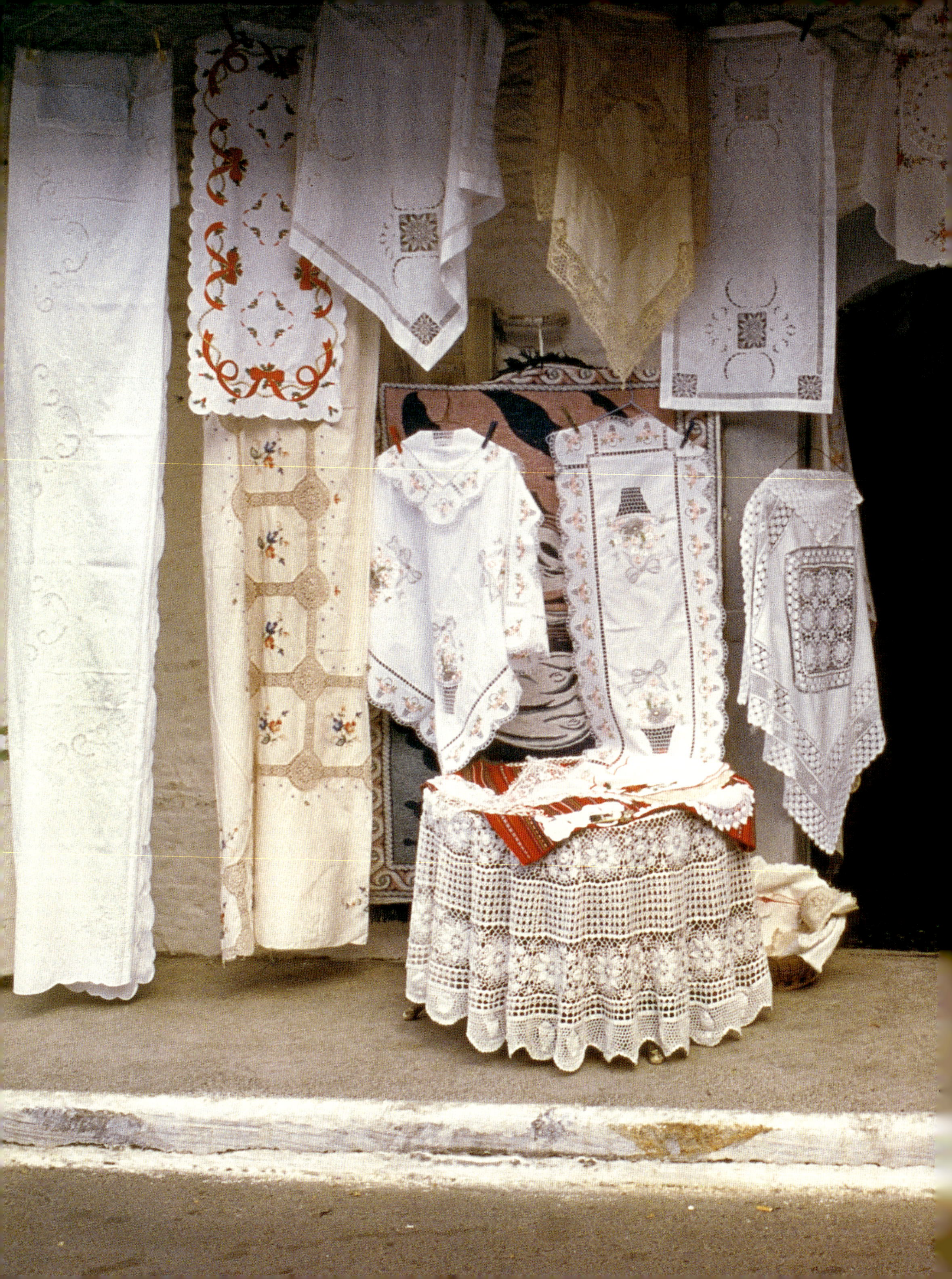

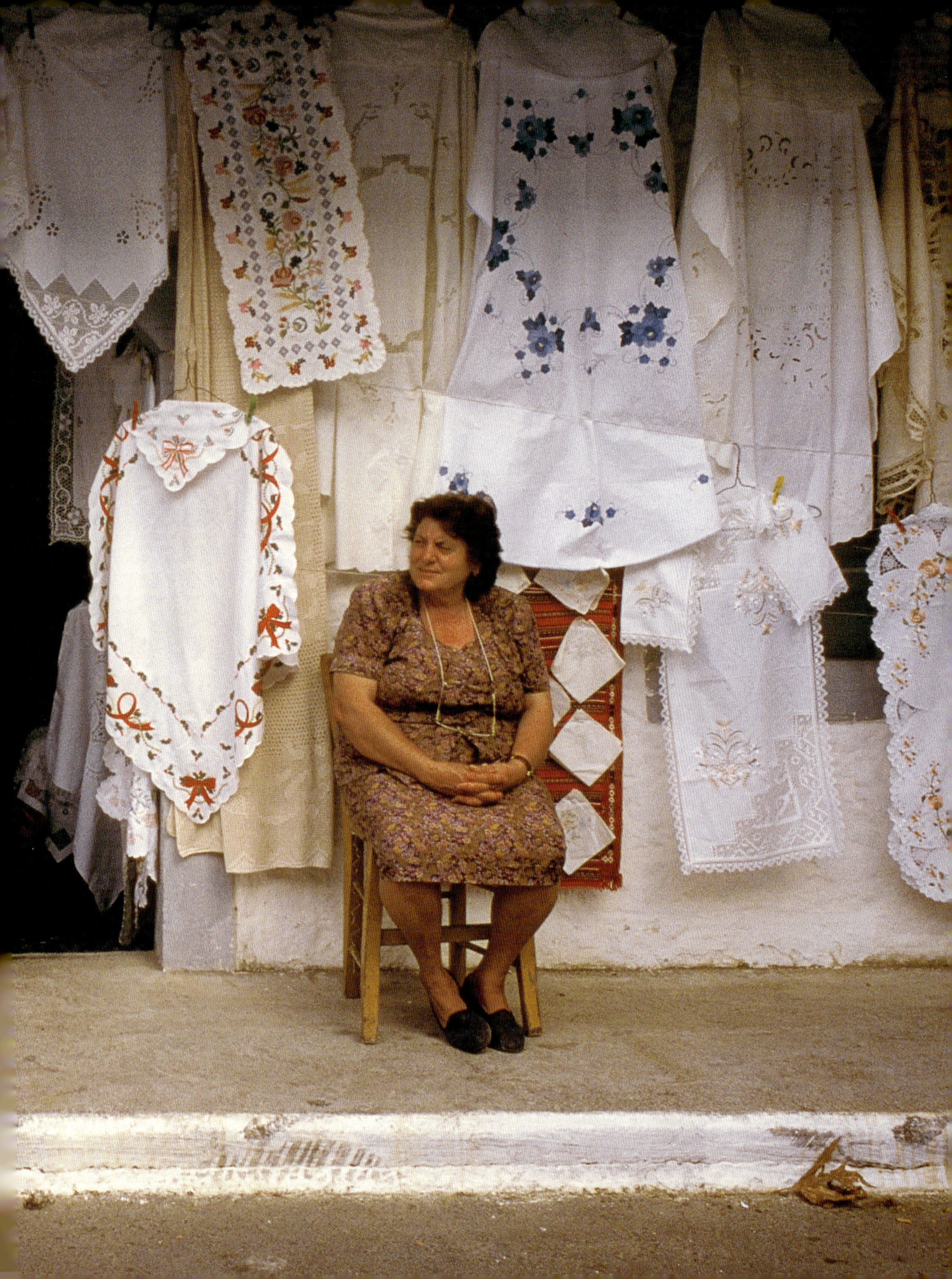

baked stuffed honey figs
síka fournóu me méli

Both purple and green figs are another favorite Greek fruit. For this recipe, use the ready-to-eat dried figs, rather than those that are compressed into a block.

SERVES 4
²/₃ **cup fresh orange juice**
6 tbsp Greek honey
12 ready-to-eat dried figs
¼ **cup shelled pistachio nuts, chopped finely**
¼ **cup ready-to-eat dried apricots, chopped very finely**
1 tsp sesame seeds
authentic Greek yogurt, to serve

1 Put the orange juice and 5 tablespoons of the honey in a saucepan and heat gently until the honey has dissolved. Add the figs and simmer for 10 minutes, until softened. Remove from the heat and let cool in the liquid.

2 Meanwhile, prepare the filling. Put the nuts, apricots, sesame seeds, and remaining tablespoon of honey in a bowl and mix well.

3 Using a slotted spoon, remove the figs from the cooking liquid and reserve. Cut a slit at the top of each fig, where the stem joins. Using your fingers, plump up the figs and stuff each fig with about 1 teaspoon of the filling mixture. Close the top of each fig and place in an ovenproof dish. Pour over the reserved cooking liquid.

4 Bake the figs in a preheated oven, 325°F/170°C, for 10 minutes, until hot. Serve warm or cold, with the sauce and Greek yogurt.

greek shortbread cookies
kourambiédes

These are the national cookies of the Greeks. Although traditionally eaten at Christmas and New Year, they are delicious at any time.

MAKES 24

8 oz/225 g butter, softened
½ cup confectioners' sugar
1 egg yolk
1 tbsp ouzo or brandy
2½ cups all-purpose flour
1 cup ground almonds
confectioners' sugar, for dredging

1. Put the butter and confectioners' sugar in a large bowl and beat until pale and fluffy. Beat in the egg yolk and ouzo or brandy and then the flour and almonds to form a soft, firm dough. Using your hands, quickly bind the mixture together.

2. Cut the dough into 24 pieces then roll each piece into a ball and then into a sausage shape measuring about 3 inches/7.5 cm long. Place the sausage over one finger and press down on the ends to form a plump moon shape. Place on baking trays, allowing room for them to spread slightly.

3. Bake in a preheated oven, 350°F/180°C, for 15 minutes, until firm to the touch and light golden brown. Meanwhile, sift a layer of confectioners' sugar into a large roasting pan.

4. When baked, allow the biscuits to cool slightly then place in the pan in a single layer, as close together as possible. Sift confectioners' sugar generously on top and let cool for 3–4 hours. Store the biscuits in an airtight tin with any remaining confectioners' sugar, so that the biscuits remain coated.

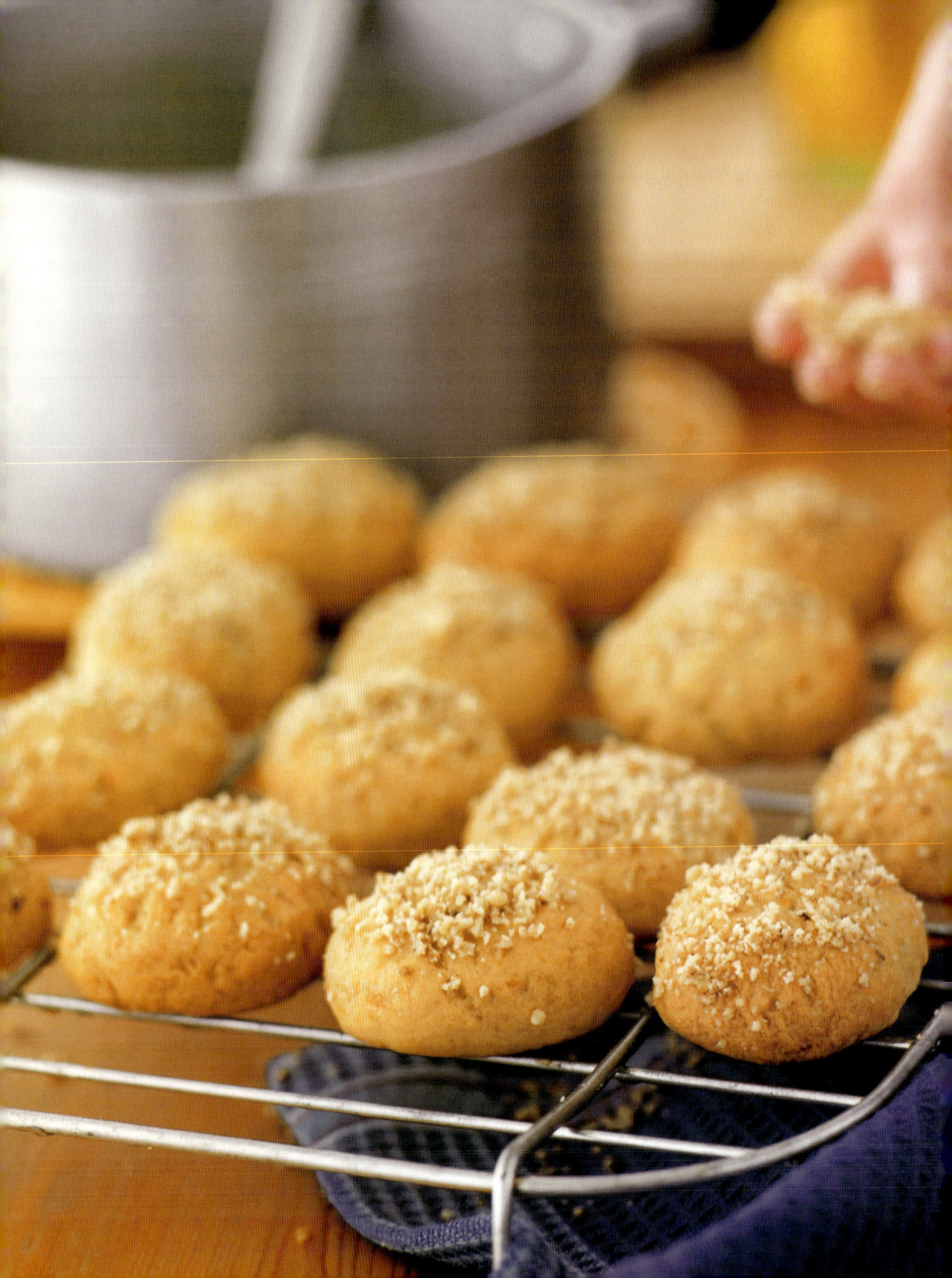

orange and walnut cakes
melomakárona

These delicately spiced orange-flavored cakes, also known as Finikia, *are made by Greek families during the week preceding Christmas. After baking, they are dipped in a hot honey syrup and sprinkled with chopped walnuts.*

MAKES ABOUT 18

3 cups self-rising flour
½ tsp baking soda
½ tsp ground cinnamon
¼ tsp ground cloves
pinch of grated nutmeg
pinch of salt
1¼ cups olive oil
⅓ cup superfine sugar
finely grated rind and juice of 1 large orange
2 tbsp brandy

for the topping
¼ cup walnut pieces, chopped finely
½ tsp ground cinnamon

for the syrup
½ cup Greek honey
½ cup water
juice of 1 small lemon
juice of 1 small orange or 1 tbsp orange flower water

1. Sift together the flour, baking soda, cinnamon, cloves, nutmeg, and salt.

2. Put the oil and sugar in a bowl and beat together. Add the orange rind and juice then gradually beat in the flour mixture. Turn the mixture onto a lightly floured surface and knead for 2–3 minutes, until smooth.

3. Take small, egg-size pieces of dough and shape into ovals. Place on baking trays, allowing room for spreading and, with the back of a fork, press the top of each twice to make a criss-cross design.

4. Bake the cakes in a preheated oven, 350°F/180°C, for about 20 minutes, until lightly browned. Transfer to a wire rack and let cool.

5. Meanwhile, make the topping by mixing together the walnuts and cinnamon. To make the syrup, put the honey and water in a saucepan, bring to the boil, then simmer for 5 minutes. Remove from the heat and add the lemon juice and orange juice or orange flower water.

6. When the cakes have almost cooled, using a slotted spoon, submerge each cake in the hot syrup and leave for about 1 minute. Place on a tray and top each with the walnut mixture. Let cool completely before serving.

variation
These small cakes, soaked in honey syrup, are intensely sweet but you can omit this if you don't think it will suit your taste.

butter cookies
koulourákia

These cookies are traditionally baked at Easter in Greece and, although they can now be found in a variety of different shapes, they were originally shaped like small snakes, because the Cretans worshipped the snake for its healing powers.

MAKES ABOUT 36

6 oz/175 g butter

¾ cup superfine sugar

1 egg

2 cups self-rising flour

finely grated rind of 1 lemon

3 tbsp slivered almonds (optional)

1 Put the butter and sugar in a bowl and whisk until light and fluffy. Whisk in the egg then fold in the flour and lemon rind.

2 Turn out the dough onto a lightly floured surface and knead gently until smooth. Form the mixture into rolls the thickness of a finger then cut into 4-inch/10-cm lengths. Shape each roll into an S shape and place on baking sheets, allowing room for spreading. If desired, stud with a few slivered almonds.

3 Bake the cookies in a preheated oven, 350°F/180°C, for about 15 minutes, until lightly browned. Cool on a wire rack. Store the cookies in an airtight tin.

The traditional way of life continues in many Greek communities, which may be isolated by mountain or sea

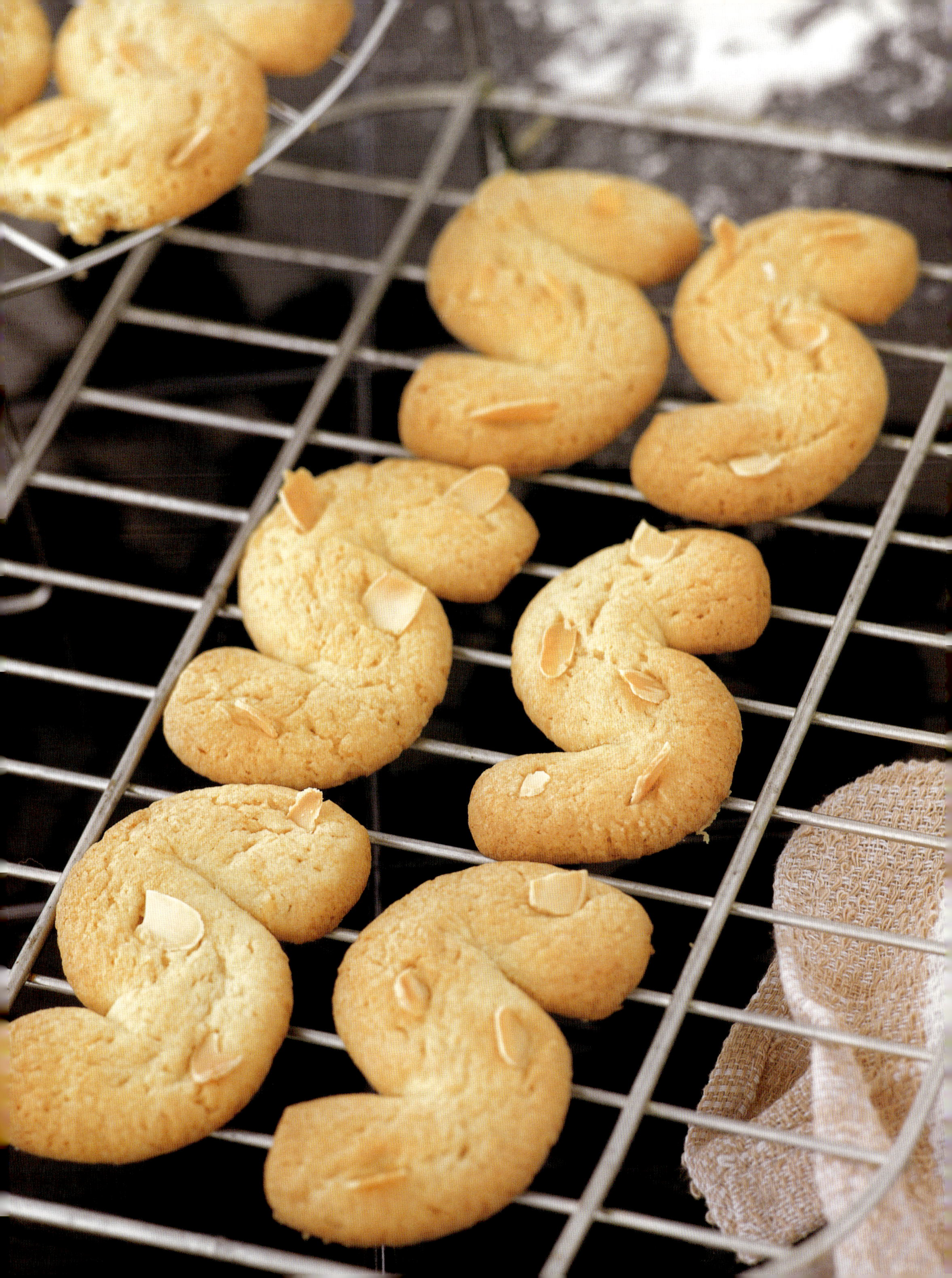

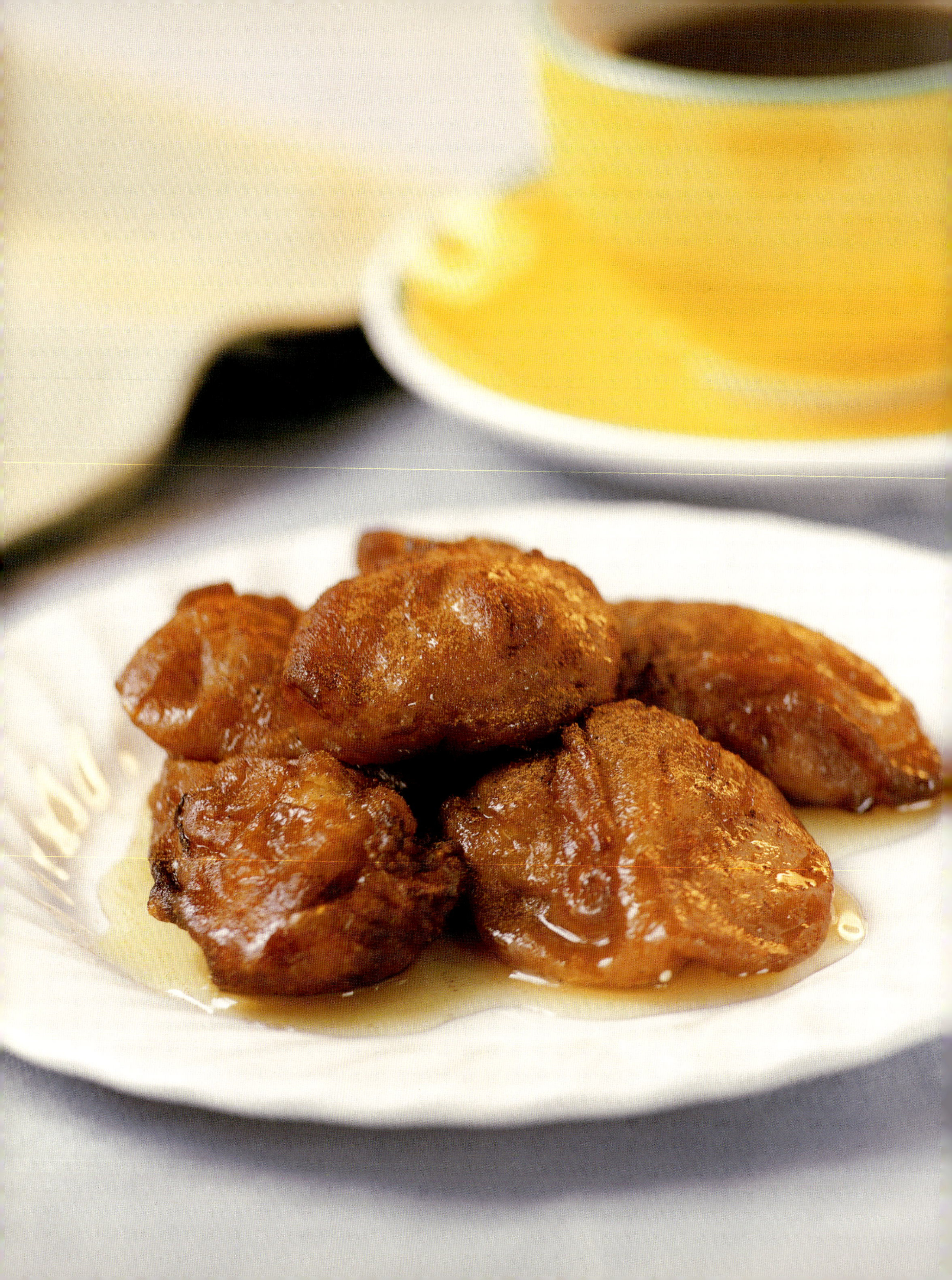

sweet things

doughnuts in honey syrup
loukoumádes

These little fritters are delicious served as a dessert or as an afternoon snack—especially for children. They are sold in every café throughout Greece.

SERVES 6

2 cups plus 2 tbsp all-purpose flour
1 tsp salt
finely grated rind of 1 orange
1 envelope dried yeast
1¼ cups warm water
⅓ cup Greek honey
1 tsp lemon juice
sunflower oil, for deep-frying
ground cinnamon

1. Put the flour, salt, and orange rind in the bowl of an electric mixer fitted with a dough hook and sprinkle in the yeast. Gradually add the water and whisk for 10 minutes to form a thick batter. Alternatively make the batter in a large bowl using a whisk.

2. Cover the bowl with a clean dish towel and leave in a warm place for 2 hours, until risen with lots of bubbles.

3. Meanwhile, make the honey syrup. Put the honey, lemon juice, and 1 tablespoon water in a saucepan and simmer until combined. Set aside.

4. When the batter has risen, heat the oil in a deep-fat fryer to 350°F/180°C or until a cube of bread, dropped into the fat, turns brown in 1 minute. Using 2 teaspoons (one to scoop and one to push), dip the spoons in cold water to prevent the batter from sticking and drop small amounts of the batter into the hot oil. Cook about 5 at a time, for 2–3 minutes, turning with a slotted spoon, until they puff up and are golden brown. Remove from the fryer and drain on paper towels.

5. Serve about 5 hot doughnuts per person, spoon over the warm honey syrup, and sprinkle with cinnamon.

Sunset across the water viewed from the top of a church

walnut custard tarts
tártes karidión

1. Melt the butter. Brush 4 deep 4-inch/10-cm tartlet pans with a little of the butter. Cut the sheets of phyllo pastry in half to make 16 rough squares.

2. Take 1 square of pastry and cover the remaining squares with a damp dish towel. Brush the square with a little of the melted butter and use to line 1 of the pans. Repeat with 3 more pastry squares, placing each of them at a different angle. Repeat with the remaining pastry to line the remaining 3 pans. Place the tins on a baking tray.

3. To make the filling, finely chop 2 tablespoons of walnuts. Put the yogurt, honey, cream, sugar, eggs, and vanilla extract in a bowl and beat together. Stir in the chopped walnuts until well mixed.

4. Pour the yogurt filling into the pastry shells. Coarsely break the remaining walnuts and scatter over the top. Bake in a preheated oven, 350°F/180°C, for 25–30 minutes until the filling is firm to the touch.

5. Let the tartlets cool, then carefully remove from the pans and dust with confectioners' sugar. Serve with a bowl of yogurt, if desired.

Custard-filled phyllo pastries, like these, are often eaten in Greece at Easter, after the traditional roast lamb.

SERVES 4

1½ oz/40 g butter
8 sheets authentic Greek phyllo pastry
¼ cup walnut halves
scant ⅔ cup authentic Greek yogurt
4 tbsp Greek honey
⅔ cup heavy cream
2 tbsp superfine sugar
2 eggs
1 tsp vanilla extract
confectioners' sugar, for dusting
authentic Greek yogurt, to serve

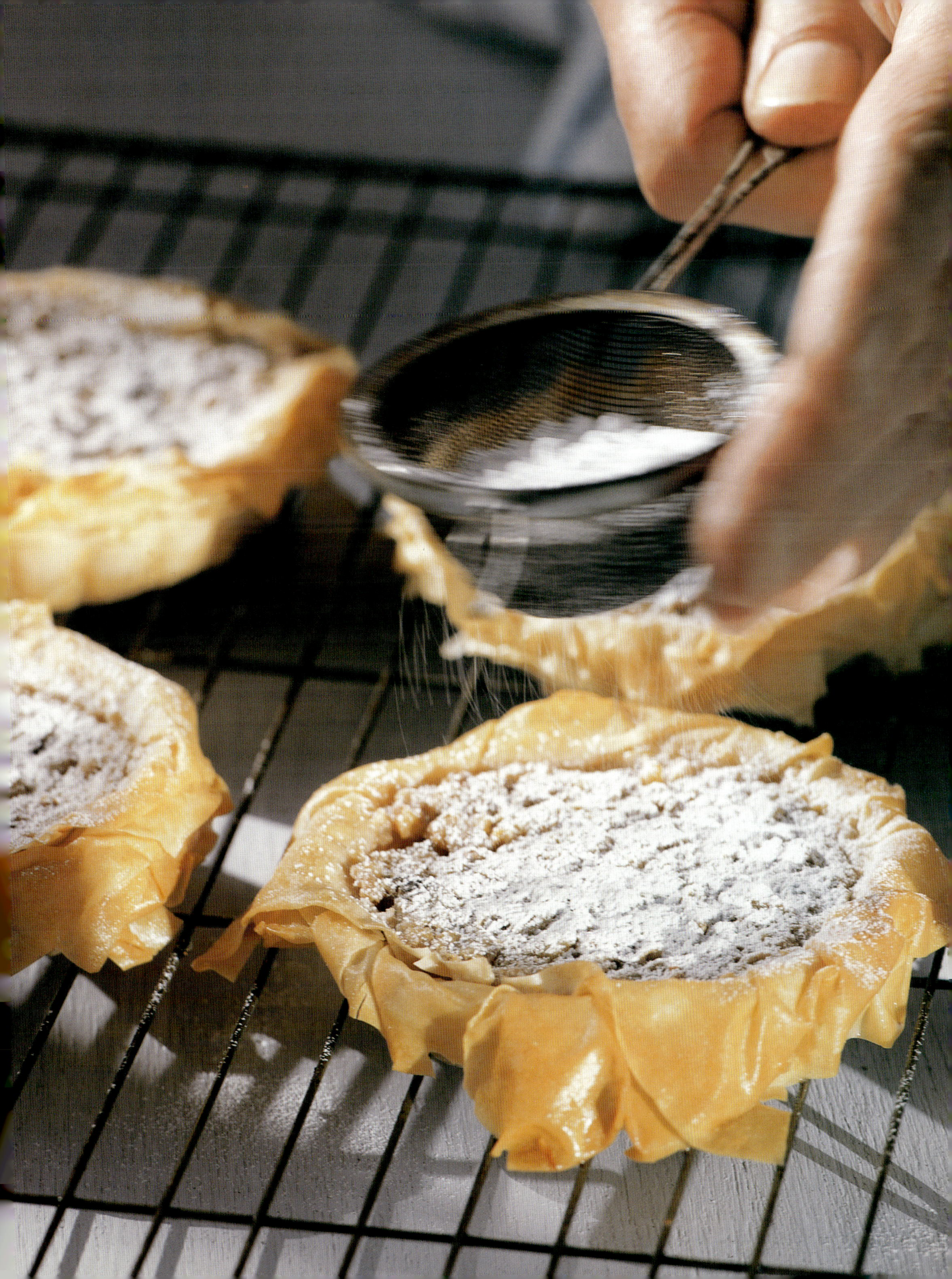

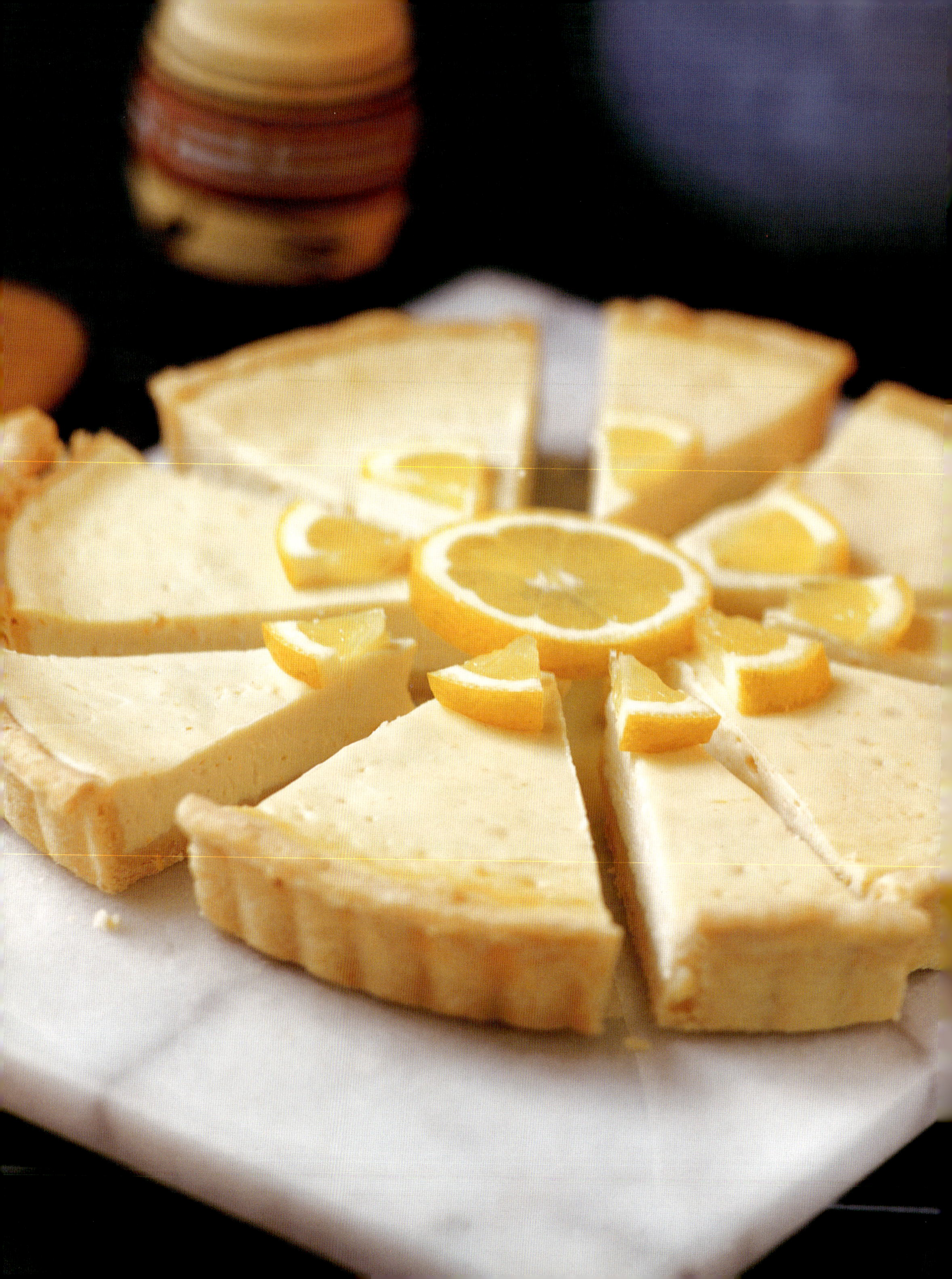

honey and lemon tart
siphnópitta

In Greece, a soft, sweet cheese, known as manoúri, *would be used in this tart, but cottage cheese makes a suitable alternative. Alternatively, you could use cream cheese or Italian ricotta. Choose an aromatic honey such as Hymettus or orange blossom, for a good flavor.*

SERVES 8-12

1 1/2 cups plus 3 tbsp all-purpose flour
pinch of salt
1 1/2 tsp superfine sugar
5 1/2 oz/150 g butter
3-4 tbsp cold water
1 1/3 cups cottage cheese, cream cheese, or ricotta
6 tbsp Greek honey
3 eggs, beaten
1/2 tsp cinnamon
grated rind and juice of 1 lemon

1 To make the pastry, put the flour, salt, sugar, and butter, cut into cubes, in a food processor. Mix in short bursts, until the mixture resembles fine breadcrumbs. Sprinkle over the water and mix until the mixture forms a smooth dough. Alternatively, make the pastry in a bowl and rub in with your hands. The pastry can be used right away but is better if allowed to rest in the fridge, wrapped in waxed paper or foil, for about 30 minutes before use.

2 Meanwhile, make the filling. If using cottage cheese, push the cheese through a sieve into a bowl. Add the honey to the cheese and beat until smooth. Add the eggs, cinnamon, lemon rind, and juice, and mix well together.

3 On a lightly floured surface, roll out the pastry and use to line a 9-inch/23-cm tart pan. Place on a baking sheet and line with waxed paper. Weigh down with pie weights and bake in a preheated oven, 400°F/200°C, for 15 minutes. Remove the waxed paper and weights and bake for a further 5 minutes, until the base is firm but not brown.

4 Reduce the oven temperature to 350°F/180°C. Pour the filling into the pastry shell and bake in the oven for about 30 minutes until set. Serve cold.

The painted dome of this chapel is in perfect harmony with the color of the sea beyond

orange cheesecake with caramelized lemon slices
cheesecake portokáli me karameloméno lemóni

In Greece, mizíthra cheese, a by-product from making feta cheese, would be used for this delicious cheesecake. It is similar to cottage cheese, which makes an ideal substitute, as does Italian ricotta. The caramelized lemons are a stunning decoration and can also be used to decorate the other cake recipes in this book.

SERVES 8

1 1/2 **cups cottage cheese or ricotta cheese**
4 **egg yolks**
2/3 **cup superfine sugar**
finely grated rind of 1 orange
1/4 **cup fresh orange juice**
1/2 **cup ground almonds**

for the caramelized lemons
2 **lemons, sliced thinly**
2/3 **cup superfine sugar**
2/3 **cup water**

authentic Greek yogurt, to serve

1. Grease and line the base of a 8-inch/20-cm loose-bottomed cake pan with waxed paper.

2. If using cottage cheese, push the cheese through a sieve into a bowl. Gradually beat the egg yolks into the cheese then add the sugar, orange rind, and orange juice and beat until smooth. Carefully fold in the ground almonds.

3. Turn the mixture into the prepared pan and bake in a preheated oven, 350°F/180°C, for about 35 minutes, until set. When cooked, turn off the oven, open the oven door, and leave ajar. Allow the cheesecake to remain in the oven for 2–3 hours to cool.

4. Meanwhile, make the caramelized lemons. Put the lemon slices, discarding any pips, the sugar, and water in a small saucepan and bring to the boil, then simmer for about 45 minutes, shaking the pan occasionally, until most of the liquid has evaporated and the lemons have caramelized. Watch very carefully toward the end of cooking that the lemons do not burn. Drain the lemon slices on a wire rack.

5. When the cheesecake has cooled, carefully remove from the pan and decorate with the caramelized lemons. Serve accompanied with Greek yogurt.

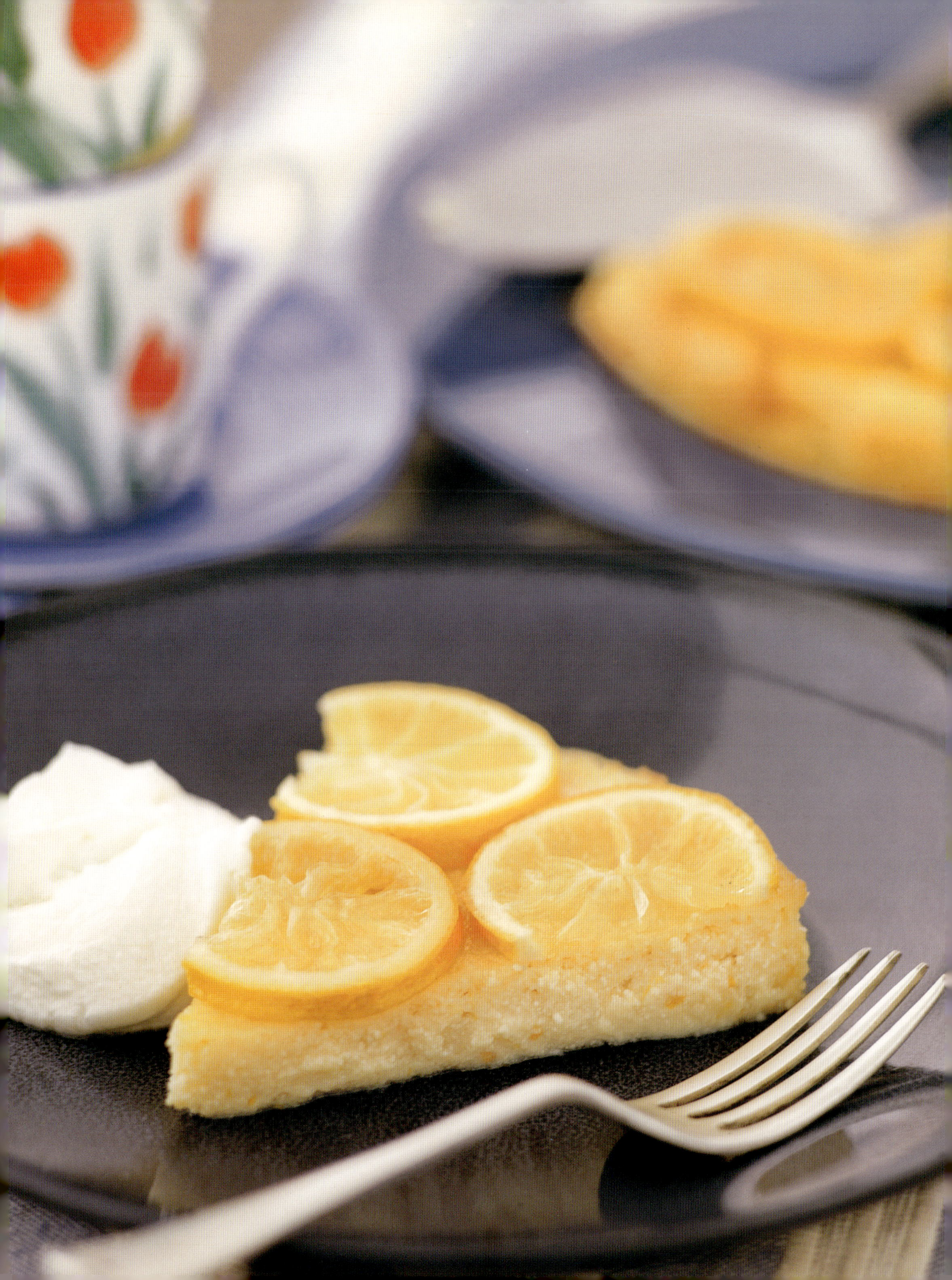

greek rice pudding
rizógalo

Greek rice pudding is always made by first cooking the rice in water before adding the milk. The result is thick and creamy and quite unlike any other rice pudding. In Greece it is always served cold and is often eaten for breakfast as well as for dessert.

SERVES 4

2/3 **cup short-grain rice**
1 1/4 **cups water**
1 **tbsp cornstarch**
2 1/2 **cups whole milk**
1/3 **cup superfine sugar**
1 **tsp vanilla extract or finely grated rind of 1 large lemon**
ground cinnamon

1 Put the rice in a saucepan and add the water. Bring to the boil then simmer for 12–15 minutes, stirring occasionally, until the water has been absorbed. Meanwhile, in a small bowl, blend the cornstarch with 2 tablespoons of the milk.

2 Add the remaining milk to the rice, return to the boil then simmer for 20–25 minutes, stirring frequently, until the rice is very soft and most of the liquid has been absorbed. Stir in the sugar, vanilla or lemon rind, and the cornstarch mixture, return to the boil then simmer for a further 5 minutes, stirring.

3 Spoon the rice mixture into individual serving dishes and let cool. Serve cold, sprinkled generously with cinnamon.

sweet things

oranges in caramel sauce
portokaliá karameloméno

Fresh fruit is the logical conclusion to a Greek meal. Oranges can be sliced and sprinkled very lightly with orange flower water or, as in this recipe, served in a simple caramel sauce with the addition of honey.

SERVES 6

9 oranges

¾ cup water

1⅓ cup white granulated sugar

3 tbsp Greek honey

1. Using a zester, remove the zest from the oranges and put in a small saucepan. Add the water and leave to soak for 1 hour.

2. When the orange zest has soaked, simmer for 20 minutes. Strain any remaining liquid, reserving the zest, into a measuring cup and make up to ¾ cup with water.

3. Using a sharp knife, remove the peel from the oranges, discarding all the white pith. Cut the flesh widthwise into ¼-inch/5-mm slices and arrange in a glass serving dish, scattered with a little of the orange zest. Reserve most of the zest to decorate.

4. Put the measured water and the sugar in a saucepan and heat until the sugar has dissolved, then bring to the boil and boil rapidly until it turns a pale golden color. Immediately remove from the heat, stir in the honey until dissolved, and then add the reserved orange zest. Let cool slightly then pour the caramel sauce over the oranges. Chill in the fridge for at least 3 hours before serving, decorated with the reserved zest.

lemon ice cream in an ice bowl
pagotó lemóni se bol apo págo

This truly delicious, refreshing ice cream is made with Greek yogurt and looks stunning served in an ice bowl. Your guests will comment on how attractive your bowl is and will then be amazed that it is made of ice. They will certainly request the instructions for making it!

SERVES 4–6

for the ice bowl

2 lemons

water

4¼ cups authentic Greek yogurt

⅔ cup heavy cream

⅔ cup superfine sugar

6 tbsp lemon juice

1. To make the ice bowl, thinly slice the lemons and discard the pips. Use the lemon slices to line the base and sides of a 1½-quart/1.5-litre freezer-proof bowl. Insert a 1-quart/1-litre freezerproof bowl inside and fill the space between the two bowls with water. Immediately place a plate and heavy weight on top. Transfer to the freezer and freeze for at least 4 hours, until frozen.

2. Turn on an ice cream maker or set the freezer to its lowest setting. To make the ice cream, put the yogurt, cream, sugar, and lemon juice in a bowl and mix well together. Pour the mixture into an ice cream maker and freeze according to the manufacturer's instructions.

3. Alternatively, pour the mixture into a shallow freezer container and freeze, uncovered, for 1–2 hours, until beginning to set around the edges. Turn the mixture into a bowl and, with a fork, stir until smooth. Return to the freezer container, cover, and freeze for a further 2–3 hours, until firm.

4. To use the ice bowl, remove the weight and plate and quickly run the bowls under hot water until they loosen then remove the ice bowl. Quickly transfer the ice bowl to a serving plate and return to the freezer.

5. About 30 minutes before serving the ice cream, remove it from the freezer and leave at room temperature to allow it to soften slightly. Spoon into the ice bowl and serve.

*variation

Instead of just sliced lemons, the ice bowl can be lined with a variety of additional ingredients. Fresh mint leaves or lemon geranium leaves look particularly attractive.

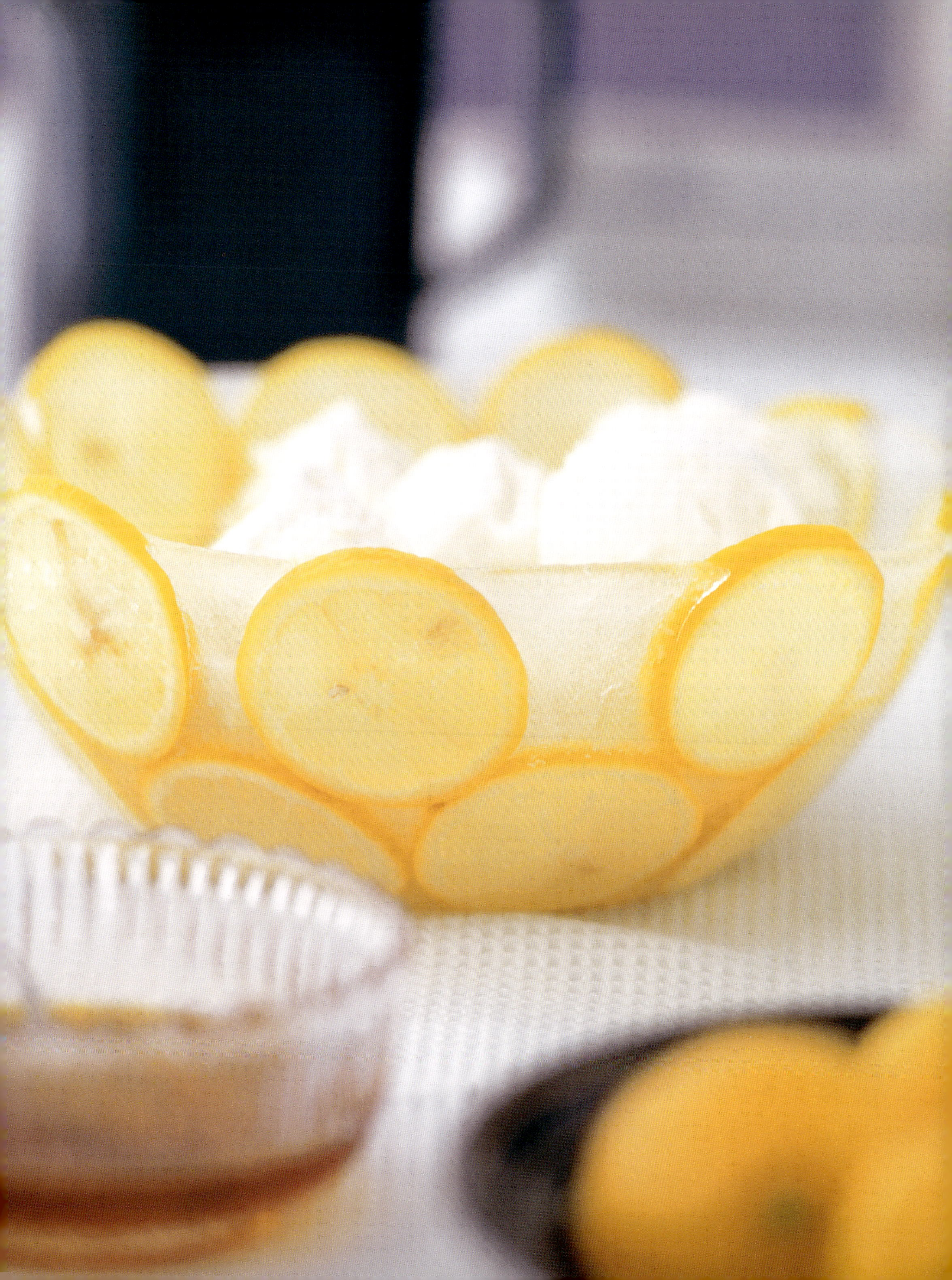

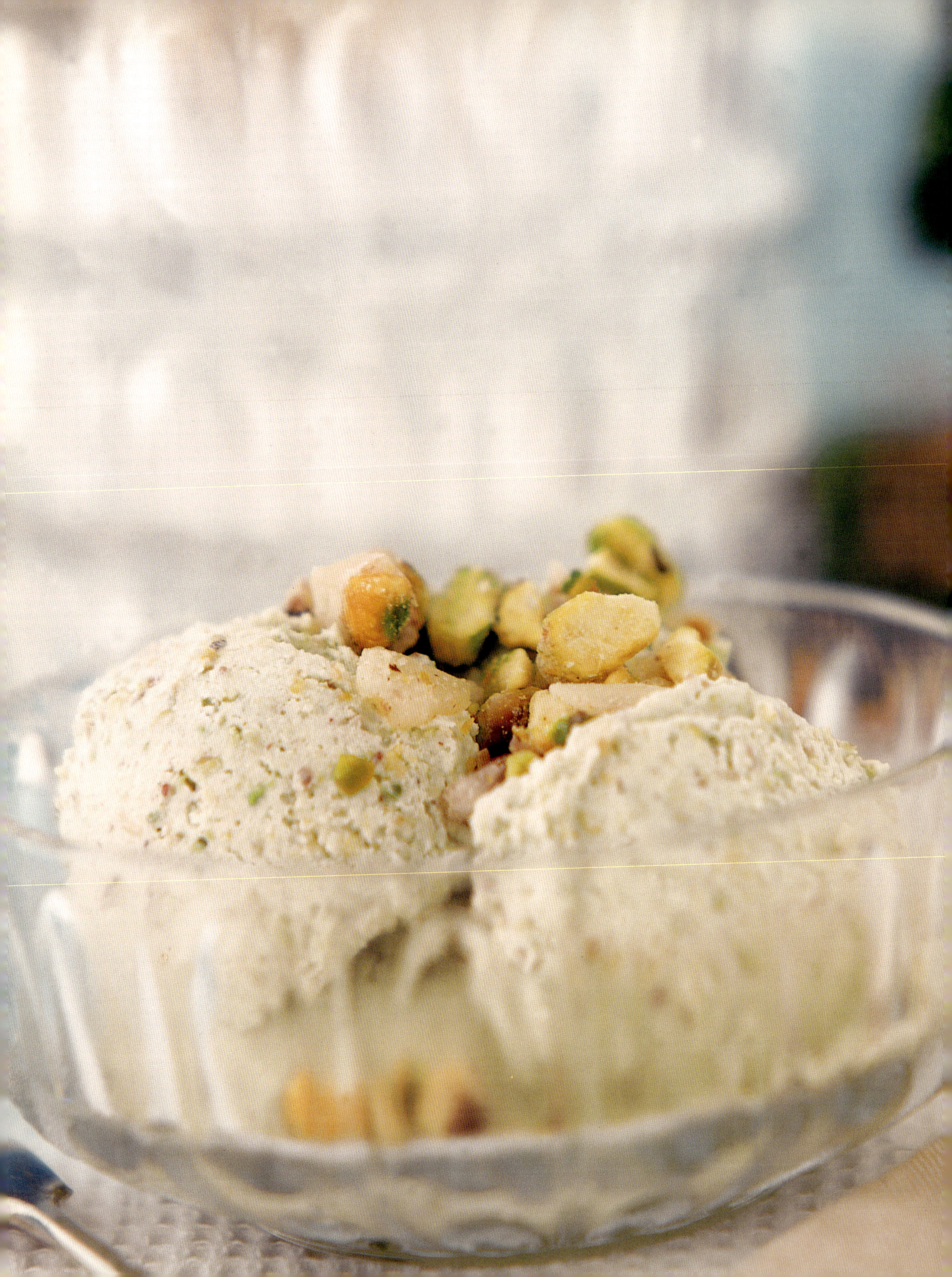

pistachio ice cream
pagotó fistíkia

Pistachios are probably the Greeks' favorite nut, and combined in an ice cream make for a very popular flavor. The pistachio praline is an optional extra. An almond or pine nut ice cream can be made in the same way by simply replacing the pistachios with the appropriate nut.

SERVES 4

1¼ cups heavy cream

⅔ cup authentic Greek yogurt

2 tbsp milk

3 tbsp Greek honey

green food coloring

⅔ cup shelled unsalted pistachio nuts

for the pistachio praline

oil, for brushing

¾ cup granulated sugar

3 tbsp water

⅔ cup shelled, whole, unsalted pistachio nuts

1 Turn on an ice cream maker or set the freezer to its lowest setting. Put the cream, yogurt, milk, and honey in a bowl and mix together. Add a few drops of green food coloring to tint the mixture pale green and stir in well. Pour the mixture into an ice cream maker and freeze according to the manufacturer's instructions.

2 Meanwhile, put the pistachio nuts for the ice cream in a food processor and very finely chop. Stir the nuts into the ice cream just before it freezes firmly.

3 Alternatively, pour the ice cream mixture into a shallow freezer container and freeze, uncovered, for 1–2 hours, until beginning to set around the edges. Turn the mixture into a bowl and, with a fork, stir until smooth then stir in the pistachio nuts. Return to the freezer container, cover, and freeze for a further 2–3 hours, until firm.

4 To make the pistachio praline, brush a baking sheet with oil. Put the sugar and water in a saucepan and heat gently, stirring, until the sugar has dissolved then allow to bubble gently, without stirring, for 6–10 minutes, until lightly golden brown.

5 Remove the pan from the heat and stir in the pistachio nuts. Immediately pour the mixture onto the baking sheet and spread out evenly. Let stand in a cool place for about 1 hour, until cold and hardened.

6 When the praline is hard, crush it in a food processor or in a plastic bag with a hammer.

7 About 30 minutes before serving the ice cream, remove it from the freezer and let stand at room temperature to allow it to soften slightly.

8 Scatter the pistachio praline over the ice cream before serving. Store any remaining pistachio praline in an airtight jar.

Overleaf *Misty islands create a nostalgic setting*

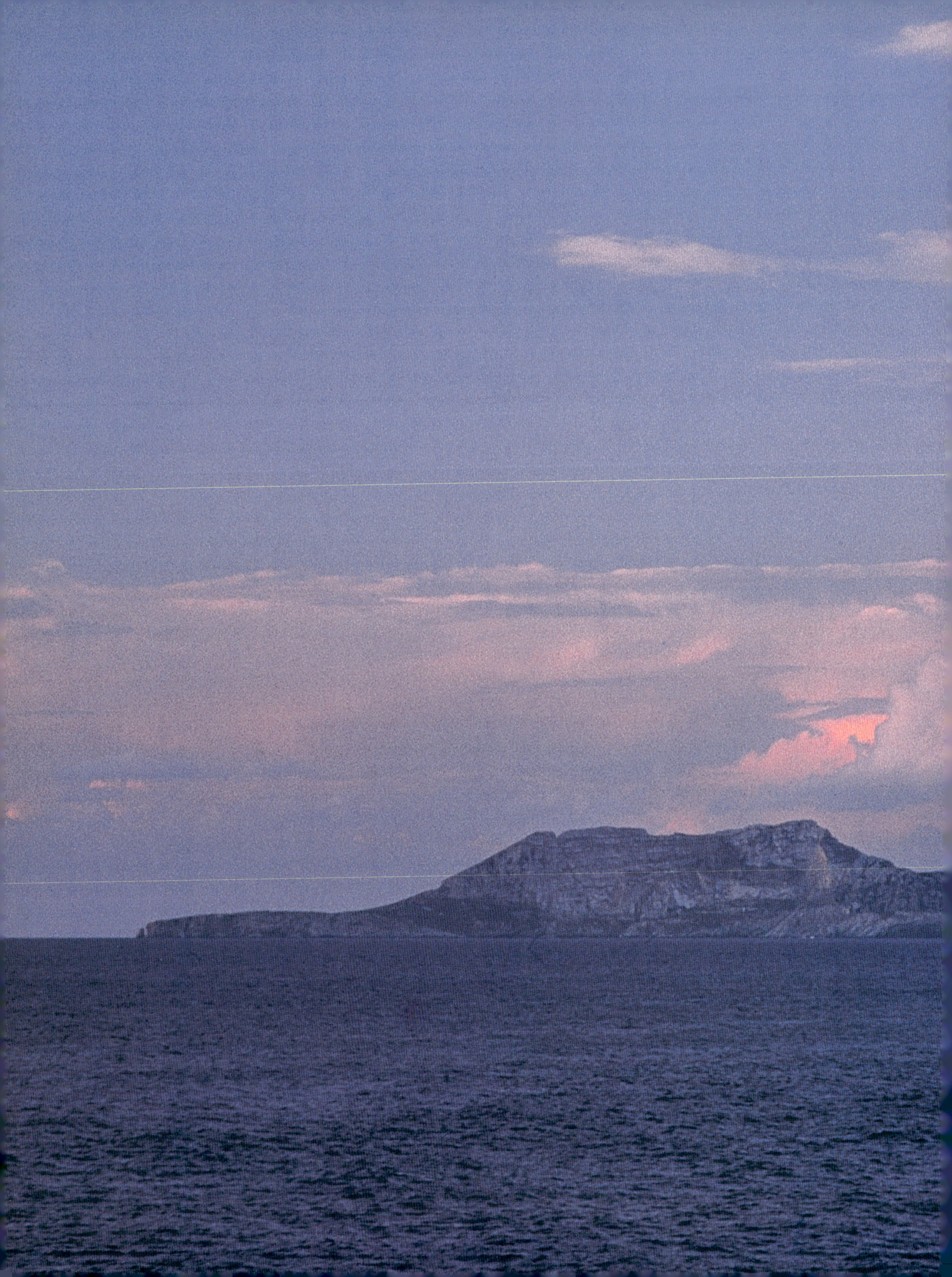

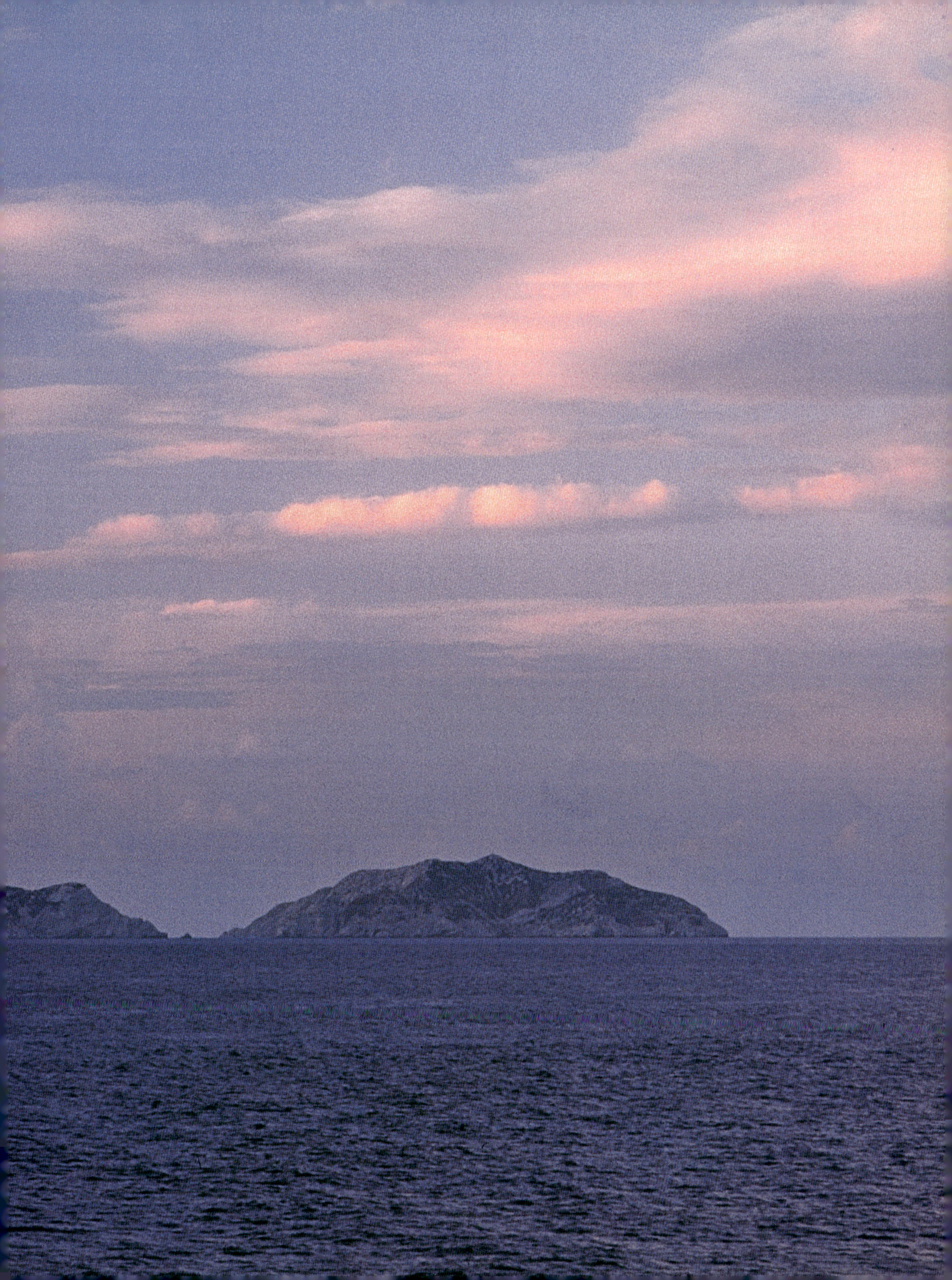

walnut pastries
baklavás

MAKES ABOUT 12

3 1/2 oz/100 g butter

2 1/2 cups walnut pieces, chopped finely

1/3 cup superfine sugar

1 tsp ground cinnamon

1/2 tsp ground cloves

8 oz/225 g authentic Greek phyllo pastry

3/4 cup Greek honey

2 tsp lemon juice

2/3 cup water

This is Greece's most famous dessert, whether it is eaten as an afternoon snack or on special occasions.

1. Melt the butter and use a little to lightly grease a deep 10 x 7-inch/25 x 18-cm metal baking pan.

2. To make the filling, put the walnuts, sugar, cinnamon, and cloves in a bowl and mix well together.

3. Cut the pastry sheets in half widthwise. Take 1 sheet of pastry and use to line the pan. Cover the remaining sheets with a damp dish towel. Brush the sheet with a little of the melted butter. Repeat with half of the pastry sheets then sprinkle over the walnut filling. Top with the remaining pastry sheets, brushing each with butter and tucking down the edges. Using a sharp knife, cut the top layers of the pastry into 12 diamond or square shapes.

4. Bake in a preheated oven, 425°F/220°C, for 10 minutes then reduce the oven temperature to 350°F/180°C and bake for a further 20 minutes, until golden brown.

5. Just before the pastries have cooked, make the honey syrup. Put the honey, lemon juice, and the water in a saucepan and simmer for about 5 minutes, until combined. Set aside.

6. When the pastries are cooked, remove from the oven and evenly pour over the honey syrup. Let cool. Before serving, cut along the marked lines again to divide into pieces.

Church bells provide a memorable silhouette at nightfall

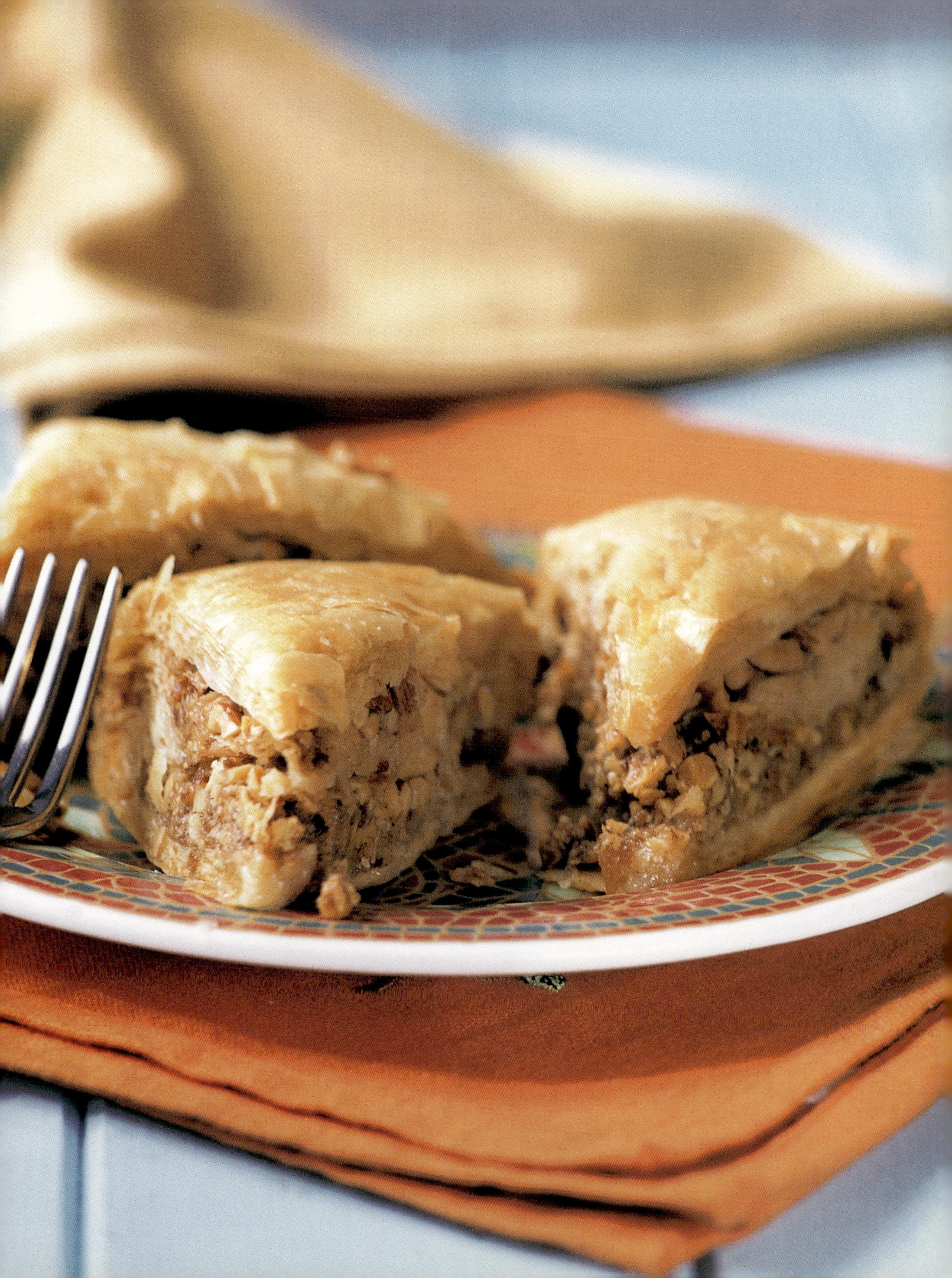

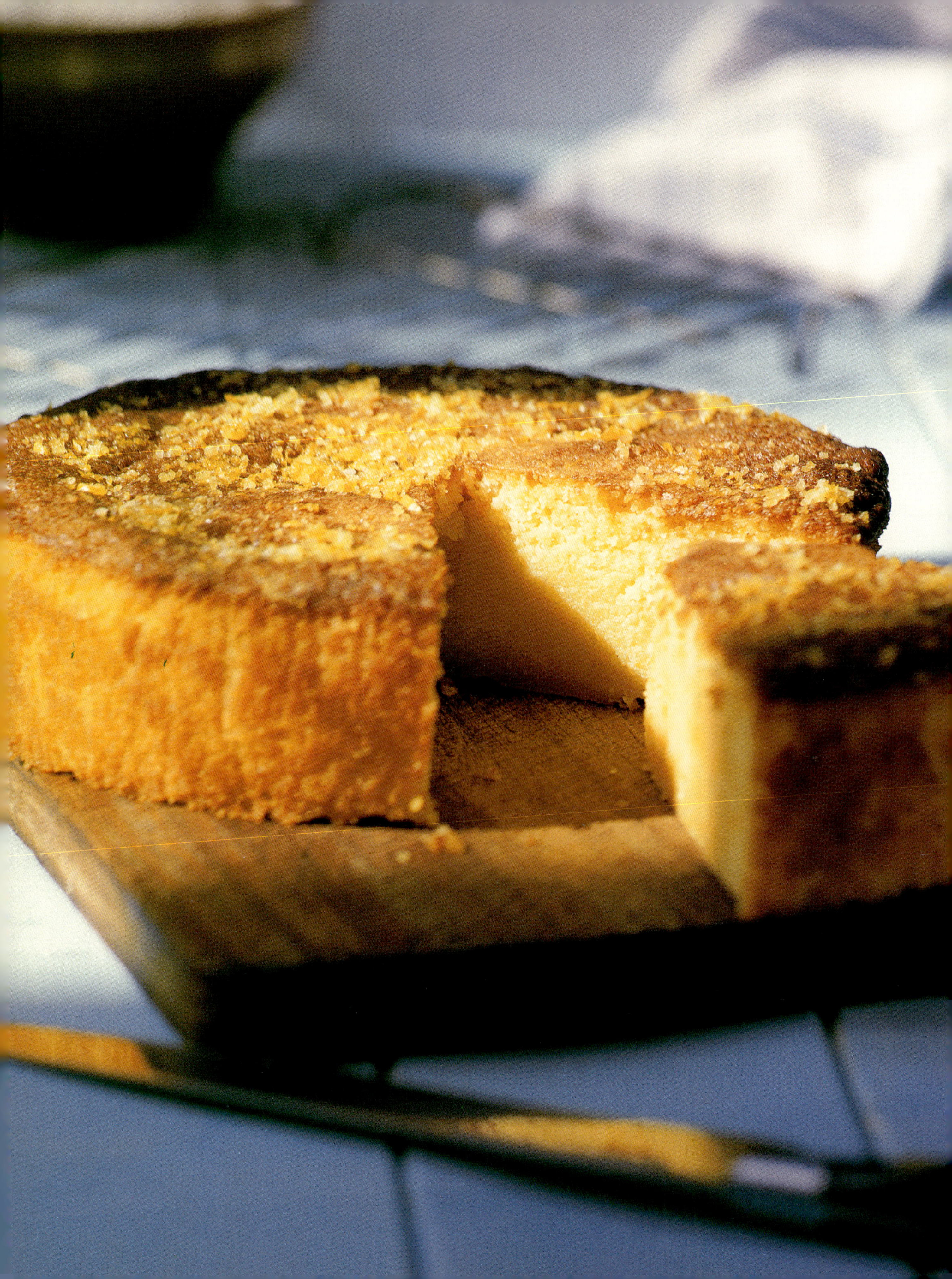

semolina and almond cake
halvás

Halvás is usually associated with the rich blocks of sesame seeds but it is also the name of this orange- and lemon-flavored semolina cake.

SERVES 8-12

8 oz/225 g butter, softened

1 cup superfine sugar

6 eggs, separated

¾ cup plus 2 tbsp fine ground semolina

1½ cups ground almonds

finely grated rind and juice of 3 oranges

⅔ cup white granulated sugar

¼ cup water

1 cinnamon stick

finely grated rind and juice of 2 lemons

1. Grease and line a round, loose-bottomed 9-inch/23-cm cake tin with waxed paper.

2. Put the butter and superfine sugar in a large bowl and beat together until light and fluffy. Add the egg yolks, one at a time, beating well after each addition. Add the semolina, ground almonds, orange rind and juice and mix well together.

3. Whisk the egg whites until stiff then fold into the mixture. Turn the mixture into the prepared pan and bake in a preheated oven, 350°F/180°C, for 50 minutes–1 hour, until golden brown and firm to the touch.

4. Put the granulated sugar, water, and the cinnamon stick in a saucepan and heat gently until the sugar has dissolved. Bring to the boil and boil for 4 minutes, until the mixture begins to thicken. Remove from the heat and add the lemon rind. Strain in the lemon juice.

5. When the cake is cooked, let stand in the pan for 5 minutes then carefully remove from the pan and place on a wire cooling rack, set over a cookie sheet. Prick the top of the cake all over with a fine skewer. Remove the cinnamon stick from the lemon syrup and, if necessary, reheat the syrup. Spoon the hot syrup and lemon rind over the warm cake, and let cool.

apricot and pistachio cake
kéik me eginís kai veríkoko

This is a moist cake, bursting with the flavors of some of Greece's favorite ingredients, and is ideal served as a dessert.

SERVES 8–10

½ cup ready-to-eat dried apricots
finely grated rind and juice of 1 large orange
6 oz/175 g butter
¾ cup plus 2 tbsp superfine sugar
4 eggs, separated
1⅔ cups fine ground semolina
1 scant cup ground almonds

for the syrup

¾ cup Greek honey
⅓ cup orange juice
2 tsp lemon juice

for the topping

1¼ cups authentic Greek yogurt
⅓ cup shelled unsalted pistachio nuts, chopped

1. Put the apricots, orange rind and juice in a bowl and let soak for 12 hours. Transfer the apricots and juice to a food processor and blend until smooth.

2. Grease and line a round, 9-inch/23-cm loose-bottomed cake pan with waxed paper.

3. Put the butter and sugar in a large bowl and beat together until light and fluffy. Add the egg yolks, one at a time, beating well after each addition. Add the semolina and ground almonds and mix well together. Fold in the apricot purée.

4. Whisk the egg whites until stiff then fold into the mixture. Turn the mixture into the prepared pan and bake in a preheated oven, 350°F/180°C, for about 45 minutes, until light golden brown and firm to the touch.

5. Meanwhile, make the syrup. Put the honey, orange juice, and lemon juice in a saucepan, bring to the boil, then simmer for 2–3 minutes, until combined. Set aside.

6. When the cake is cooked, let stand in the pan for 5 minutes then remove from the pan and place on a wire rack, set over a cookie sheet. Prick the top of the cake all over with a fine skewer. If necessary, reheat the syrup. Spoon the hot syrup over the warm cake and leave on the wire rack to cool.

7. When the cake is cold, remove from the pan. Just before serving, spread the yogurt over the cake and sprinkle over the pistachio nuts.

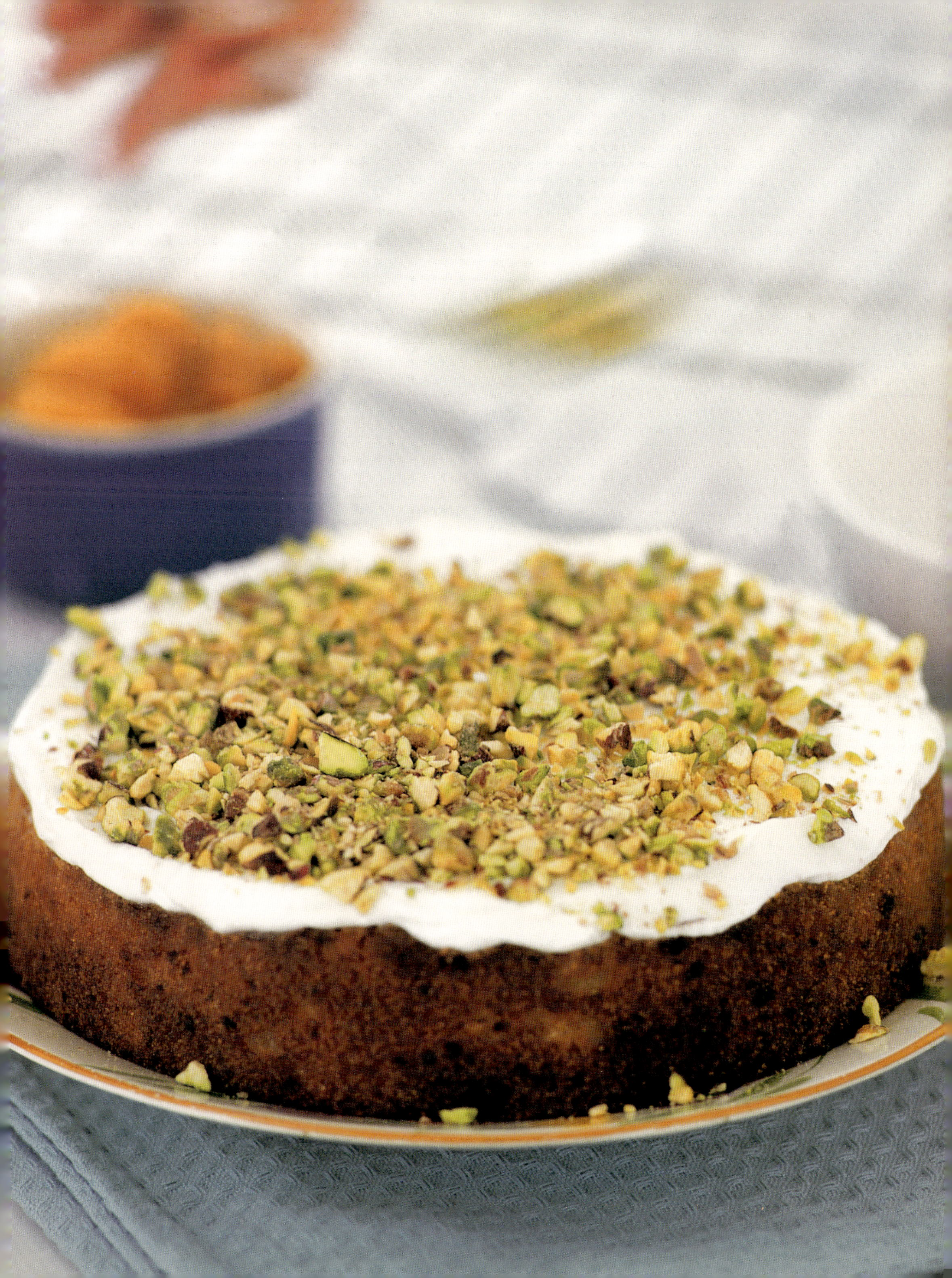

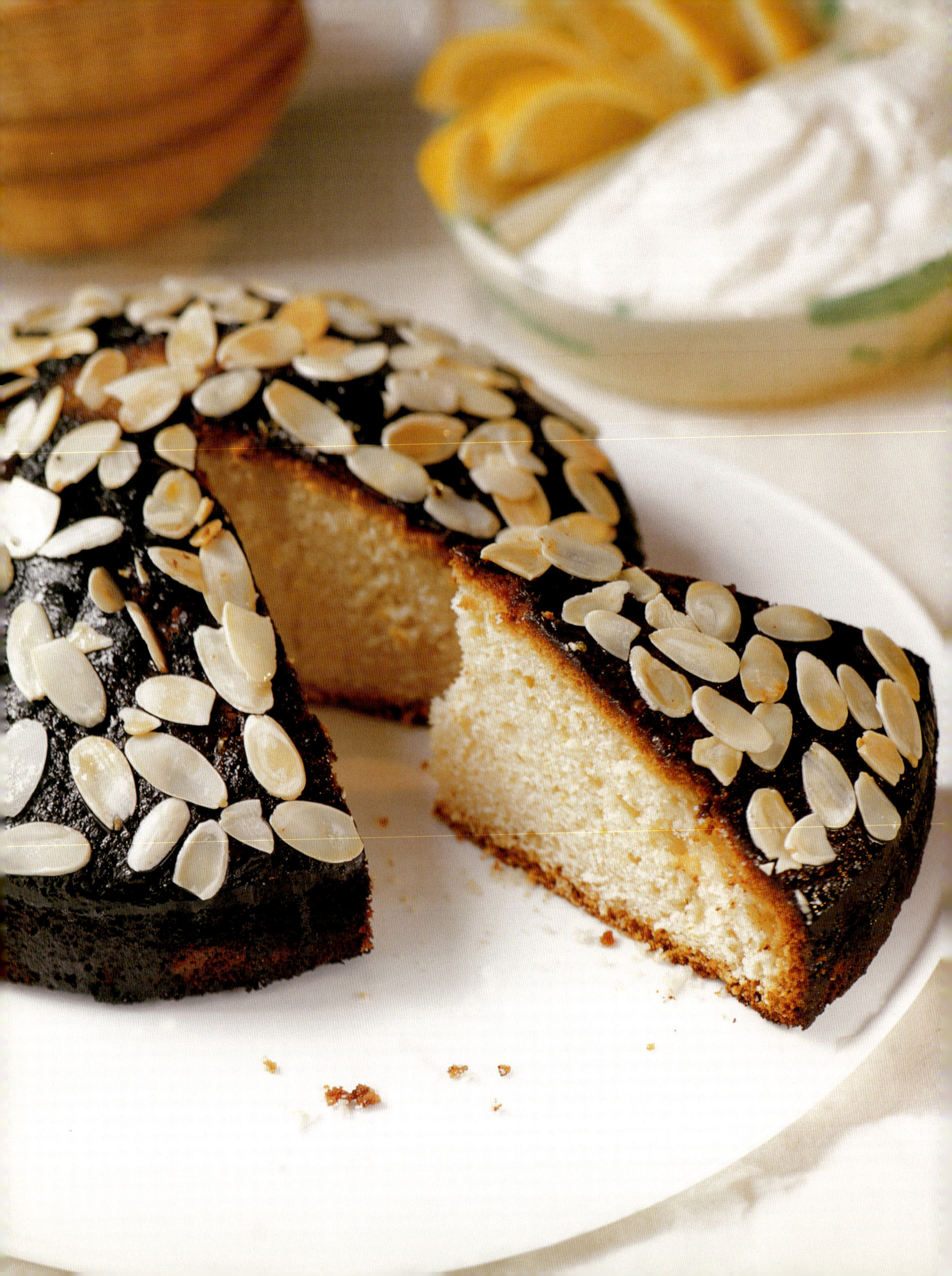

yogurt cake
yaourtópita

This is a light, moist cake, finished with a tangy lemon and honey syrup.

SERVES 8

2/3 cup authentic Greek yogurt

1/2 cup plus 1 tbsp sunflower or corn oil

1 1/2 cups superfine sugar

1 3/4 cups self-rising flour

2 eggs

finely grated rind and juice of 2 large lemons

1/3 cup white granulated sugar

2 tbsp Greek honey

1/4 cup toasted slivered almonds, to decorate

authentic Greek yogurt, to serve

1. Grease and line a round, 8-inch/20-cm loose-bottomed cake pan with waxed paper.

2. Put the yogurt, oil, superfine sugar, flour, eggs, and lemon rind in a large bowl or food processor and whisk together until smooth.

3. Turn the mixture into the prepared cake pan and bake in a preheated oven, 350°F/180°C, for about 1 1/4 hours until golden brown and a skewer, inserted in the center, comes out clean.

4. Meanwhile, put the lemon juice and granulated sugar in a saucepan and heat gently until the sugar has dissolved. Bring to the boil then simmer for 2–3 minutes. Stir in the honey.

5. When the cake is cooked, carefully remove from the pan and place on a wire cooling rack, set over a cookie sheet. Prick the top of the cake all over with a fine skewer. If necessary, reheat the lemon syrup then pour the hot syrup over the warm cake and let cool. Scatter over the slivered almonds to decorate, before serving. Serve with Greek yogurt.

walnut cake
karidópita

This very popular Greek dessert is a moist cake made with walnuts, which grow in abundance in Greece. It is topped with a fragrant orange- and brandy-flavored syrup.

1. Grease and line the bottom of a deep metal baking pan measuring 10 x 7 inches/25 x 18 cm with waxed paper.

2. Sift together the flour, cinnamon, and cloves. Put the butter and superfine sugar in a large bowl and beat together until light and fluffy. Add the eggs, one at a time, beating well after each addition. Using a metal spoon, fold in the sifted flour then fold in the walnuts.

3. Turn the mixture into the prepared pan and bake in a preheated oven, 375°F/190°C, for 30 minutes, until risen and firm to the touch.

4. Meanwhile, put the orange juice in a measuring cup and make up to $2/3$ cup with water. Pour into a saucepan, add the granulated sugar and the pared orange rind, and heat gently until the sugar has dissolved. Bring to the boil and boil for 6 minutes until the mixture begins to thicken. Remove from the heat and stir in the brandy.

5. When the cake is cooked, prick the surface all over with a fine skewer then strain the hot syrup over the top of the cake. Leave in the pan for at least 4 hours before serving.

SERVES 12

- 3/4 cup plus 2 tbsp self-rising flour
- 1/2 tsp ground cinnamon
- 1/4 tsp ground cloves
- 4 oz/115 g butter, softened
- 2/3 cup superfine sugar
- 4 eggs
- 1 1/2 cups walnut pieces, chopped finely
- pared rind and juice of 1 orange
- 2/3 cup white granulated sugar
- 2 tbsp brandy

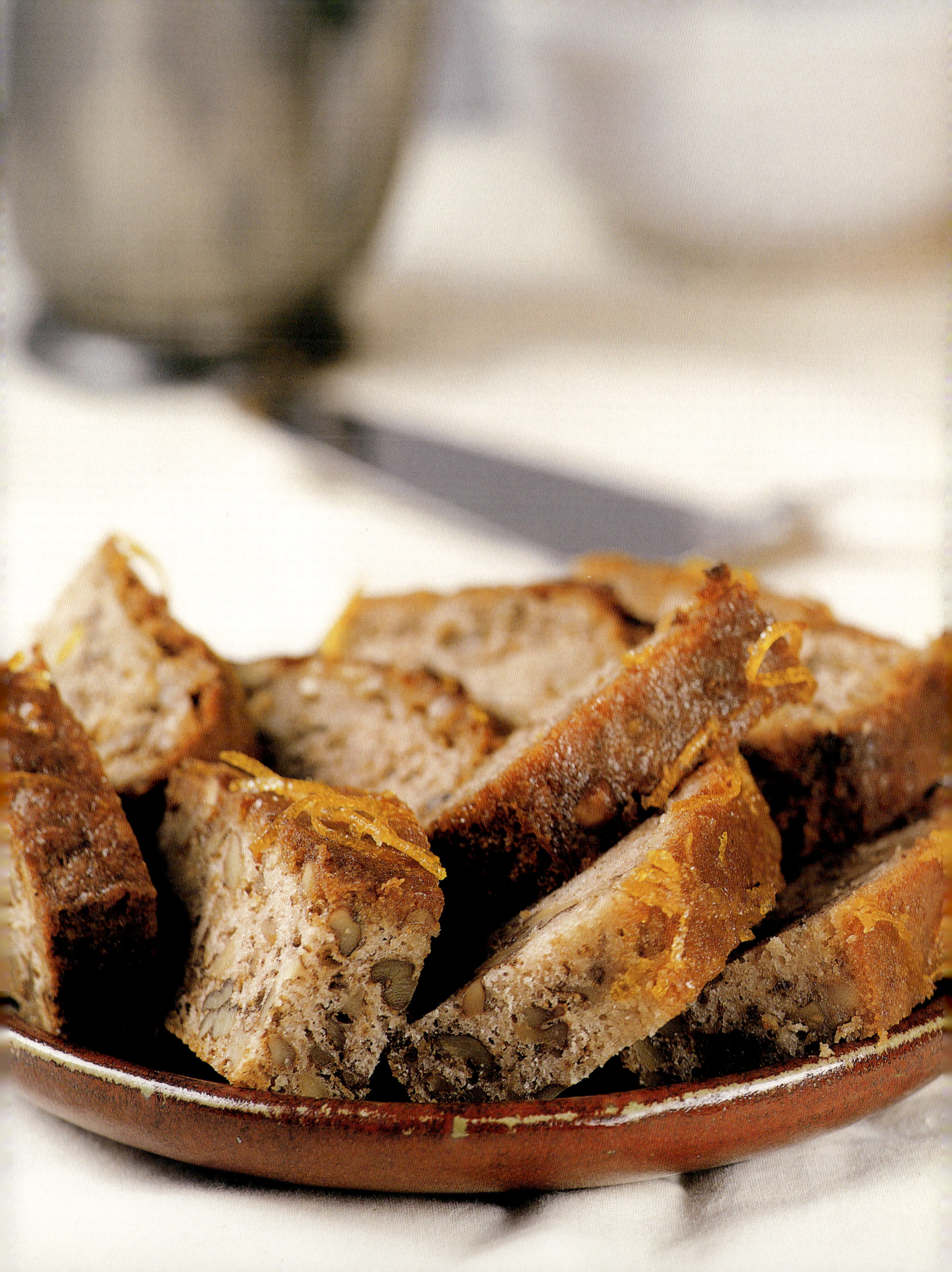

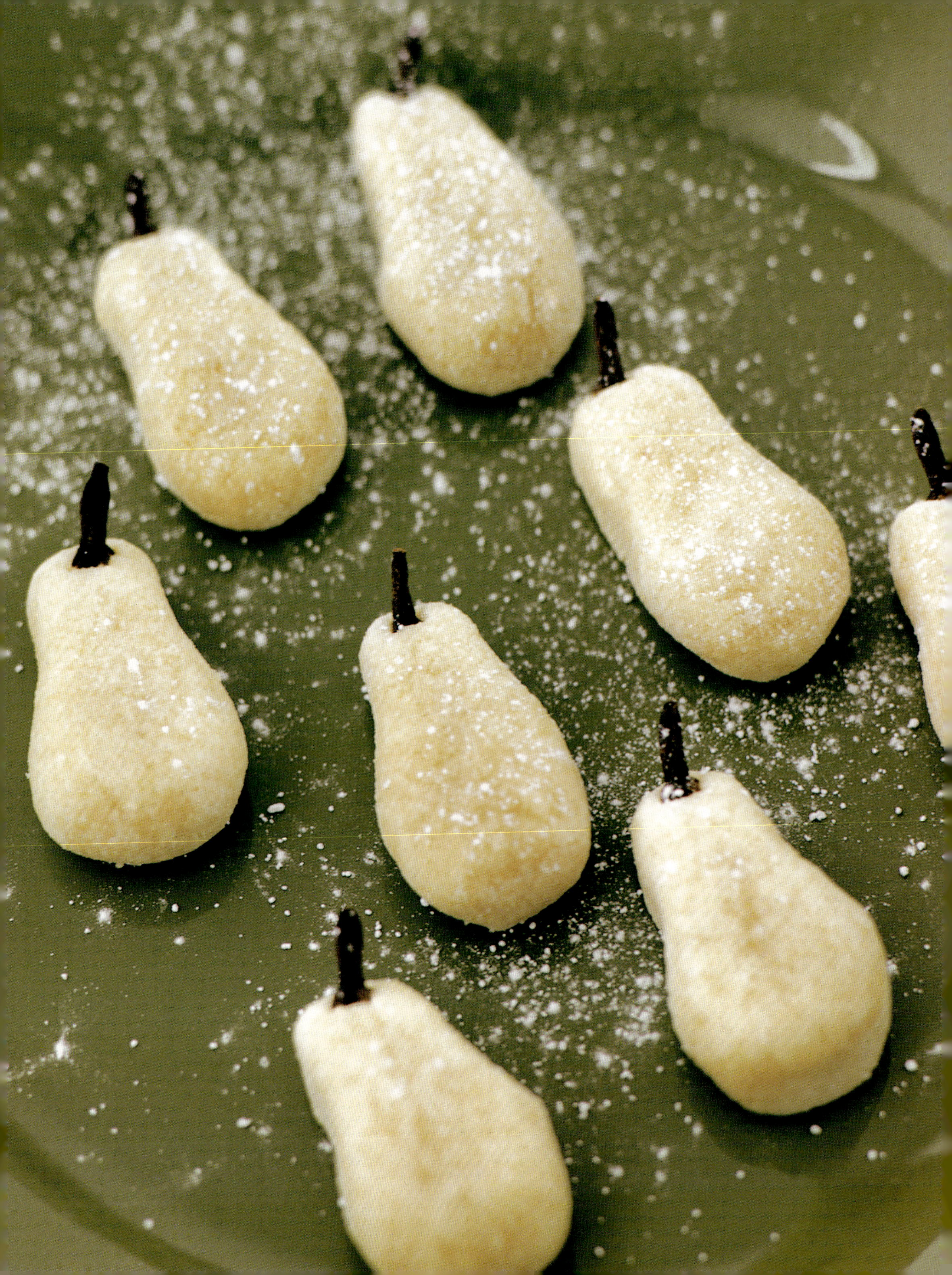

almond paste pears
achládia apo pólto amýgdalou

These pear-shaped cakes are served as a sweetmeat and are a specialty of the island of Hydra.

MAKES ABOUT 20

oil, for greasing

1¾ cups ground almonds

½ cup superfine sugar

2 tbsp fine ground semolina

1 egg, beaten

1 tsp orange flower water or rosewater, plus extra for brushing

about 15 whole cloves

confectioners' sugar, for dusting

1 Oil a baking tray. Put the ground almonds, superfine sugar, and semolina in a bowl and mix together. Stir in the egg and orange flower water or rosewater and knead to a smooth dough.

2 Break off small pieces of the mixture, about the size of a walnut, and form into pear shapes. Insert a clove in the top of each to form a stem. Place on the baking sheet.

3 Bake the almond pears in a preheated oven, 300°F/150°C, for about 20 minutes, until lightly colored. Let cool.

4 When the almond pears are cold, brush lightly with orange flower water or rosewater and then dust with sifted confectioners' sugar.

Simple Greek buildings in exposed sites have small windows to keep out the heat of the day

lemonade
lemonáda

Lemons grow and are used in abundance in Greece so lemonade is an obvious, popular drink.

MAKES ABOUT 2½ CUPS FOR ABOUT 16 SERVINGS

pared rind and juice of 3 large lemons

2¼ cups white granulated sugar

⅔ cup water

1 cinnamon stick

to serve

still or sparkling water

ice cubes

1 Put the pared lemon rind, the sugar, water, and cinnamon in a saucepan. Bring to the boil, stirring until the sugar has dissolved, and then simmer for 5 minutes, without allowing the syrup to color. Let cool.

2 When cool, strain the syrup then strain in the lemon juice. Pour into a clean bottle and seal. Label and store in the fridge for up to 2 weeks.

3 To serve, pour the lemonade into a glass, add ice cubes and dilute with still or sparkling water, allowing 1 part lemonade to 3 parts water or according to taste.

sweet things

greek coffee
ellinikós kafés

Coffee is the most popular drink in Greece and is drunk at all hours of the day at home or in cafés. It is made in a *bríki*, which is a small, long-handled brass pot with a narrow top and broad lip. Sugar is added to taste and when you order a coffee you will be asked how you would like it, as sugar is added to the coffee grounds at the same time as the water. You must ask for *métrio* if you want a medium-sweet coffee, *skéto* if you don't want sugar in it and *varies glyko* if you want it very sweet.

SERVES 2

¾ **cup cold water**
2 tsp sugar for medium sweetness, or according to taste
2 heaping tsp fine-ground coffee
glasses of ice water, to serve

1 Put the water and the sugar, according to taste, in a *bríki* or small enamel saucepan. Bring to the boil then, before it overflows, remove from the heat and stir in the coffee.

2 Return to the heat and as soon at the coffee forms a foam and boils to the top of the *bríki* immediately remove from the heat and tap the sides of the *bríki* with a teaspoon, until the coffee subsides a little.

3 Repeat the boiling of the coffee and tapping of the *bríki* for a second time.

4 Return to the heat for a third time and just before the coffee boils over, remove from the heat and, using a teaspoon, spoon the foam into 2 coffee cups. Pour the coffee into the cups, being careful not to disturb the foam on top of each cup. Serve with glasses of ice water.

index

Achládia apo Pólto Amýgdalou 251
Aginares me Koukiá 194
Almirá me Sousámi 78
Almonds 28, 40, 64, 219, 243, 251
Anari 28
Angourósoupa 42, 71
Apricot and Pistachio Cake 244
Arní me Dendrolívano se Fílo 141
Arní me Domátes, Anginares, kai Eliés 133
Arní me Giouvétsi 138
Arní me Kanéla 136
Arní me Kolokíthia 129
Arní me Melitzána kai Eliés 142
Artichokes 133, 194
Avgolémono 107, 123

Baked Dishes 90, 93, 99, 144, 184, 218
Baklavás 240
Bámies Kokkinístes 176
Baroúnia me Ambelófila 113
Basil 28, 163
Beans 28, 35, 42, 50-1, 70, 170, 194, 198, 204
Beef 55, 118, 149
Bell Peppers 36, 54, 197, 209
Bread 42, 77
Butter Cookies 222

Cabbage Leaves, Stuffed 182
Cakes 214, 221, 243-8
Capers 28
Carrots à la Grecque 187
Casseroles 133, 136, 149
Cephalopods 56, 84
Charred Bell Pepper Salad 209
Cheese
    Chicken with Goat Cheese and Basil 163
    Feta 28, 60, 81, 190, 195, 202-3
    Hallóumi 30, 197
    Hot Cheese Pastries 60
    types of 28, 30-1, 229-30
    Walnut Cheese Wafers 81
Cheesecake Portokáli me Karaloméno Lemóni 230
Chicken 118, 123
    with Goat Cheese and Basil 163
    Grilled Chicken with Lemon 156
    Kabobs with Yogurt Sauce 123, 160
    Phyllo Chicken Pie 159
    Roast Chicken with Oregano 123, 165
    Spicy Aromatic Chicken 157
    with Walnut Sauce 123, 164
Chickpea and Sesame Dip 51
Cinnamon Lamb Casserole 136
Cod 48, 85
Coffee 214, 253
Consommé with Egg and Lemon Sauce 66
Cookies 212, 219, 222

Cottage Cheese 229-30
Crispy Roasted Fennel 179
Cucumbers 47, 71
Custard Tarts 226
Cuttlefish 84-5

Desserts 212-51
Dips 28, 40, 42, 47-54, 64
Dolmádes 40, 59, 182
Domatasaláta me Féta 202
Doughnuts in Honey Syrup 225

Egg and Lemon Sauce 66, 107, 155
Eggplants
    Baked Stuffed 184
    and Garlic Dip 53
    Lamb and Eggplant Moussaka 130
    Lamb with Eggplant and Olive Sauce 142
    Roasted Vegetable Moussaka 189
    Roasted Vegetable Soup 69
Eliótsomo 77
Ellinkós Kafés 253

Fasoláda 70
Fasólia Yahní 198
Fáva 28, 50
Fava Beans 194, 204
Fennel 153, 179
Feta Cheese 28, 60, 81, 190, 195, 202-3
Figs 29, 218
Finíkia 221
Fish 10, 48, 56, 72, 82-115
    in Egg and Lemon Sauce 107
    Fritters with Greek Garlic Sauce 104
Fishermen's Soup 41-2, 72
Fresh Herb Soup 75
Fruit 212

Garídes Piláfi 114
Garlic Sauce 40, 64, 104, 177
Glyká tou Koutalioú 212
Goat Cheese 163
Green Salad 206
Gufrétes me Tirí kai Karídia 81

Hallóumi Cheese 30, 197
Halvás 36, 243
Herbs 28, 31-2, 34, 36, 75, 171
Hirinó Avgolémono 155
Hirinó me Aníthos 153
Honey 31, 212, 214, 218, 221, 225
    Honey and Lemon Tart 229
Hórta me Ladolémono 206
Húmmous kai Tachíni 36, 40, 51

Ice Cream 234, 237
Imam Baildi 184

Kabobs 100, 123, 135, 160
Kaccaviá 41–2, 72
Kalamarákia 56
Karidópita 248
Karóta à la Grecque 187
Keftédes 128
Kéik me Eginís kai Veríkoko 244
Kolokíthia Gemistá 195
Kolokíthia me Skordaliá 177
Kolokithópita 181
Kotópita 159
Kotópoulo me Karídia 164
Kotópoulo me Rígani 165
Kotópoulo me Tirí Próvio kai Vasilikó 163
Kotópoulo Pikántiko 157
Kotópoulo Scharás me Lemóni 156
Kotópoulo Souvláki me Sáltsa Yaóurti 160
Koulourákia 222
Kounéli me Domáta kai Mirodiká 166
Kourambiédes 212, 219

Láhano Dolmádes 182
Lamb
    Cinnamon Lamb Casserole 136
    with Eggplant and Black Olive Sauce 142
    and Eggplant Moussaka 130
    Marinated Lamb and Vegetable Kabobs 135
    Roast Lamb with Orzo 124, 138
    Rosemary Lamb in Phyllo Pastry 141
    with Tomatoes, Artichokes, and Olives 133
Lamb's Liver in Red Wine and Orange Sauce 143
Lemonáda 252
Lemons
    Caramelized 230
    Egg and Lemon Sauce 66, 107, 155
    with Fish 87, 93, 107, 109
    Grilled Chicken with Lemon 156
    Honey and Lemon Tart 229
    Lemon Dressing 172, 206
    Lemon Ice Cream in an Ice Bowl 234
    Lemonade 252
Lettuce, Romaine 28, 155
Liver, Lamb's 143
Loukánika 55, 118
Loukoumádes 225

Mackerel, Stuffed 99
Makarónia me Thalasiná 111
Makarónia me Thalasiná kai Koukounária 95
Manoúri Cheese 31, 229
Mastic (*Mastíha*) 32
Meat 10, 116–67
Meatballs, Grecian 128
Melitzánes Gémistes 184
Melitzanosaláta 53
Melomakárona 221
Mezzes 40–1, 46–64, 77–81, 85
Monkfish and Shrimp Kabobs 100
Moshári me Kókkino Krasí 150

Moussaká 118, 130
Moussakás Lahanikón 189
Mustard and Caper Sauce 108

Nuts 46, 214, 237
    see also Almonds; Pistachios; Walnuts

Octopus 84
Okra 32, 176
Olive Bread 42, 77
Olive Oil 10, 13, 32
Olives 13, 32–3, 133, 142, 202–3, 207
Orange
    Cheesecake with Caramelized Lemon Slices 230
    Flower Water 34
    and Olive Salad 207
    and Red Wine Sauce 143
    and Walnut Cakes 221
Oranges in Caramel Sauce 233
Oregano 35, 93, 123, 165
Orzo 35, 124, 138
Ouzo 35

Pagotó Fistíkia 237
Pagotó Lemóni se Bol apo Págo 234
Pan-fried Fish with Lemon 109
Pása Témpos 40, 46
Pasta Dishes 95, 111, 124, 138, 144
Pastítsio 118, 144
Pastry *see* Phyllo Pastry Dishes; Honey and Lemon Tart
Pears 251
Phyllo Pastry Dishes 29–30
    Baklavás 214, 240
    Phyllo Chicken Pie 159
    Rabbit, Roast Tomato, and Sage Pie 166
    Rosemary Lamb in Phyllo Pastry 141
    Spinach and Feta Pie 190
    Walnut Custard Tarts 226
    Zucchini Pie 181
Pies *see* Phyllo Pastry Dishes
Pilaf 114, 170–1, 200
Piláfi me Domáta 200
Pine Nuts 35, 95, 99
Piperiá Kapnistí 54
Pipéries Gemistés me Hallóumi 197
Pistachios 35, 237, 244
Pita Bread 42
Pork 55, 153, 155
Portokaliá Karamelomèno 233
Psári Avgolémono 107
Psári me Moustárda kai Cápari 108
Psári me Skordaliá 104
Psári Plakí 90
Psári Skordáto 92
Psária Spetsiótika 96
Psári Tiganitó me Lemóni 109
Psitó Traganistó Aníthos 179

Quince 35

255

Rabbit, Roast Tomato, and Sage Pie 166
Red Mullet Wrapped in Vine Leaves 113
Red Snapper, Broiled with Garlic 92
Religious Festivals 16, 86-7, 123-4, 170, 212
Retsina 35
Rice 170-1
    Greek Rice Pudding 232
    Shrimp Pilaf 114
    Stuffed Vine Leaves 59
    Tomato Pilaf 201
Ricotta Cheese 229-30
Rígani 16, 35
Rizógalo 232
Roasted Fish from Spatsae Island 96
Roasted Vegetables 36, 69, 189, 197
Romaine Lettuce 28, 155
Rose Flower Water 35
Rosemary Lamb in Phyllo Pastry 141

Sage 35, 166
Salads 171-2, 202-9
Saláta Horiátiki 203
Saláta me Koukiá 204
Saláta me Portokali kai Eliés 207
Santorini 13, 28
Sardéles me Rígani 93
Sardines (Fresh) Baked with Lemon and Oregano 93
Sausages 55, 127
Scallops, with Pasta and Pine Nuts 95
Sea Urchins 85
Seafood 111, 114
Semolina and Almond Cake 243
Sesame Seeds 36, 51, 78
Shortbread Cookies 212, 219
Shrimp and Monkfish Kabobs 100
Shrimp Pilaf 114
Síka Fournóu me Méli 218
Sikotakiá me Sáltsa 143
Siphnópitta 229
Skate in Mustard and Caper Sauce 108
Skordaliá 40, 64, 104, 177
Skoubriá Gemistá 99
Smoked Cod Roe Dip 48
Smyrna Sausages in Tomato Sauce 127
Soudzoukákia 127
Soúpa Avgolémono 41, 66
Soúpa me Freska Mirodiká 75
Soúpa Psitón Lahanikón 69
Soúpa tou Psará 72
Soúpa Yaoúrti-Domáta 65
Soups 41-2, 65-75
Souvlákia 40, 123, 135
Souvlákia me Psári kai Garides 100
Spanakópita 40, 190
Spices 28, 144, 157
Spinach and Feta Pie 190
Split Peas 28, 50
"Spoon Sweets" 212
Squid 56, 84

Stifádo 118, 149
Stuffed Dishes 59, 99, 182, 218
    Vegetables 170, 184, 195
Sweetmeats 251

Tahini Paste 36, 51
Taramasaláta 40, 48
Tartes Karidión 226
Tirópites 60
Tomatoes 13, 36
    Braised with Okra 176
    with Fish 87, 96
    with Lamb 129, 133
    Pilaf 201
    Rabbit Pie 166
    Roasted Vegetable Soup 69
    Salad with Fried Feta 202
    Smyrna Sausages in Tomato Sauce 127
    Yogurt and Tomato Soup 65
Traditional Greek Salad 203
Tzatzíki 40, 47

Veal 118, 150
Vegetables 168-209
    Moussaka 189
    Soup 69, 70
Vine Leaves 37, 59, 113

Walnuts 37
    Cake 248
    Cheese Wafers 81
    Chicken with Walnut Sauce 123, 164
    Chilled Cucumber Soup 71
    Custard Tarts 226
    Orange and Walnut Cakes 221
    Pastries 240
    Stuffed Zucchini 195
Wine 143, 150

Yaourtópita 247
Yogurt 37
    Cake 247
    Chicken Kabobs with Yogurt Sauce 123, 160
    Chilled Cucumber Soup 71
    Cucumber and Yogurt Dip 47
    Eggplant and Garlic Dip 53
    Fresh Herb Soup 75
    Lemon Ice Cream 234
    Tomato Soup 65

Zucchini
    Lamb with Zucchini and Tomatoes 129
    Roasted Vegetable Moussaka 189
    Sliced with Greek Garlic Sauce 177
    Stuffed with Walnuts and Feta 195
    Zucchini Pie 181